GREAT
PERFORMANCES

SECOND EDITION

Larry **LEWIN** | Betty Jean **SHOEMAKER**

GREAT
PERFORMANCES

SECOND EDITION

CREATING

CLASSROOM-BASED

ASSESSMENT TASKS

ASCD | Alexandria, Virginia USA

1703 N. Beauregard St. • Alexandria, VA 22311-1714 USA
Phone: 800-933-2723 or 703-578-9600 • Fax: 703-575-5400
Website: www.ascd.org • E-mail: member@ascd.org
Author guidelines: www.ascd.org/write

Gene R. Carter, *Executive Director;* Judy Zimny, *Chief Program Development Officer;* Nancy Modrak, *Publisher;* Scott Willis, *Director, Book Acquisitions & Development;* Carolyn Pool, *Acquisitions Editor;* Julie Houtz, *Director, Book Editing & Production;* Deborah Siegel, *Editor;* Sima Nasr, *Senior Graphic Designer;* Mike Kalyan, *Production Manager;* Keith Demmons, *Desktop Publishing Specialist*

Printed in the United States of America. Cover art © 2011 by ASCD. ASCD publications present a variety of viewpoints. The views expressed or implied in this book should not be interpreted as official positions of the Association.

All web links in this book are correct as of the publication date below but may have become inactive or otherwise modified since that time. If you notice a deactivated or changed link, please e-mail books@ascd.org with the words "Link Update" in the subject line. In your message, please specify the web link, the book title, and the page number on which the link appears.

PAPERBACK ISBN: 978-1-4166-1177-6   ASCD product #110038   n6/11
Also available as an e-book (see Books in Print for the ISBNs).

Quantity discounts for the paperback edition only: 10–49 copies, 10%; 50+ copies, 15%; for 1,000 or more copies, call 800-933-2723, ext. 5634, or 703-575-5634. For desk copies: member@ascd.org.

Library of Congress Cataloging-in-Publication Data
Lewin, Larry, 1949-
  Great performances : creating classroom-based assessment tasks / Larry Lewin and Betty Jean Shoemaker. – 2nd ed.
       p. cm.
  Includes bibliographical references and index.
  ISBN 978-1-4166-1177-6 (pbk. : alk. paper) 1. Educational tests and measurements–United States. 2. Grading and marking (Students)–United States. I. Shoemaker, Betty Jean, 1946- II. Title.
  LB3051.L462 2010
  371.27'1–dc22
                    2010053668

20 19 18 17 16 15 14 13 12 11   1 2 3 4 5 6 7 8 9 10 11 12

To Betty,
Coauthor, colleague, passionate advocate,
and provider of tea and pastries
during our editing sessions.

—LL

I have been blessed to be surrounded by smart and competent teachers in my career. These teachers have profoundly influenced my thinking and pedagogy. This group includes

- my coauthor, Larry Lewin, whose efforts to refine both the science and art of teaching have been a beacon for many;

- my husband, George Shoemaker, who has the largest vocabulary and most refined use of language of anyone I know;

- Barbara Shirk, Michelle Markus, Mary McKrola, and Roberta Fair, my teaching colleagues, and our students at Ida Patterson Elementary School in Eugene, Oregon, with whom I have engaged in the most exciting teaching and learning community;

- my colleagues in the Instruction Department in Eugene Public Schools, including Dr. Martha Harris, Dr. William Kentta, and Ms. Denise Gudger, among others;

- my friends and colleagues with whom I have consulted in many settings—Paul Weill, Karen Antikajian, and Yvonne Fasold; and, of course,

- my children, Timothy Carlos Shoemaker and Theresa Elena Shoemaker, who have taught me, grounded me, and loved me through the completion of my dissertation, through absences from home for numerous consulting trips, and through many a project in which I "tried it out" on them first, before bringing it to the classroom!

—BJS

great performances

Creating Classroom-Based Assessment Tasks

List of Figures

Preface: Teaching and Assessing Meaningfully in a Standards-Based World

Betty's Story

When I was in the 3rd grade, my aunt and uncle sent me several packets of flower seeds. I was thrilled about the potential of creating something that could be both beautiful and utilitarian. I don't remember how I came up with the idea of creating a flower bed in front of my school. I immediately set to work on putting my plan in place. I would revitalize the front of my drab, red brick elementary school with rows of black-eyed Susans, red poppies, Shasta Daisies, and zinnia Lilliputs.

First, I asked my teacher, Mrs. Hedberg, what she thought of the idea. She loved it and paved the way for me to get started on the project during recess soon after the spring thaw. I rounded up a few of my friends to help me, and we began to prepare the ground for planting. Throughout the process, Mrs. H. kept providing us with reading material about planting and maintaining flower gardens and about the types of gardens that attract birds to one's neighborhood.

About six weeks into the work, when the seeds had sprouted and we began to see the fruit of our labors, we arrived at school one day to see the local florist bringing in planter boxes to place in front of the school. My feelings were surprise, concern, and then shock! What was going on?

I rushed into my classroom. Mrs. Hedberg explained to me that the Parent Teacher Association had noticed my small plot and decided that it was time for them to start a "beautification initiative" for the entire school as a result of my efforts. When recess came, my crew and I headed out to see the new "stuff." To our horror, a couple of the 6th grade girls (one whose mother was the president of the PTA) were actively pulling out our tender starts. They laughed at us and stated that our "puny" plants would not amount to much and that they were charged by the PTA to remove them in order to prepare for the much nicer boxes loaded with hardy nursery plants. I was enraged—livid! I don't remember deciding to hit her, but I swung my fist around and slugged her. I DO remember sitting in the classroom the rest of the week for the infraction. My heightened sense of justice just could not conceive of someone else taking my initiative and turning it into something that I would have then called "highfalutin."

Now why would we share this story in this revision of *Great Performances?* When we wrote the first edition, Larry and I held a *classroom-based* worldview of performance assessment. That is, we saw the value in having assessment tools that would

* help you figure out what students know/don't know and can/can't do in relation to specific academic tasks;
* help individual students in your class know in what areas their performance is strong and in what areas their performance is weak and what they can do to improve their performance;
* help you know how to adjust and improve your instruction so that students have the tools to improve their performances.

We continue to view performance assessment as an effective classroom-based endeavor. However, in workshops we have presented over the last few years, some educators have expressed concerns that policymakers have "hijacked" the use of performance assessment data solely for accountability purposes. That is, assessment scores in some cases are being used to determine whether a school has made AYP (adequate yearly progress), and schools are threatened with either the loss of funding or the state taking over the school.

Teachers have shared that—in some settings—their district's or state's entire standards-based system has been implemented to the detriment of the whole performance-based effort. It is their impression that performance assessment is not for teaching and learning anymore, but just used to segregate schools and neighborhoods into successful and unsuccessful places.

Did a hijacking occur? It helps us here to remember the flower garden. In general, teachers initiated this movement from a classroom-based worldview and perceive that policymakers see the movement from an accountability worldview. Just as Betty could not understand why someone would so cruelly usurp her flower project, some educators cannot conceive of performance assessment being used for high-stakes, large-scale accountability!

This discussion also brings to mind a statement made by esteemed educator and author Dr. Arthur L. Costa at an annual ASCD conference: "Teaching and assessing *solely* by number is about as effective as painting by number." All of us who continue to be engaged in the performance assessment movement, whether policymakers or educators, need to avoid getting polarized into camps about this. However, we believe that those who find themselves embracing something with such passion that it becomes rigid and formulaic *need help*.

Let's be reminded again of the fundamental notions with which we started the first edition (1998) of *Great Performances*. We wanted

* to teach rich integrated, thematic units of instruction where students grapple with meaty conceptual ideas and use the processes of reading, writing, problem solving, and investigation as effective strategy users.
* to avoid standards-based systems that force teachers to teach a narrow band of targets and where students cough up the answers they think the test requires.
* to share with our readers a range of assessment strategies, from short and specific to lengthy and substantive.

As we present this new edition, we trust that you will continue to find here effective assessment devices that can be easily implemented in your classroom, that enhance and inform your instruction, that improve the performance of students, and that reflect the depth and complexity of the challenging academic content you teach. We hold that you MUST continue to teach *meaningfully* in a standards-based world.

When educators rightfully ask, "Are current performance-based assessment systems becoming so unwieldy that they will implode upon themselves, and if so, what will we have left?" our answer is strong and clear: keep your "eyes on the prize." Focus on the students in your classrooms. What happens when you interact with students in YOUR class is what makes the difference. Let go of the rest!

chapter 1

Great Performances: Our Journey Begins

Do You Recognize This Place?

Betty's Sad Story

As someone who takes pride in my oral reading skills, I attempt to read in a dramatic way that engages the entire class with the text. On this occasion, I was reading *Charlotte's Web* (White, 1952) to my combined 1st and 2nd grade class. As I neared the end of this popular book, my voice deepened and my words became dignified:

Suddenly a voice was heard on the loudspeaker. "Attention, please!" it said. "Will Mr. Homer Zuckerman bring his famous pig to the judges' booth in front of the grandstand. A special award will be made there in twenty minutes."

One of my freckle-faced 1st graders looked quizzically at me and asked, "You mean *Wilbur's* the pig? I thought Charlotte was the pig!"

Larry's Sadder Story

During the debriefing of our three-week in-depth study of Jamestown Colony, an 8th grader in my U.S. history/language arts class raised her hand and stated:

I feel like I really get it all now, about Jamestown, and the English colonists coming over on the ships, and trying to survive during the "Starving Time." And the Pocahontas–John Smith thing—you know, the argument over if they had a romance and if she really saved his life. I get all that, but one thing: was Lincoln still the president back then?

Betty's Saddest Story

A few years ago I was concerned that my 4th and 5th graders were consistently using stereotypical language to refer to people of color. This concern led me to develop and teach a six-week unit with the goal of unlearning stereotypes about Native Americans, Asian Americans, and Hispanics/Latinos.

Students read widely from multiple perspectives, analyzed representations of people of color in the media, and interacted with Asian, Hispanic/Latino, and Native American guests in the classroom. At the end of the unit, we invited a local Native American community leader to class. "What do you know about Native Americans?" this leader asked students. One 10-year-old politely raised her hand, was called on, and earnestly replied, "They kill people."

We would like to begin this book by telling you that the above stories are true: we were there. We recognize this place. This is a place some of you may recognize also. It is a place where teachers are sometimes astounded by how little we know about what our students don't know. From here we set out on a journey. This journey has led us to embrace an integrated approach to curriculum and assessment that makes sense and works for us in the classroom. But let us not get ahead of ourselves: first things first.

Our Journey Begins

We began our journey by looking for a better way to assess our students' acquisition of content knowledge. In the past we typically conducted our assessments at the end of our units or courses. We used mostly paper-and-pencil kinds of assessments found in the teachers' guides of adopted textbooks. We also incorporated culminating projects into our units, but generally as celebratory events for students to showcase their work with little evaluation. We all felt really good about them, but did we really know who learned what? So when we were honest with ourselves, we admitted that we operated under the maxim "I taught; therefore, they learned!"

The more we talked about what we wanted to do, the more we began to develop our own notions that challenged the prevailing teaching and learning practices of which we had become a part. These ideas can be summarized as follows:

1. Instead of short "canned" units, we want to teach "meaty" units, where in-depth study takes place and students gain a grasp of major conceptual ideas.

2. In spite of our best attempts, we still have trouble helping students comprehend basic core knowledge facts, concepts, and generalizations. We want to teach in such a way that students really "get it."

3. We cannot assume that all students coming into our classes have the skills needed to process the important content information we are teaching.

4. We are concerned that moving to a standards-based system will compel teachers to teach to a narrow band of targets and will compel students to produce the answers they think teachers want.

5. We want to incorporate the newer, more time-consuming performance assessment methods (while continuing to use some traditional methods), but we wrestle with how to pull off the logistics in the classroom.

6. We must expand the opportunities for our students to show what they have learned through various modes, not exclusively through paper-and-pencil activities.

7. Our repertoire of assessment strategies needs to include a range of evaluations—from short and specific to lengthy and substantive.

8. Our assessments must arise naturally out of our teaching. They cannot be awkward add-ons to the units or, even worse, irrelevant assessments imposed from the outside.

9. We want to have confidence that how we teach students and assess their work actually contributes to their achievement.

10. We want to embrace methods that assess student work not only at the end of the unit, but also at the beginning and middle.

We know that we are not alone. Many of our colleagues also share these beliefs. Using these ideas as guideposts, we will lead you on a journey through the world of classroom-based assessments. We will share what we've learned about developing performance tasks that measure students' understandings of the content matter we teach them daily in our classrooms. And we promise to be honest with you. Our focus is on the practical, the doable. You can learn from our mistakes. When we as colleagues share with one another, we all improve our abilities to design and elicit great performances from our students.

To help you better understand the assessment procedures we will be describing in this book, let's briefly look at the integrative model from which they come.

The Coin Model: What Do We Teach?

It doesn't matter whether we teach kindergarten or high school, science or language arts, in urban or rural environments. We all teach two things: knowledge and know-how—sometimes called content and skills. We teach core knowledge content to our students, such as the seasons as a cycle, the separation of powers in the U.S. Constitution, and facts about the cardiovascular system. And we also teach them key skills, strategies, and processes such as how to read, write, and problem solve.

To help you understand this idea of teaching and assessing these two different kinds of knowledge, we use the metaphor of a coin (Shoemaker & Lewin, 1993). (See Figure 1.1.)

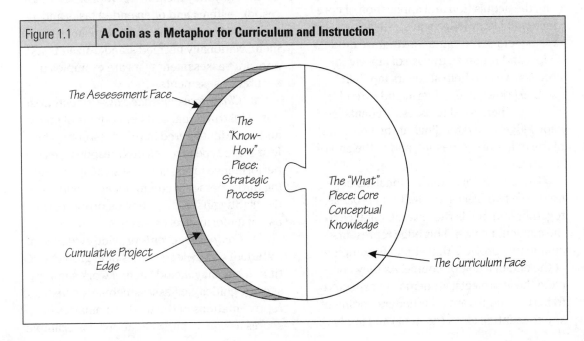

| Figure 1.1 | A Coin as a Metaphor for Curriculum and Instruction |

The Assessment Face

The "Know-How" Piece: Strategic Process

The "What" Piece: Core Conceptual Knowledge

Cumulative Project Edge

The Curriculum Face

One face of the coin represents curriculum and the other face assessment. Curriculum and assessment, like the two faces of a coin, are inseparably fused and directly related to each other.

Visualize a coin cut down the center into two interlocking puzzle pieces. One piece describes the "what" of the curriculum—core conceptual knowledge—which most folks call "content." The other piece describes the "know-how" of the curriculum—strategic processes—which most folks simply call "skills." In our model, we define core knowledge, sometimes referred to as declarative knowledge (Marzano, 1994), as "meaty" conceptual ideas, as opposed to rote factual knowledge. A strategic process, sometimes called procedural knowledge, is a set or a series of interconnected actions that combine skills or strategies to produce a particular result or condition—such as comprehending a difficult passage of a book or problem solving to construct a toothpick bridge.

We teach and assess both pieces of the coin, the acquisition and application of core conceptual knowledge and strategic processes. And in the same way that we model, shape, and routinize the use of any given process, we also help students tap their existing knowledge, refine it, and extend it. Thus, teachers need to assess students' core knowledge understandings at the beginning of the unit, during the unit, and at the end of the unit.

Our coin is three-dimensional. Its edge holds the two pieces, content and process, together and melds the assessment face to the curriculum face. This edge represents cumulative projects that students complete at the end of a unit or course. As they complete these projects, students are expected to both demonstrate their understanding of key conceptual ideas (content) and apply the strategic processes (skills) taught in the unit or course. Culminating projects are orchestrated efforts to apply core conceptual understandings and strategic processes to create personally meaningful new knowledge.

Let's look closer at the assessment face.

An Introduction to Assessment

Strong assessment systems incorporate four critical elements:

1. *Validations* emerge from adult judgments about whether a student has met, not yet met, or exceeded the performance standard. They are based on a number of data sources, including direct observations, performances on tasks, student self-assessments, tests, and traditional classroom work. They reflect performance over time.

2. *Secured assessments* are administered under controlled conditions (during a certain window of time), where no help is given. They may include traditional selected-response items and open-ended tasks and are scored outside the classroom environment. Nationally normed standardized tests and state assessment tests are examples of secured assessments.

3. *Classroom-embedded assessments* arise out of instructional units or courses of study and are administered in the classroom. The four basic types are selected response, essay, performance tasks, and assessments involving direct personal communication with students (Stiggins, 1997). They incorporate the use of uniform, overt scoring systems.

4. *Composite records* provide evidence of a student's knowledge, skills, and growth over time. They may include actual work samples, scoring guides, self-assessments—or, instead, representations of the work, summaries of scores assigned, and validations, for example.

Classroom Assessments with Overt Scoring Systems

As teachers we use all four of the assessment elements just described. However, it is the third for which we are most directly responsible. We create classroom assessments. We rely upon them far more than the other elements. And we know that we need to do a better job working with them.

As just noted, Stiggins (1997) suggests that classroom assessments take four basic forms. Here's how we understand the four types:

1. *Selected-response assessments* are traditional paper-and-pencil tasks in which the teacher selects the questions and students must respond. A student picks from multiple choices or true/false items, matches items, and fills in short answers.

2. *Essay assessments* require a student to produce a longer written response to a teacher prompt.

3. *Performance assessments* call for the student to construct a response within a context. Popular performance tasks include story writing, science lab experiments, and debates. Evaluation criteria are clearly identified in the form of dimensions or traits, and the focus of evaluation is on both the product and the process used to produce it.

4. *Personal communications as assessment* include substantive dialogue between the teacher and students during instruction, interviews, conferences, conversations, and oral examinations.

In this book we are going to zero in on the third type, performance assessments. Why? Because they work for us. They allow us to assess content and process simultaneously. They are more engaging for students. They give us feedback that helps us improve our instruction.

And now the big question: Just what exactly are *performance assessments*? Performance assessments encompass a range from short and specific to lengthy and substantive; from *mini,* which open a window into a student's developmental thinking early in a unit, to *maxi,* which paint a picture of a student's overall thinking at the end of the unit. Performance tasks fall within this broad range.

In our definition, a performance *task* has the following key characteristics:

1. Students have some choice in selecting or shaping the task.

2. The task requires both the elaboration of core knowledge content and the use of key processes.

3. The task has an explicit scoring system.

4. The task is designed for an audience larger than the teacher; others outside the classroom would find value in the work.

5. The task is carefully crafted to measure what it purports to measure.

In summary, a performance task can be completed in different lengths of time: in one class period—a *mini*; in two or three class periods—a *midi*; in a week or more—a *maxi.*

A Snapshot of Chapter 1

In this chapter, we provided a big-picture overview of why we set out on our assessment journey. We shared with you the 10 key notions we used to develop our new assessments, as well as the central elements of our integrative "coin" model: content, process, and product. We also explored the four essential elements of a strong assessment program and four types of classroom-based assessments.

We are interested in a continuing dialogue with teachers on this journey. Please share your thoughts and reactions with us.

A Preview of Coming Attractions

In the chapters that follow, we offer a close-up look at our view of classroom-based assessments—the assessment face of our coin.

In Chapter 2, we provide you with background on how students acquire content knowledge—*Info In*—using the key learning processes of reading, listening, manipulating, and viewing. We also introduce the *Prepare, First Dare, Repair, and Share* approach to teaching these key processes. In addition, we examine the four modes that *Info Out* can take—graphic, written, oral, and constructions. Students use these vehicles to make their content understanding explicit to teachers and other adults for evaluation.

In Chapter 3, we will explore the first Info Out mode, *visual representations,* in which students share their content knowledge through graphic organizers, comic strips, electronic slide shows, and the like.

In Chapters 4, 5, and 6, we examine three additional Info Out modes: *writing* (for example, a historical persuasive letter and

a parent advisory brochure); *oral presentations* (such as round-robin mini-speeches and debates); and *large-scale substantive projects/ performances* (including museum exhibits and models and prototypes).

In Chapter 7, a new chapter in this edition, we zero in on classroom-based reading assessments. We explore a number of currently available schoolwide or districtwide assessment measures that districts and states are encouraging teachers to use and provide some of our insights into their use. We reference RTI (Response to Intervention) in relationship to these reading assessments, helping teachers understand how RTI fits into the bigger scheme of classroom assessment.

In the final chapter, we summarize several strengths and weaknesses of classroom-based performance assessments. And in this new edition, we address the daunting issue of how to convert performance assessment scores into traditional letter grades.

Also in this second edition, we have tried to update the examples and streamline the scoring guides throughout the chapters. In particular, we want to share performance tasks that we have designed and used with students as an integral part of an existing unit or course of study. These tasks vary in length and complexity and take various forms. They can be used as assessments at the beginning of the unit, during the unit, and at the end of the unit.

chapter 2

Info In: How Students Learn New Content Information

Larry's Story

As my students filed into the classroom for 5th period Reading and Lit, each brightened up upon noticing the TV cart parked in front of the room.

"Are we watching a movie today?" each wanted to know. When I replied affirmatively, they beamed with contentment. However, no one bothered to ask me about the topic of the movie or why I was going to show it. All they needed to know was that something, anything, would be flickering on a screen.

After taking attendance, collecting homework, and laying out the goals of the period—including the chief goal of "comparing the video version to the book version"—I dimmed the lights and hit "play."

Sadly, the educational goal of the film was forgotten by many, so the next day when I led a class discussion on comparing and contrasting the film and text versions, few students had something to say other than "Huh??"

My teaching career spanned 24 years at elementary, middle, and high school, and regardless of the grade level, I vividly recall that DVD viewing (preceded by VHS tapes, 16mm films and even nonsound filmstrips early in my career—does this date me?) were often misperceived by a number of my students. That is, they misunderstood the purpose for viewing the film: when the lights went down, so did their heads. Has anyone else experienced students taking a break from learning instead of engaging in the intended Info-In experience? Or what about students secretly socializing or attempting to finish homework for another class while the video, DVD, or podcast plays on uselessly?

Because of a variety of in- and out-of-school factors, too many learners are unable to effectively apply the learning processes—like viewing—to take in new content information. We cannot assume all students are skilled at "Info Inning." As with any Info In learning process, the viewing process must be taught.

Info In: Learning New Content

This book, obviously, is about assessment—it even says so in the title. But this present chapter is about what happens *before we assess* our students' learning; it is about *instruction*. More specifically, this chapter is about the results of our instruction—students taking in the content information we teach.

We believe:

Before you can assess what students have learned, you have to teach them something; we call instruction "Info In."

Students "Info In" using four modes: reading, listening, viewing/observing, and manipulating/hands-on experiences.

Next, our students must show us what they learned as a result of our instruction; we call assessment "Info Out."

Students Info Out using four modes: writing, illustrating/visual representations, speaking, and large-scale project/performances.

It is very useful to organize both Info Inning and Info Outing into a four-step process approach template; we call it "Prepare, First Dare, Repair, and Share."

Let's be clear about where we are headed. This chapter is about Info In; Chapters 3, 4, 5, and 6 are about Info Out. Before addressing how we assess student learning of content, we must first consider how they learn that content. The purposes of this chapter are

- to introduce you to Info In: how learners use key learning processes to acquire content knowledge
- to show you how we teach Info In processes to students

Of the four Info In modes listed above, we have chosen to focus on the third and fourth—viewing and manipulating (sometimes called hands-on projects)—in this chapter for four important reasons:

Video/DVD/online-streaming viewing and hands-on manipulating are increasingly popular in our schools.

Students may often misperceive both viewing and hands-on learning time as kick-back, do-nothing time.

Teachers typically don't instruct students on how to effectively watch videos or participate in hands-on activities.

The unfortunate results are often either widespread boredom or, worse, the potential for mass chaos.

First, we will illustrate how a 6th grade language arts middle school class applied the viewing process to actively gain expertise about folk and fairy tales in a literature unit. Then we will follow with an elementary-level example of using manipulatives in a science experiment to help students gain expertise about the transmission of viruses and bacteria.

The Viewing Process: A 6th Grade Language Arts Class Watches Folk/Fairy Tales

Teacher Tom Cantwell at Cal Young Middle School in Eugene, Oregon, guided his 6th grade language arts class successfully through a unit on folk and fairy tales. He introduced the unit by showing a video clip of a Native American folk tale version of Cinderella, titled *Turkey Girl;* then he assigned a Vietnamese version of the tale, *The Story of Tam and Cam* (McDougal Littell, 2001), from their course literature anthology text, making comparisons that ultimately were expressed in a compare/contrast essay.

The content of this literature unit, as with all Info In, has to be connected to our teaching objectives, most notably the state or school district standards. Tom's objectives for this unit, beyond the obvious importance and enjoyment of reading folk tales, come from his state's 6th Grade Language Arts Standards:

> EL.06.LI.03 Identify and/or summarize sequence of events, main ideas, and supporting details in literary selections.

> EL.06.LI.01 Listen to text and read text to make connections and respond to historically or culturally significant works of literature that enhance the study of other subjects.

> EL.06.RE.29 Connect and clarify main ideas by identifying their relationships to multiple sources, known information and ideas, and related topics.

> Source: Oregon Department of Education, http://www.ode.state.or.us/teachlearn/real/standards/sbd.aspx

These standards are perfectly addressed in folk and fairy tales due to the consistency of story structure and the wide variety of different versions of the same tale across different cultures.

Getting Ready to View

Before firing up the video clip of the Native American version of the folk tale, Tom wisely decided to have his students tap their prior knowledge by employing a visual device called the Open Mind to help his students think about what they already know about folk tales, particularly Cinderella. This handout is simply the outline of a human head with lots of room inside for students to write, draw, or both in response to a teacher prompt. Combining visual representations (drawing) and text (writing) increases achievement. This effectiveness of combining linguistic and nonlinguistic expression is backed up by research. Robert Marzano states, in *Building*

Cinderella in Different Cultures

For an excellent listing of folk tales and myths with the same theme, check out *Children's Literature in the Elementary School* (1987) by Charlotte Huck, Susan Hepler, and Janet Hickman.

Cinderella stories listed are as follows:
- "Tattercoats" from England
- "Aschenputtel" from Germany
- "The Princess on the Glass Hill" from Norway
- "Nomi and the Magic Fish" from Africa
- "Yeh-Shen" from China
- Cinderella in Native American lore
- "Vasilisa the Beautiful" from Russia
- "The Brocaded Slipper" from Vietnam

Several websites offer various versions
— Teacher John Pennisi at Auburn High School, Alabama, provides a synopsis of six versions at http://auburnschools.org/AHS/jpennisi/aaEnglish%20Files/cinderella.htm.
— Professor D. L. Ashliman, retired from the University of Pittsburgh, offers the text of 15 versions at www.pitt.edu/%7Edash/type0510a.html.

Background Knowledge for Academic Achievement (2004):

> In addition to a linguistic form, our memory packets have a nonlinguistic form. In other words, our memory packets are bimodal. . . . The realization that background knowledge is stored in bimodal packets with linguistic and nonlinguistic components greatly informs any attempt to indirectly enhance academic background knowledge. Specifically, such attempts should involve activities

designed to enhance students' linguistic representations of the target information and their imagery of the targeted information. (pp. 19, 21)

Tom modified the basic Open Mind by instructing his students to draw a line through the middle of the head outline from top to bottom. On the left side he prompted them to conduct a memory search on Cinderella—that is, to tap into their prior knowledge about this famous fairy tale. (See Figure 2.1.) The right side was used the next day for a different purpose.

Why use an Open Mind for a memory search instead of just a regular piece of notebook paper? Why not? It's far more engaging to kids because it is novel, it's more visual, and it's more fun. As teachers, we do whatever we can to inspire Info Inning, right?

It should be noted that Tom employed other Info In modes in his unit. In fact, he opted to use three of the four: Not only did his 6th graders *view* videos, they also *read* folk tales, including a Vietnamese version of the Cinderella story, and the class *listened* to several of his mini-lectures on the common story structure of folk tales, the overlap of folk tales across cultures, and how authors develop characters. He could have opted to include the fourth mode (*manipulating*) as well, if he had an activity that required hands-on, tactile learning—perhaps constructing miniature characters for a puppet show contemporary version of the tale. But he did not for a simple reason: He didn't have the time or the energy. No teacher is required to use all the modes all the time. Rather, we pick and choose—making sure to use them all at some time during the semester, differentiating our instruction and assessment so that all learners have a good chance at succeeding in meeting the course's standards.

A Four-Step Generic Process Approach: Prepare, First Dare, Repair, and Share

What Tom was doing at the beginning of his unit with the Open Mind was *preparing* his students for Info In. By conducting a memory search of prior knowledge about Cinderella,

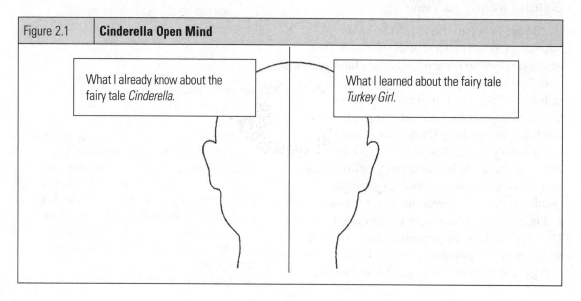

Figure 2.1	**Cinderella Open Mind**

What I already know about the fairy tale *Cinderella*.

What I learned about the fairy tale *Turkey Girl*.

the kids were *getting ready to learn* new content information coming up in the unit.

Betty and I call this first stage of the Info In learning process *Prepare*. All teachers know the importance of getting students ready to learn. Some educators call it establishing the "anticipatory set." And because we cannot assume that all of our students have already mastered skills such as checking out the materials in advance of using them, tapping prior knowledge, anticipating new information, generating guiding questions, or establishing a purpose for learning, we have to guide students in the right direction. Otherwise, we might find ourselves *committing assumicide* (a nifty phrase from Anita Archer that points up the danger of assuming that students can independently prepare, only to discover later that they did not, and thereby killing the lesson).

Important Aside: Lots of Options

As successful as the Open Mind activity was for Tom's class, there are lots of other possible preparation activities he could have used in this unit. For example, he could have opted to lead his class to

1. review the difference between folk and fairy tales;
2. read or listen to two different versions of a fairy tale other than Cinderella and compare them with a Venn diagram;
3. brainstorm/predict possible endings to the video clip—in this case, *Turkey Girl*.

All or any of these would have been useful in setting up students to successfully Info In. Variety is the key; we would never want to use and reuse the same activities over and over.

The *Prepare* stage is followed by the *First Dare, Repair,* and *Share* stages. The *First Dare* is a learner's first attempt to access that new information, to gather as much info as possible in an initial try. It can be thought of as a first try or a first attempt at learning something new.

Repair recognizes the need to return to the information source in order to fine-tune, upgrade, or correct the initial (First Dare) understanding. It is sometimes thought of as revision, rethinking, or relearning.

And last, *Share* allows the learner to reveal what he or she has learned. It is the demonstration of knowledge or skills, and we can make this stage very attractive and motivating to kids. It is often referred to as the presentation.

We like this generic four-step process—Prepare, First Dare, Repair, and Share—for three important reasons: (1) it is easy to remember; (2) it is generic, so it can be applied to a number of different learning processes; and (3) it provides a *temporary place holder scaffold* to support students who need it.

As proud as we are of this, it is important to realize that both the number of steps and the labels applied to them are arbitrary. That is, a learner could easily invent a three-step learning process, or a five- or even six-stepper, and the labels could be anything that works. For example, the classic writing process uses four steps that are labeled *Pre-writing, First Drafting, Revising,* and *Publishing* (this is the genesis of our four steps). The scientific investigative process, on the other hand, typically employs five steps: 1. *Hypothesize; 2. Gather materials and equipment; 3. Conduct experiment, analyze data and control for variable(s); 4. Re-conduct experiment;* and 5. *Report findings.* And as another example, the math problem-solving process is 1. *Read the problem carefully; 2. Cross out unnecessary information; 3. Show your work. Don't do it in your head; 4. Don't erase your mistakes. Cross out errors instead; 5. Re-read your problem and check your answers; 6. Draw a picture that illustrates the problem; 7. Write in your own words how you got your answer* (ABCTeach, Solving Word Problems Chart, n.d.).

Of course, there are many different versions of all of these processes, but clearly they have much in common. The key to this process approach, any process approach—whether it is a generic four-step process as we describe here or a more specific process—is that it mitigates the dreaded "one and done" syndrome. This is where the learner short-circuits the process when he assumes that he has produced one draft and he is, therefore, done! Our colleague and friend, Paul Weill, refers to this as "punting on first down."

While it is very useful for learners to follow formulas like those above, we believe that the ultimate goal is for each learner to develop her or his own personal learning processes and be facile in using them. Meanwhile, a generic process is useful until students adapt their own personalized Info In learning process.

Here is a handy chart showing in more detail a set of strategy families that kids need to learn tied to our four-step process template (see Figure 2.2).

First Dare Viewing

Let's move on to First Dare and Tom's folk tale unit. The next day, following the introductory Open Mind memory search activity, I volunteered to help out by presenting a different version of the Cinderella tale

Figure 2.2	A List of Strategy Families Tied to Various Steps in a Process
Prepare Strategies	
Surveying:	Used to take stock of presented information and relationships
Retrieving:	Used to tap prior knowledge about a topic from one's memory
Planning:	Used to complete an assignment or a project in a timely manner
Forecasting:	Used to anticipate potential learning through predicting or questioning
First Dare Strategies	
Focusing:	Used to selectively attend to significant information
Information gathering:	Used to acquire needed new information
Self-regulating:	Used to monitor one's own construction of meaning (metacognition)
Generating:	Used to produce new information, meanings, or ideas
Organizing:	Used to track data, construct meaning, and enhance retention
Repair Strategies	
Fixing up:	Used to resolve any cognitive dissonance
Evaluating:	Used to assess the value, quality, or significance of ideas
Analyzing:	Used to examine essential features as parts of the whole
Perspective taking:	Used to examine other points of view
Share Strategies	
Integrating:	Used to synthesize, connect, and combine information meaningfully
Organizing:	Used to structure large amounts of data meaningfully for presentations
Presenting:	Used to develop a final product using various media

to the class via the Internet. Tom's school district owned a site license to the online educational video resource Unitedstreaming.com. Therefore, we were able to go there and search for Cinderella digitalized videos, and sure enough, I found *Turkey Girl*, a Native American folk tale that parallels the Cinderella story. With Unitedstreaming, educators can either stream selected videos or shorter video clips in real time to the class using a computer projector or SmartBoard, or alternatively, download it to the computer's hard drive for later viewing. Because Tom's school has a speedy T-1 bandwidth, we decided to stream the four short video clip segments of *Turkey Girl* for his class to watch.

Please note that I was not practicing "reading welfare" here—the substitution of an easier learning mode for the difficult one of reading. I was using online video clips to introduce reading—not to replace it. Video viewing is a legitimate Info In mode, and it was the only format I had for this version of the fairy tale.

Even though students routinely watch videos (online, on TV, with an iPod, etc.), not all of them are skilled at video viewing *for academic purposes*. No surprise, of course, so Tom and I built in a note-taking activity to support their First Dare view. I gave the kids these instructions: "Take out your Open Mind from yesterday and review on the left-hand side what you wrote about Cinderella from memory." I called on some students to read aloud what they had written.

Next I said, "OK, today you're going to use the other half of your Open Minds. In the right-hand column you will jot down or make a quick sketch of any important new information you get from this video version of the Cinderella story. But I must tell you that this version is somewhat different from the one you know. I will pause the video once

in a while (at the end of each of the four segments) to give you a chance to write, draw, or both. Who's ready to watch *Turkey Girl*?"

This prompt alerted them to address the first state standard listed above, "Identify and/or summarize sequence of events, main ideas, and supporting details in literary selections." It's nice having an activity like the Open Mind that can be used in multiple ways.

Variations on Note Taking During a First Dare Video Viewing

Now, in retrospect, to support students' Info In, I could have opted to provide Tom's class with a Venn diagram template instead of the Split Open Mind. Because the two versions of Cinderella have both similarities and differences, the Venn may have been a good choice to help them track comparisons and contrasts. Even though this device has been around for about 130 years, it still works well. It may well be the first graphic organizer ever invented.

Alternatively, I could have employed another classic note-taking device, the two-columned T-sheet, sometimes called the Double Entry Two-Columned Note Taker. Students draw a straight line across the top of their paper and then another line down the center to make a large T. They label the left side at the top "Quotes," prompting them to record any important lines from the film. The top right side is labeled "Notes," and this is where students jot a note (in their own words) reacting to the quote. Other versions of this two-columned sheet have been adapted with replacement prompts at the top, like "What It Said" and "What I Think." In Reading Apprenticeship, the two columns are labeled "Evidence" (what the student saw, heard, or read in the text) and "Interpretation" (what the student wondered or thought). In all versions, the left side is for literal-level tracking of incoming information, and the right side is for the interpretative and evaluative responses.

Third, I might have decided to use the SnapShots note-taking activity, where students take a mental picture of what they are seeing by drawing a quick visualization. This activity is very powerful, and I've used it for years with great success, but Tom and I opted to save it for a reading assignment later in the unit.

Last, the Folded File Folder (FFF) activity would have worked for this purpose. Playing off the metaphor of file folders for the mental categories humans create in their memories (schemata), the FFF teaches students some important comprehension strategies. The teacher distributes 8½ by 11-inch papers (colored paper, to get their attention) and instructs the students to fold them in half, leaving a 1/2- to 1-inch tab on top (see Figure A.1 in the Appendix).

After labeling the tab with the topic about to be viewed—in this case, "*Turkey Girl* Folk Tale"—students open the Folded File Folder and use the top inside section (between the tab and fold) to tap their prior knowledge by jotting down anything they already know or think they know about the topic. The teacher tells students that tapping prior knowledge is a key strategy for synthesizing new information while viewing a video.

In the middle, right on top of the fold, the teacher instructs students to quickly predict what they think the video might tell them. Because some students are hesitant to mispredict, assure them that there is no such thing as a "bad" prediction. Many researchers have identified the strategy of prediction as very important for successful comprehension building.

The bottom portion of the FFF is reserved for taking notes on new information that was

"Info In-ed" during the viewing, fostering more active viewing.

If you are thinking, "Hmmm, this seems familiar to the KWL Sheet," you are right. The FFF is an adaptation of this classic reading strategy practice activity invented nearly 25 years ago by Donna Ogle (1986). We modified it into a folded file folder just to add some variety to our instruction and avoid overuse of KWL.

In *Dimensions of Learning,* Bob Marzano and colleagues (1997) recommend that we "create classroom tasks that relate to students' interests and goals [because] students are more likely to perceive tasks as valuable if the tasks somehow relate to their interests and goals." The questions we would ask ourselves are, Are we able to connect the curriculum to our students' interests and goals? And can we come up with devices to measure their achievement that inspire interest and energy?

So does the Open Mind, the Venn diagram, the T-sheet, SnapShots, or the FFF turn kids on enough to inspire them to try their hardest? That is, do any of them spark interest and seem valuable? If not, then we must go back to the drawing board and invent, borrow, or adapt a technique that does. Suffice it to say, when students have a variety of ways of expressing their thinking about whatever topic, they tend to stay more engaged than if they "do the same old thing" (like "read the chapter and answer the questions") over and over and over again.

Repairing Initial Understanding

The third stage of the learning process, *Repair,* provides learners with another chance. They are given the opportunity to go back and reconsider what they learned. Repair is not just for fixing mistakes—it is for boosting overall understanding.

The strategy families chart in Figure 2.2 lists four important ones: fixing up, evaluating, analyzing, and perspective taking. For example, in the writing process, Repair means to revisit your rough draft (First Dare) and scrutinize it for places in need of improvement, both evaluating and analyzing content and fixing up any errors in spelling, punctuation, or grammar. In the case of the viewing process, students would be given the opportunity to review the video (or selected scenes) to troubleshoot any confusion or misunderstanding.

Because there is no hard-and-fast rule that requires a learner to repair all assigned work, Tom skipped this stage. This is totally fine. No one expects every learner on every assignment to go through all the steps of the process. So Tom decided, based on looking over the students' notes on the right side of their Open Minds, that all the kids did just fine viewing the video. Not every one of them understood every single element, but for our purposes, the mission was accomplished—they got the gist.

Likewise, sometimes in the writing process, a rough draft of a writing assignment is sufficient. Other times, revising a draft is essential, especially when the final work will be presented to an audience; it all depends on the objective of the lesson.

Sharing What You Learned

This last stage of the process shifts us from Info In to Info Out; that is, Prepare, First Dare, and Repair are all about taking in information. Share, however, is all about integrating and synthesizing the new information and imparting it back out. Sharing is the opportunity for students to pull these pieces together into some meaningful whole and communicate the results with an audience. Three key

share strategies are integrating, organizing, and presenting. (See Figure 2.2.)

Good news: there is no shortage of possibilities for sharing. Three come quickly to mind: Sharing with Classmates, Big-Time Sharing Options, and Sharing with the Teacher.

- *Sharing with Classmates.* Tom could simply assemble his students into pairs, trios, quads, or groups of five and ask students to show each other their work on their Open Mind Sheets. This is a common approach, and it has merit. To make sure the sharing goes well, it makes sense for the teacher to establish some simple guidelines. For instance, Tom could establish the order of group members' sharing, the amount of time allocated, how to appropriately respond to each other's work, and of course, how to determine who shares with whom. Students are then free to add ideas they acquired from others' Open Minds to expand their own thinking. The Share stage of the process makes student work into "public property," which is used to help advance the community of learners' understanding. Alternatively, Tom could simply post the Open Minds on a bulletin board, so all students could see their classmates' work and consider which ones work well.

- *Big-Time Sharing.* If time allowed (and he was feeling like Super Teacher), Tom could elevate the Share stage into some sort of celebration. The Open Minds could be collected and stapled into a booklet with a volunteer creating a nice cover. Maybe Tom could invite the principal to class and have the kids present the booklet, and explain how they did their Open Minds. In this scenario, it would, no doubt, be a good idea to reinsert the Repair stage into the process and instruct the students to double-check their work for accuracy and neatness, and perhaps even provide them with time to add color.

Or he could scan the Open Minds into digitized images and paste them into a slide show for the class. Of course, this is time-consuming and may be overkill, but if it so happened that a Parent Night or Open House were scheduled soon, he may find the extra energy. Again, if the Sharing involves an audience, then the Repair stage is critically important.

Other Share options can bubble up in the teacher's mind. It's nice to be creative and spice up the classroom atmosphere. Not all Shares can be big-time celebrations, nor do they need to be. But it is important to remember that a good Share idea can generate the enthusiasm and energy required to complete a successful assignment. It makes the hard work of Prepare, First Dare, and Repair worth it.

• *Sharing with the Teacher.* More commonly, the students simply share their work with the teacher, who collects and scores them. This is the traditional, standard Share routine, and it is a viable option. As we mentioned above, the Open Minds were deemed by the teacher to be satisfactory demonstrations of taking in the important pieces of the video. But what if the teacher needs to discern more formally just how well each student performed on the Open Minds? What could a teacher do with these Open Minds to assess them more completely than just give them a quick look-over?

The simplest way to score students' Open Minds, of course, is for the teacher to assign some overall point value for the assignment; for example, this Open Mind would be worth 15 points, and this student earned 10 points.

Alternatively, the teacher could identify some advanced set of criteria to measure student performance against. Typically, this involves creating (or borrowing) a scoring rubric. A rubric, as we all have learned over our careers, is a scoring mechanism that provides students (performers) and teachers (judges) two critical elements: a set of criteria that are essential to the assignment, called traits, and a scoring scale usually in the form of a point scale (often 4, 3, 2, and 1.) This assessment option would help elevate the activity into a *task*. (The difference between an activity and a performance task will be addressed momentarily.)

A Scenic Detour: Routine Assignments vs. Performance Tasks

Before we move on here, we think that it is important to clarify the difference between a routine classroom activity and a performance task. Quite simply, assignments are for instructional purposes, and tasks are for assessment purposes.

In our minds, an activity is some regular assignment that teachers use in the classroom to support the taking in of information about the topic and constructing of meaning —Info In.

A performance task, on the other hand, is somewhat more formal and is designed to elicit student construction of meaning around the topic and the sharing of that meaning— Info Out.

The question now becomes, Is the Open Mind an activity or a performance task? Well, it depends on the purpose we have for assigning it. Like all of the activities described above, it can be used as a performance task— if it is employed as an assessment of student ability. An activity is simply an assignment in class, or for homework, that is used to help students learn key content or skills. We like to think of activities as practices. Tasks, on the other hand, are more like show time— the time to perform at a high level—and are judged accordingly, usually with an accompanying rubric.

So in this case, the Open Mind—or the alternative Venn diagrams, T-sheets, and SnapShots—serve to facilitate Info In through note-taking practice, while simultaneously revealing the level of student understanding of the video. They serve a dual purpose: support Info In *and* reveal Info Out. It is up to the teacher to decide which is more important, or if both are important, then how to score them as assessments.

But to qualify as a performance task, they must meet the five characteristics we listed in Chapter 1:

- Students have some choice in selecting or creating the task.
- The task requires both the elaboration of core knowledge and the use of key processes.
- The task has an explicit scoring system.
- The task is designed for an audience larger than the teacher; others outside the classroom would find value in the work.
- The task is carefully crafted to measure what it purports to measure.

The Open Mind does not meet characteristics 1 (some student choice), 3 (has accompanying scoring device), and 4 (for a larger audience), so it falls short of a performance task. But because it becomes far more than a routine assignment by meeting criteria 2 and 5, we choose to call it a *performance assessment,* or for short, a *mini performance.* (See below.)

It all comes down to how much data the teacher needs to collect from the Open Minds:

- If we have students keep them as note-taking devices, they serve as assignments.
- If we look them over quickly and check them off, they serve as assignments.

- If we award credit to them with points, they serve as assignments.
- If we score them with a rubric, they serve as performance assessments, or a mini performance.

So Tom, our 6th grade teacher, opted to use Open Minds as a note-taking assignment, and he merely looked them over to get a general sense of how the class as a whole took in the video. Of course, later in the unit (after plenty of practice), he could reassign the Open Mind for a different video viewing and use it to assess the content acquisition that they acquired from the video clip. To elevate it to a performance task, two things would have to occur: his students would need to be notified that the purpose now is to measure their ability, not just to practice, and he would have to redesign the task to meet the five characteristics above.

Mini, Midi, and Maxi Performance Tasks

Mini Performance Assessments

Mini assessments, like the Open Mind above, are performance *assessments.* They don't qualify as maxi or midi performance *tasks* but are effective mini assessment tools. They help learners acquire important content information, move students closer and closer to the targeted outcomes, and simultaneously provide their teachers with important feedback on that learning. And they are quick: mini tasks are designed to take a single class period or less. They have become a cornerstone of our instruction because we know that short, quick, ongoing assessment strongly informs our instruction.

Midi Performance Tasks

Midis do incorporate all five of the key characteristics of performance tasks, as do the maxi tasks. The difference is in the amount of time they require for students to complete them. Generally speaking, midi tasks take up to two to three periods to perform, while maxis require more than three classes.

Examples of midi tasks are

• Writing a postcard to an author expressing an opinion about the assigned reading, with specific examples as support, and repairing the postcard to get it to a high level worthy of the author.

• Drawing a SnapShots photo album to help track a reading assignment by employing visualization. This one is an all-time favorite of teachers, so we will zoom in on it in a moment.

Maxi Performance Tasks

Maxi tasks, finally, require more than three class periods (or part of each period) to complete, and they are considered the substantive culminating projects that typically come at the end of a unit of study.

Examples of maxi performance tasks are

• Drawing an 8- to 10-panel comic strip, editing it for accuracy and sequence, and coloring it.

• Selecting and acting out a scene, complete with rehearsal, props, and performance.

• Writing a historical fiction short story set in the historical period being studied, including real historical figures and events as well as realistic, believable, fictional ones.

• Creating a scrapbook of findings in a science unit on germ transmission titled "Becoming Disease Detectives" (described later in this chapter).

First Dare Reading with SnapShots

As mentioned earlier, not only did Tom's class view a video folk tale, they also read one in their textbooks. To facilitate their first reads (First Dares), Tom opted to provide them with a during-reading activity that uses drawing and captioning called SnapShots, a midi task that took two class periods for students to draw a quick representation of what they were seeing—in this case, in their "mind's eye"—as they read. While the tale did include some pictures of scenes to accompany the text, the students were responsible for visualizing all the scenes and actions by translating the author's words into mental images. The ability to do this greatly supports comprehension, and clearly some students can already do this. (See Figure 2.3.)

Of course, not every word or sentence in the tale warrants a SnapShot, nor does every paragraph. The challenge in this midi task is to determine which scenes deserve to be illustrated. In other words, the 6th graders needed to apply the key strategies of focusing (used to selectively attend to significant information), information gathering (used to acquire needed new information), self-regulating (used to monitor one's own construction of meaning), generating (used to produce new information, meanings, or ideas), and organizing (used to track data, construct meaning, and enhance retention). (See Figure 2.2.) Lots going on here, which makes this midi task so useful.

Now, as popular as this SnapShot midi task is at all grade levels, some students may initially reject it due to fear of drawing. Not to worry, though, because in Chapter 3 we have some ideas for you on how to reassure non-artists that representing visualizations is not an art project.

| Figure 2.3 | **Fairy Tale SnapShots** |

Wait a Minute... What About Prepare?

Before Tom launched his class into First Dare reading with the SnapShots task, he needed to help them get ready to read, right?

To prepare his students for Info In with reading, Tom guided them in a "flip through" of the folk tale's pages to practice good getting-ready-to-read strategies. First, they found the story in their books and read the title and looked at the picture on the page. They speculated on what the story might be about. They read the opening sentence, which began with "Once upon a time"—a dead giveaway that it was a fairy tale. Next, Tom instructed them to flip through the story to see what they noticed about the way the text was laid out (the text features). Responses included the recognition of footnotes at the bottom of some pages, the names of the key characters, the total length, a two-column layout, more illustrations, and some author information at the end. Tom discussed these findings with the class, showing students how these features might help them as they read to boost their interest in and confidence with reading the story independently. Additionally, he introduced them to a few key vocabulary words that he expected to be troublesome even with the footnote definitions, and they reviewed the genre by answering his question "What do we know about fairy tales?" All this preparation took about 15 minutes, time that was not spent actually reading but in preparing for reading. It's money in the bank. Now the students were ready to read the folk tale and take some SnapShots.

Assessing Student SnapShots

The SnapShots activity is designed not only to facilitate student reading comprehension but also to assess that comprehension.

Tom and I elevated it from an activity into a performance task by providing his students with a task summary and a scoring device.

Here is the Task Summary for SnapShots: On sticky notes, take mental snapshots (quick sketches) of what you are seeing in your mind's eye as you read the story. You cannot take SnapShots of every word, sentence, or even paragraph. Instead, you must decide how many to take by deciding which character's actions and thoughts, which setting(s), and which problems facing the characters are the *most important* to the story— and don't forget the ending! Additionally, your SnapShots should go beyond these basic story elements and include the more advanced connections you see between this story and another story you read, or even a movie, TV show, or personal experience. And you should include a SnapShot of what you see as the author's message (the theme). We will send your SnapShots to the author (or the illustrator).

Tom used a Holistic ChecBric (see Figure 2.4) instead of a traditional rubric. A ChecBric combines a checklist (for the students) with a rubric (for the teacher). We prefer the two-columned ChecBric to a rubric for several important reasons, which we look forward to sharing with you in detail in the next chapter. Meanwhile, take a look at this one, and see if you can predict why we like it better than a rubric.

Sharing student understandings is what this book is about. In fact, the chapters that follow deal with alternative modes for the Share stage. Chapter 3 is Assessing Students' Understanding with Visual Representations; Chapter 4 is Assessing Students' Understanding Using the Written Mode; Chapter 5 is Assessing Students'

Figure 2.4	**SnapShots Holistic ChecBric**
Student Checklist	**Teacher Rubric**

Student Checklist

1. On my own, I could not find the story basics or the more complicated story ideas, but **with help**

____ I identified the story's characters.
____ I identified the story's setting.
____ I identified the story's problem.
____ I identified the story's ending.

2. On my own, I was not able to find the more complicated story ideas, but I could find the **story basics**:

____ I identified the story's characters.
____ I identified the story's setting.
____ I identified the story's problem.
____ I identified the story's ending.

3. On my own, I could find both the story basics, **plus** the more complicated story ideas:

____ I identified the story's characters, setting, problem, and the ending.

PLUS

____ I made connections in the story that were not directly stated by characters or the narrator.
____ I figured out the author's message.

4. On my own, I could do all of 3, plus I was able **to go beyond** what was taught because

____ I made connections from events in the story to events outside of the story, like other stories, movies, or personal experiences.
____ I figured out how the author's life may have affected the writing of the story.
____ I commented on the author's style of writing, the author's strengths and weaknesses.

Teacher Rubric

Score 1: With help, the student demonstrates a partial understanding of **some of the simpler**, basic story components and **some of the more complex**, complicated elements.

Score 2: Student **independently** makes no major errors or omissions regarding the simpler, basic story components.

Score 3: Student **independently** identifies the **basic** and the more **complicated** story elements that were explicitly taught with no major errors or omissions.

Score 4: In addition to a 3 performance, student **independently exceeds** what was taught by adding additional information, ideas, or commentary.

Source: from Based on Scoring Scale, *Classroom Assessment and Grading That Work*, by R. Mazano, 2006, Alexandria, VA: ASCD. ChecBric ©2007 Larry Lewin Educ. Consulting, larry@larrylewin.com.

Understanding Through Oral Presentations; and Chapter 6 is Assessing Students' Understanding Through Large-Scale Projects or Performances. In these chapters, we will share numerous mini, midi, and maxi performance assessments for use before, during, and at the end of a course of study.

But first, we want to walk you through another example of a teacher Info Inning her students—this time, an elementary teacher using the hands-on learning process to teach 3rd graders about germs.

The Manipulating Process: From Betty's Primary Grade Perspective

Next let's explore how to use the generic process approach—Prepare, First Dare, Repair, and Share—to teach young students to take in information through hands-on manipulation activities. As an example, I (Betty) will show you how I taught primary students to conduct a simple scientific investigation.

The formal scientific process, we should note, is the "granddaddy" of process approaches. From this centuries-old scientific method come other process approaches, including our generic four-step approach. Figure 2.5 shows this relationship.

What we are saying is that you really can teach the process approach—whether it is scientific investigation, writing, reading, viewing, presenting orally, or problem solving—using Prepare, First Dare, Repair, and Share. But can it be done successfully with 1st and 2nd graders?

Our district's content standards for health include the following:

• Knows essential concepts about the prevention and control of communicable and noncommunicable diseases.
• Demonstrates ways to avoid unsafe situations and practice healthy behaviors.
• Demonstrates self-management and advocacy skills while understanding the relationships among health behavior and prevention of disease.

Figure 2.5	**Comparing Prepare, First Dare, Repair, and Share with Other Process Approaches**	
Our Four-Step Process Approach	**The Formal Scientific Method**	**The Writing Process**
1. Prepare: Get ready to process new information.	1. State the problem and form a hypothesis.	1. Prewriting
2. First Dare: Try out something and begin to make sense of it.	2. Observe and experiment.	2. Drafting
3. Repair: Return to the information; improve on your initial understanding.	3. Interpret data. Identify variables. Reexperiment.	3. Revising and editing
4. Share: Share what you have learned.	4. Draw and state conclusions.	4. Publishing a final draft

Grade 3 has these benchmark expectations:

• Knows signs and symptoms of common diseases and how to prevent them.

• Knows ways to prevent or reduce the risk of disease.

• Knows and practices good self-care.

Because of my interest in teaching young students the formal scientific method in such a way as to involve them in a hands-on activity, I developed a unit titled "How to Catch a Cold."

Prepare: Becoming Disease Detectives

At the time, a number of my students had been out with colds and flu. Several were just returning after missing several days. "What is causing this cold and flu epidemic?" I asked the class on the first day of the unit.

Nearly in unison, students proclaimed, "Germs!"

I responded, "What are germs? Where can we find germs? How can we find them? I can't see any around here. How do we know germs are around us?"

Looking puzzled, several students attempted to explain: "You can't see them. They are too tiny to be seen. But they are here." After a few minutes of probing, one student volunteered that a doctor had used a swab to scrape germs out of the back of his mouth and then rubbed the swab into a little plastic dish. He didn't know any more about the process, but he knew that doctors did those kinds of things.

I then took the class to the boys' and girls' restrooms and asked them to read the prominently displayed signs by the sinks: "Hand washing prevents infection." I asked, "Is this true? Does hand washing prevent infection? What does hand washing have to

do with germs? Can we prove that this statement is true?"

Back in class, I introduced students to the formal scientific method through an activity I called "Let's Investigate: Disease Detectives." I walked them through the following directions:

In the next week, we will all become special scientists called epidemiologists—scientists who study diseases, especially contagious ones that affect communities. Epidemiologists use the scientific method to uncover the causes of infectious diseases, and they teach people in a community how to prevent the spread of germs that cause diseases like strep throat and flu. How do epidemiologists approach their work? They use the process approach!

Next, I explained the steps:

1. They Prepare: Epidemiologists identify a problem. They ask questions. They think about what they already know about the topic. They come up with a possible explanation.

2. They First Dare: Epidemiologists set up experiments and observe what happens.

3. They Repair: Epidemiologists study the data (the information they obtain from the experiment). Then they rerun the experiment to make sure they have considered all of the important factors that might affect their results.

4. They Share: Epidemiologists pull together their research and share what they have learned with others, usually by writing a paper about their work.

Before I taught this unit, the district's Assessment Task Force (Eugene Public School District 4J, 1995) developed a list of Prepare, First Dare, Repair, and Share strategies that scientists would likely use to conduct a scientific investigation. After setting up the simulation using the above process, I gave each student a copy of the following menu of strategies to improve their use of the scientific investigation process:

1. Prepare: How well do I get ready to do a scientific investigation?
    a. I know why I am doing this experiment and what I want to find out.
    b. I think about everything I already know about this topic.
    c. I gather the equipment and materials I need to do the experiment.
    d. I get help from others if needed.
    e. I make a hypothesis and set up an experiment to test it.

2. First Dare: How well do I handle the beginning work on a scientific investigation?
    a. I conduct an experiment.
    b. I observe and record what happens.
    c. I see if my experiment proves or disproves my hypothesis.

3. Repair: How well do I use revising strategies to improve my scientific investigation?
    a. I make a new hypothesis if appropriate.
    b. I redo the experiment.
    c. I record the results.
    d. I check for any mistakes.

4. Share: How well do I share the results of my scientific investigation?
    a. I present my results to others.
    b. I listen to comments.
    c. I compare my findings with those of others who did the same experiment.
    d. I think about another experiment I might do.

When I first developed this unit, there were no requirements from the Oregon Department of Education (ODE) for producing and scoring science or health work samples.

However, starting in the fall of 2009, the Oregon Department of Education requires the collection of work samples in science and has developed near final drafts of its scientific inquiry scoring guides (rubrics). I'm sure this is true in many other states as well. And I know that teachers must work from a standards-based system for two reasons. One, it helps us focus on common critical elements in producing and scoring tasks, and two, we have no choice—accountability is here to stay. So I encourage teachers to begin incorporating language from the Scientific Inquiry Scoring Guide for grade 3 into their discussions with students.

The dimensions of the Scientific Inquiry Scoring Guide for teachers in the State of Oregon include

*   forming a question or hypothesis,
*   designing an investigation,
*   collecting and presenting data, and
*   analyzing and interpreting results.

See how nicely our process approach (Prepare, First Dare, Repair, and Share) matches these dimensions? I paired Prepare with "form a question or hypothesis"; First Dare with "design an investigation"; and so forth. Remember, these students were in 1st and 2nd grade. I didn't need to follow the official grade 3 scoring guide yet, but I wanted students to become familiar with the language on the scoring guide.

In addition, for those of us in Oregon, the criteria that make up each dimension are anchored with three different threads that describe important organizing components of scientific inquiry. The threads include

*   application of scientific knowledge— the importance of connecting inquiry to scientific concepts and principles found in the examination of scientific phenomena;

- nature of scientific inquiry—the need for the development of evidence-based explanations by students as they engage in answering questions about those scientific phenomena; and
- communication—the importance of developing students' abilities to communicate clearly about results and explanations, especially in light of alternative explanations that might be generated.

To help teachers understand how this might look with students, the Oregon Department of Education shares a chart comparing the relationship of the above threads to the dimensions in the 2005–2007 Scientific Inquiry Scoring Guide. It keeps the focus, benchmark by benchmark, on the big picture of what we are after here. (See Figure A.2 in the Appendix.)

As the teacher, I would keep these dimensions and threads in mind as I talked to students and modeled the process with the class. See the entire set of scoring guides for benchmarks 1 (grade 3), 2 (grade 5), 3 (grade 8), and high school (grade 10) at www.ode. state.or.us/search/page/?=1414.

To continue to prepare for our study, the class discussed what we thought we knew about germs. Following our discussion, each student constructed a scrapbook in which to record his or her thoughts, using a combination of pictures and labels. Scrapbooks are one more technique for tapping prior knowledge, like the Folded File Folder for older students described earlier in this chapter.

You can introduce the use of a scrapbook by sharing a photo album of a personal trip. Remind students that one constructs a scrapbook before, during, or after a trip as a way to remember special experiences from the journey. In this case, ask students to begin constructing a scrapbook of what they think they know about germs—anything that comes to mind. Throughout the unit they will add new learnings based on their experiences.

Info In via the Listening Mode

On day two, to further prepare for our scientific investigation, we invited a local health care professional to the classroom to discuss bacteria and viruses and how they are spread. She walked students through the process of taking a throat culture, explaining what doctors use as a medium in which to grow bacteria. She pointed out that viruses, bacteria, and fungi can be grown in petri dishes.

On day three, I set up stations in the classroom staffed by high school science and visual art students from our nearby high school. I worked with students at Station Four. The groups and their focus of study included

- Station One: What can we learn about germs (microorganisms)?
- Station Two: How can we use a microscope to view bacteria and fungi?
- Station Three: How can we keep track of our data through observational drawings?
- Station Four: How do we ask questions and form hypotheses?
- Station Five: How can we keep track of our data with charts and graphs?

Students rotated from station to station during one afternoon. They spent about 25 minutes at each station and participated in hands-on activities at each.

The following day, as we continued to prepare to move into the First Dare stage, I gave the class a list of questions generated at Station Four. We agreed as a class to pursue the question "Does hand washing prevent infection?" Question asking is an excellent prepare-to-learn strategy. We developed the following hypothesis: Washing your hands will remove most of the germs from your hands. If this is true, then fewer germs will grow in the petri dishes of students who have washed their hands.

We also completed another manipulative activity—one that I borrowed from my friend and colleague Barbara Shirk. I devised a way to use it to involve students in learning key content using a hands-on approach. Students constructed an origami "fortune teller," a folded paper toy. They then recorded basic information on each flap (the importance of hand washing, how germs are transmitted, etc.). My students then taught other students at school the basics of hand washing.

First Dare: Is Our Hypothesis True?

We used the same method that medical personnel use to grow germs from throat cultures. A local medical laboratory donated 60 prepared petri dishes for our project. I didn't mind the heartburn from gobbling my lunch in the car as I sped over to pick them up.

On day four, we started the experiment after morning recess. We formed four experimental groups:

- Group One: One-third of the class who did not wash their hands.
- Group Two: One-third of the class who washed their hands with cold water and no soap.
- Group Three: One-third of the class who washed their hands with hot water and antibacterial soap.
- Group Four: Eight teachers whom we selected at random who did not know about our hypothesis (to prevent extra hand washing).

Each student labeled the top of one petri dish with his or her name and with "washed—hot and soap," "washed—cold, no soap," or

"not washed." Everyone was careful not to lift the lids. After washers washed their hands, all groups carefully lifted their lids and tapped the balls of the fingers of one hand onto the nutrient agar prepoured in the bottom of the dishes. Lids were closed, taped shut, and placed on the counter by the sink. A few students then went around to other classrooms and asked certain teachers to touch one hand in the petri dish. They labeled these dishes "Teacher A," "Teacher B," and so forth. They asked those teachers how recently they had washed their hands with soap and water. The students recorded these times on the lids of the dishes as well.

Back in the classroom, students finished their first observational drawings of the experiment. Each student completed a drawing of his or her own dish plus one dish from another group for their scrapbooks. This important recording of "information coming in" mirrors the suggested use of Venn diagramming while viewing a video in the middle grade language arts class.

Right before the end of the school day, students completed another observational drawing of the same dishes. At the same time on each following day, they drew observations of the same dishes. I encouraged my students to write any comments they deemed appropriate.

Share: The Results

Wait! What happened to Repair? I deliberately skipped it this time and went straight to Share. Just remember that the generic template (Prepare, First Dare, Repair, and Share) is recursive: you can move easily forward and backward as needed, in and out of stages. The better you get at the process, the more easily and efficiently you will move through the stages.

And sometimes, depending on your proficiency, you can skip a stage altogether. For example, if I tried to fix plumbing by myself, believe me, I would labor through each stage of the process due to my lack of plumbing problem-solving experience. A plumber, however, could move much more efficiently from stage to stage—maybe even skipping or abbreviating a stage!

So, in the afternoon of day three, we all gathered around the petri dishes and observed various colonies of bacteria and fungi. We listed our findings on chart paper. As you can predict, the hand washers' dishes were clearer than those of nonwashers. Students chose from the listed phrases on the chart paper to craft their own conclusions, which they recorded and placed in their scrapbooks. I instructed them to start with

- Our hypothesis was . . .
- This experiment proved our hypothesis to be true/untrue for these reasons . . .
- I continue to have questions about . . .

Back to Repair: Reruns

The cultures in some dishes, however, seemed to support a different conclusion. Bacteria were growing in dishes where hand washing had occurred—not to the extent of the nonwashers', but enough to make one wonder. I took this opportunity to introduce the notion of Repair.

I suggested that there must have been something else going on in those dishes. We hypothesized what that might be. I added to the student variable list and instructed students to partner with a classmate to redo the experiment (Repair), controlling for one of the following variables:

- Hands with long fingernails and hands with short fingernails.
- Hands washed in cold water and hands washed in hot water.
- Hands washed for 30 seconds and hands washed for two minutes.
- Hands on which someone had recently coughed and hands that had been in one's mouth.
- Hands recently run through hair or hands rubbed over clothing.
- Petri dishes stored in a dark, moist place and those stored in a dry, bright place.

You may be able to think of other variables you would like to add to this list. My directions are shown in Figure 2.6.

Share: Working with Each Team

Each team was expected to bring its scrapbook to an interview with me. Of course, I also used other Info Out options (for example, graphic representations, observational drawings) and written descriptions. I chose to add the oral option, interviewing, because of its developmental appropriateness for 1st and 2nd graders.

For each interview, I used Piaget's clinical interview format (Ginsburg & Opper, 1988) to review the work of the team. I asked the following questions:

- What variables did you decide to study?
- What was your hypothesis?
- How did you conduct your experiment?
- What were your results?
- Did anyone else in the class study the same variables, and were their results similar?
- What questions do you still have?
- What gives you confidence that your work is accurate?

Figure 2.6	**Follow-up Hand Washing Experiment: Controlling for Variables**

Partner Names _____ and _____

Follow this process, step-by-step. Keep this form in your scrapbook. Put your initials in the box on the left when you have completed each step of the scientific investigation process.

Initial Here:	Step	Do This:
	Prepare	1. Write both of your names on the outside of a manila folder. This is your team scrapbook.
		2. Pick a variable that you intend to experiment with. Write it on the front cover of your album.
		3. What do you think you will find after running your experiment? Develop a hypothesis, and record it on the front cover of your album.
		4. Gather your materials. You will need two petri dishes.
		5. Label the dishes.
		6. Review the scoring guide. That is how your work will be scored.
	First Dare	1. Begin your experiment. Complete a drawing of your work and date the drawing worksheet.
		2. Complete another observational drawing right before you go home today. Put both drawings in your scrapbook.
	Repair	1. Check to see if anything unusual is happening.
		2. Complete another observational drawing.
	Share	1. Complete your last observational drawing.
		2. Complete the worksheet titled "Sharing Our Results."
		3. Be prepared to share your results with the class.

As I talked with students, I evaluated their work using the simplified Scientific Investigation Scoring Guide in Figure A.3.

Of course, my description has been a "bullet train" journey through the How to Catch a Cold unit. We did a number of other Info In activities to develop concepts and teach the use of key scientific investigation strategies. Because of the developmental level of students, we did not go into all of the variables that could influence what appears in the petri dishes. Instead, we narrowed our focus to those that students at this level would understand.

As a culmination to the Share stage, the class generated a list of key factors that contributed to or inhibited the spread of bacteria and viruses. From that list, each student created his or her own humorous pop-up book illustrating how these factors contribute to catching a cold. Students were highly motivated by this Info Out activity and by being able to share their content expertise with others.

Next time I'm going to have students work individually and then as a group to create several news articles for a class newspaper on this project. (See Chapter 4.)

I should also note that for each key process we teach, we have generated a menu of strategies just like the ones listed for the scientific investigation process. We teach these strategies explicitly to students. Having a large repertoire of strategies to use at any given stage in a process makes for good readers, writers, and scientific problem solvers!

How to Catch a Cold is our example of teaching the hands-on manipulating mode of Info In using scientific investigation and the Prepare, First Dare, Repair, and Share process in which students literally had a hands-on experience!

A Snapshot of Chapter 2

In this chapter, we

• introduced you to Info In, the use of key learning processes of reading, viewing, listening, and manipulating to acquire content knowledge;

• shared our generic template—Prepare, First Dare, Repair, and Share—for teaching the process approach to students of all ages;

• discussed the difference between mini, midi, and maxi tasks; and

• gave you two unit examples, one at the middle school level and one at the primary level.

As we have explained, the fourth stage of our four-step process approach is Share. As teachers, we may teach our students four different modes of sharing to reveal what they've learned: creating graphic representations, writing, speaking, and constructing models and performances. In the following four chapters, we will go into each of these different modes in great detail.

chapter 3

Info Out: Assessing Students' Understanding with Visual Representations

Larry's Story

An 8th grade language arts/U.S. history class was shocked to learn that Christopher Columbus's flagship, the *Santa María,* cracked open its hull and started to sink off the coast of the Caribbean island Bohio (Hispaniola, in Spanish). The students acquired this little-known historical fact by reading their history textbook's account of the events in 1492 (see Figure 3.1), which provided a cause (hit a coral reef) and the result (salvaged timbers from the ship were used to build the first Spanish settlement in the Americas).

I was determined to find out to what extent each student comprehended this important content information, so I gave them a five-question quiz asking about the cause of the accident, the setting, the key players, the sequence of events, and the results. This method, the quiz, is called a selected-response assessment option because I chose the questions to which I wanted my class to respond. As introduced in Chapter 1, short

quizzes, chapter tests, true/false tests, and fill-in-the-blank tests are all forms of selected-response assessments. They are useful for assessing students' understanding of what has been taught—for literal-level recall of information, that is.

Unbeknownst to me, in the classroom next door, my colleague, Dorothy Syfert, decided to assess her students' understanding of this same historical reading, but she elected to use a different method: she asked her class to create a historical comic strip. Guess which assessment method was more popular, engaging, and enticing.

Visual Representations

The comic strip task is an example of performance assessment in the mode of visual representations. In this chapter, we will describe a number of visual/graphic classroom performance tasks that help learners reveal their understanding of content information—that is,

| Figure 3.1 | **Christmas Day, 1492** |

An Arawak chief approaches the Spanish fort to visit Columbus at the settlement of La Navidad.

Shortly before midnight on December 25, 1492, the *Santa María* ran aground on the northern coast of Hispaniola. Christopher Columbus saw his flagship perched on a coral reef and concluded, "I saw no chance of saving my own ship. . . ."

Columbus had been on his way to meet with an American chief who claimed to know a land where there was much gold. According to Columbus's records, when the chief heard of the disaster, "He wept and at once sent his people with many canoes to the ship. So we all began to unload together. . . . He saw to it that all our goods were located near the palace . . . [and] he set two armed men to guard these both day and night."

Columbus came to believe it was God's will that he lost the *Santa María* at that exact time and place. He also took it as a sign that he should found a colony there. So he chose thirty men, many of them volunteers, to build a settlement known as La Navidad—the Village of the Nativity.

Columbus left the settlers enough supplies to last for a year. He also gave them "seed for sowing, and the ship's boat, and a caulker, a carpenter, a gunner, and a cooper." Then Columbus began his journey back to Spain on January 4, 1493, aboard the *Niña*.

When Columbus returned to Hispaniola in the fall of the same year, he found La Navidad in ashes. The first Spanish settlement in the New World had ended in failure.

For Critical Thinking

1. What events led to the founding of La Navidad? Explain the significance of its name. What does starting and naming La Navidad suggest about the personality of Columbus?

2. Use a dictionary to find out what caulkers and coopers did. What important skills would they contribute toward starting a colony?

3. Scientists try to explain a given set of facts. Each explanation is called a *hypothesis* What factors could explain the failure of La Navidad? Can your explanation, or hypothesis, be proven right or wrong? Why or why not?

4. Use the map on page 54 to locate where the *Santa María* ran aground. Through research, find out what happened to the *Santa María*, the *Niña*, and the *Pinta*.

5. Provide several examples to show that knowledge of the past can be helpful in approaching situations today.

Source: From "Christmas Day, 1492," in *A Proud Nation* (p. 38), by E.R. May, 1984, Evanston, IL: McDougal, Littell, and Company. Reprinted here with permission of the publisher. © 1984 McDougal, Littell, and Company.

to Info Out (see Chapter 2). Graphic representations are primarily visual but may include some written text. They come in many forms, including the following

• Comic strips or other series of illustrations (e.g., storyboards, SnapShots)

• Graphic organizers (webs, clusters, maps)

- Large illustrations/displays with back-up text (posters, advertisements)
- Electronic presentations (slide shows, digital movies)

We're going to introduce four visual representation performance tasks. We will explain why we selected them, how we developed them, and how we scored them.

Performance Task: The Historical Comic Strip

The first of the four visual performance tasks we'll look at is the historical comic strip. This crowd-pleaser is an example of Stiggins's (1997) third assessment option, the performance task, because Dorothy expected her students to take learned content information and apply it in a meaningful task. That is, the comic strip task required her learners to apply their knowledge and construct a personal response rather than merely regurgitate knowledge. In short, they had to *perform*— allowing both the teacher and her students to see how well they understood the events of this important historical period. The comics served as an assessment that occurred in the middle of instruction, rather than at the end of the unit.

This is formative assessment, which James Popham defines as "a planned process in which teachers or students use assessment-based evidence to adjust what they are currently doing" (2008, p. 6). This serves a different purpose than summative assessment, which "sums up" a student's work at the completion of a unit, term, or course.

Naturally, I stole Dorothy's comic strip idea to use with my class later in the year during our study of the Civil War. My students loved it too, even though it turned out to be more demanding than a test.

As much as this First Dare activity caused delight among the students, three serious design flaws emerged. First, the original directions called for five to six panels. (Note the content requirements at the top of Figure 3.2.) While this specification seemed reasonable at first, for some students, five to six panels was not sufficient space to reveal their comprehension of all the key events. This is not an atypical finding: many tasks reveal their design flaws when teachers examine actual student responses to the task.

Second, even though the task presented clear parameters to the students in the content requirements, many students did not realize that their comics would eventually be measured against these features. The scoring criteria were not explicit enough for all students to clearly understand how their comics would be evaluated. Again, this flaw is common to early task design.

Third, the extra credit component of the Share stage (stated at the bottom of the performance task sheet in Figure 3.2) made a huge difference in the performance of those students who opted for it. The decision to add extra panels and color highlights generally produced superior products. It ended up modifying the task for those students who opted for extra credit and, therefore, affected its validity—a common oversight.

Designing performance tasks for classroom assessment is a challenging process. Teachers typically find out that a great idea, like the comic strip task, will need "repairing."

Building a Better Task: Improving the Historical Comic Strip

Live and learn. Even with its flaws, the comic strip visual representation performance

Figure 3.2	**A Performance Task: 1492 Encounter "La Navidad"**

Use with History Textbook: *A Proud Nation*, page 38.[1]
Designed by Dorothy Syfert, Monroe Middle School, Eugene, Oregon

Your Task: Create a 5- to 6-panel comic strip revealing your understanding of a key event during this historical era: the shipwreck of the *Santa María*, the causes, effects, and reactions.

Content Requirements **that must be included:**

_____ 5–6 panels

_____ At least 5 characters

                _____ your Taino Indian character

                _____ a family member

                _____ at least one other native

                _____ your sailor character

                _____ at least one other sailor

_____ Character names must be identified somewhere in the comic strip

_____ Story line boxes

_____ Talking bubbles

_____ At least 1 thinking bubble

_____ The major events shown on page 38 of *A Proud Nation*.

Process Requirements **that must be included:**

Prepare Stage

• Look through the comic strip examples provided by the teacher.
• Read page 38 in *A Proud Nation*.
• Decide on the characters to include.
• On the back of this sheet, write out a rough "outline" for your story. (Optional.)

First Dare Stage

• On a sheet of notebook paper, roughly sketch out what should go in each of your comic strip panels. Include words that will be written. (DO NOT SPEND A LONG TIME ON THIS PART.)
• Staple your rough sketch to this paper.

Repair Stage

• Go over the requirements to be sure you have included everything. Be sure you can check off each item.
• Check over spelling and mechanics.

Share Stage

• Get a large sheet of plain white paper and make your final comic strip.
• When you have finished, be sure to check for any silly errors.

Extra: Additional panels and/or color added to your comic strip. Display your comic strip on the bulletin board.

[1]Focus page, Christmas Day, 1492 (1984), in *A proud nation* (p. 38) (Evanston, IL: McDougal, Littell, and Company).

task had great potential to motivate student interest and effort, as well as to reliably assess student reading comprehension. We had to polish it to ensure that it became a true performance task and not just a great activity.

Performance tasks differ from activities in two critical ways:

1. Tasks must clearly assess the targets being measured; that is, they must be valid.

2. Tasks must have clear scoring criteria, so that teachers can fairly, objectively, and, most important, consistently evaluate them; that is, tasks must have reliability.

After examining student samples of the original comic strip activity, we redesigned it to become a tighter performance task (see Figure 3.3).

Our feelings were not hurt; we understood the developmental nature of performance tasks. Tasks need to be fine-tuned, adjusted, "repaired" in order to tighten them up to reach the standards of reliability and validity. Performance tasks must have higher standards than activities because the stakes are higher: when tasks are used to measure student understanding and achievement, they must be fair and accurate indicators.

The historical comic strip now met our criteria listed in Chapter 2 in that it

1. *Involved some degree of student choice.* In the revised version, our students could determine the number of panels, the sequence of the panels, the amount of text versus graphics, and which historical figures and actions to portray. One student actually added his own choice; he decided to create his comic on the computer to mitigate his perceived lack of drawing ability. (See Figure 3.8.)

2. *Required both the elaboration of core knowledge content and the use of key processes.* The comic strip task required students to elaborate on what they had learned from reading the textbook (content) and to use both reading comprehension and project construction (processes).

3. *Included an explicit scoring system shared with learners in advance.* Students received a task sheet, a self-repair checklist, and the new hybrid scoring device that combines a checklist with a rubric (the ChecBric; see Figure 3.9) in advance. This example follows shortly.

4. *Offered an audience for the performance that is larger than the traditional audience (their teacher).* Not that their dear teacher is unimportant, but these 8th grade students were asked to communicate to 5th grade history students what happened to the *Santa María* in a more engaging and memorable manner than a 5th grade textbook.

5. *Was carefully crafted to measure what it purports to measure.* The task now more clearly assesses readers' comprehension of content information.

The revised comic strip task eliminated the earlier flaws. And with the improvements came the realization that in order for the students to perform well—that is, to reveal their understanding of the content at a high level of sophistication—they needed more time. So we expanded this from a mini task of one class period plus homework to a midi task of three class periods as follows:

Day 1: Students read the task directions, the assigned textbook section, and the ChecBric; and started preliminary sketches on 4" × 5" paper panels. (Working with individual panels made later revisions less punishing than working on one large sheet of paper. Before, students who felt as if they had made a mistake had to throw the whole thing out and start again, and again, and again!)

Day 2: Students continued panel production, completed a "Student Self-Scoring

Figure 3.3	**A Performance Task: 1864 Historical Comic Strip**

Your **task** is to create a historical comic strip about "A Fiery Plot," page 434 of your supplemental textbook.

Audience and Purpose: The purpose of this comic strip is to explain to younger students, 5th graders, what happened in this little-known historical event. Your job is to teach this event in a more interesting way than the textbook did, so that 5th graders will be inclined to understand it and to remember it.

Your comic strip should do the following:

1. Reveal your **understanding** of the event.

- Who was involved?
- What did they do?
- When did this event occur?
- Where did this event occur?
- Why did they do it? What were their motivations?
- How did it affect people?

2. Show the event in a clear and accurate **sequence.**

You may have as many panels in your comic strip as you want, but the panels should show the events in the correct order so that 5th graders won't get confused about what actually happened.

3. **Authentically** show what life was like during the Civil War era.

The characters' language and appearance and the scenery should all be realistic for the 1860s.

4. **Look like** an actual comic strip.

Don't worry: Your drawing ability is NOT important in this task. This is a history class, not an art class, so what is important is how well you understood the event "A Fiery Plot," not how well you can draw.

Stick figures are OKAY. However, you should use cartoonists' devices to show what you know about the event:

- To show dialogue, use a speech bubble.

- To show thoughts, use a thought bubble.
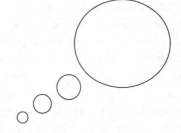

Figure 3.3	**A Performance Task: 1864 Historical Comic Strip** (*continued*)

- To show the narrator's words use a storyline box somewhere inside this panel

- To show character's reactions, use simple facial expressions

Checklist," and reread (Repaired) the text as needed to improve their comprehension.

Day 3: Students reviewed the ChecBric; placed panels in the desired sequence; colored the panels; glued them onto a large sheet of 17" × 24" paper; added name, date, and class period; and affixed their self-scoring checklist and the ChecBric to the back of the completed comic strip.

We were encouraged by the results. Students performed at a higher level than with our first attempt. While not yet rigorous enough to be an airtight assessment tool for large-scale assessments, this revised comic strip task is now a fair and accurate device for classroom-based reading comprehension assessment. We feel confident that using it in our classrooms provides a clear and accurate indicator of each student's reading comprehension of nonfiction texts.

Our Procedure for Building Better Performance Tasks

You are probably wondering if we had a process in mind when we developed this comic strip task. When we first started developing tasks, we flew by the seat of our pants. As we got better at it, we formulated a step-by-step process for building better performance tasks that we sure could have used from the beginning. Our steps now include the following:

1. Be clear about your targets. Pinpoint the skills and knowledge students must demonstrate and the standards that they will be expected to meet. (Use district or state documents to assist you.)

2. Create and describe a context for the task that will make it more meaningful and engaging. Be creative about the audience and purpose.

Figure 3.4	**Comic Strips**

Comic Strips

1. Build your page...
✓ You need a title,
✓ Your name must be easy to locate,
✓ You will need _____ squares.

2. Insert your dialogue...
✓ Print all dialogue! Neatness counts.
✓ There are three main ways to identify a speaker...
➲ **Narrator:** Storyline box above or below illustration,
➲ **Dialogue:** Words spoken out loud,
➲ **Thoughts:** Words thought but not spoken.

Use a callout to show what's being said out loud. You can use different shapes to show emotions. Just look at all the possibilities!

This is a narrator's box. No character says or thinks these words.

Use bubbles when the person is thinking, but not saying the words.

VARIATIONS IN BALLOON SHAPE ARE *MANY* AND NEW ONES ARE BEING INVENTED EVERY DAY.

I WILL BE--

AAARH!

HEE HEE HEE HEE HEE

IT'S SO QUIET!

OH, IT'S *YOU*.

TIMBER!!

ZACHA

Source: Laura Scruggs
Briggs Middle School
Springfield, OR

| Figure 3.4 | **Comic Strips** (*continued*) |

Comic Strips Part 2

3. Insert your characters...

✓ Stick figures are wonderful!

✓ Each time you draw your character, they should look the same – your reader needs to be able to tell which character is which (clothing and color help with this),

✓ Use body posture and/or facial expressions to show emotions.

4. Backdrop and Coloring...

✓ AFTER you've written the dialogue and filled in your main characters, THEN fill in the background,

✓ Include the props they would need,

✓ Remember, your reader must be able to SEE them to UNDERSTAND them,

✓ YOUR COMIC STRIP SHOULD BE IN FULL COLOR!

3. Write a short description of the task.

4. Rewrite the task in a clear and concise manner so students have unambiguous marching orders of what they are expected to do.

5. Develop (or borrow an already developed) scoring device, making sure it hits the targets identified in #1 above.

6. Develop a step-by-step work plan for students to follow. (See 6th grade teacher Laura Scrugg's comic strip four-step game plan in Figure 3.4 for an outstanding example.)

7. Introduce the task to students.

8. To show students what "good" and "not so good" look like, provide models of both strong and weak work from other classes or past years (with student names removed).

9. As a class, review the task and discuss and answer questions. Then send the students off to work, providing coaching as needed.

10. Score the task and, note any necessary revisions to improve it for next time before returning it to students.

As we provide you with more example tasks, see if you can identify these steps in use. We will elaborate on them in the following chapters and in detail in Chapter 6.

What next? Step 10 raises the next question we will pursue: how does a teacher score student performances?

Options for Scoring Systems

To ensure fairness and accuracy of scoring performance tasks, performers need clear criteria spelled out in advance. Just as Olympic divers know well in advance of the competition how they will be scored, students deserve to know in advance what "good looks like." Grant Wiggins (1995) refers to this as "demystifying the criteria for success." Classroom academic performers, just like world-class athletes, ought to be privy to the scoring system in advance of the performance.

A number of alternatives are available to teachers for scoring their students' work: rubrics, checklists, assessment lists, and scorecards, among others. Each has its own strengths in providing feedback to students and informing the teacher's instruction.

Rubrics

A rubric is simply a set of scoring guidelines for evaluating student work. Rubrics answer these questions:

• By what criteria should a performance be judged? (traits)

• What does the range in the quality of a performance look like, and where does this performance fall on this range? (point scale)

Therefore, rubrics generally contain a scoring scale and a set of descriptors for each level of performance. They can be *holistic* (including one general descriptor for performance as a whole) or *analytic* (including multiple traits, sometimes called dimensions, with each trait being scored). They can be *generic*—used in scoring several tasks—or *task specific*—crafted for a particular project or performance.

The scaling mechanism can have any number of points but generally has four, five, or six. The scale can be *longitudinal* or *relative*. On a longitudinal (sometimes referred to as an *absolute*) scale, each point describes the development of skills and concepts over time from novice to expert. On a relative scale, each point represents the range of this performance from weak to strong. Figure 3.5

Figure 3.5 | **Partial Sample Rubric for Scoring Student's Analysis of Public Issues**

Score	Content	Issue Analysis	Action Proposal or Position
	This trait refers to the ability to select, understand, and use appropriate information (facts, concepts, theories, democratic principles, etc.) to guide and support issue deliberation.	This trait refers to the ability to use critical thinking to analyze the issue from multiple perspectives.	This trait refers to taking, supporting, and communicating a position and/or proposing relevant actions through the use of argument and persuasion.
5	• The student presents a breadth and depth of relevant and accurate information and concepts applicable to the issue. This information focuses on substantive problems and themes related to the issue as opposed to facts and details only. • When applicable, the student demonstrates the relationship of particular democratic principles, including the rule of law, rights and responsibilities, liberty, justice, equality, due process, and civic participation to this issue.	• The student clearly identifies and succinctly states the central issue and its relationship to other issues. • The student analyzes the issue using several methods of inquiry from a broad range of disciplines including history, geography, economics, and political science. • The student identifies interested parties and presents their multiple perspectives on the issue. The student articulates and evaluates the reasoning, assumptions, and evidence supporting each perspective. • The student considers and clearly articulates broad public interests when deliberating on this issue.	• The student takes and communicates a position and/or proposes relevant actions. The proposal/position is creative, clear, coherent, and supported with unusually rich details. • The student explains the proposal or position and provides clear and convincing reasoning and evidence in support of it. • In a rigorous examination, the student identifies the consequences over time of taking this position or proposing this action.

This rubric was developed by Eugene Public Schools in collaboration with the Oregon Department of Education. It was originally titled Deliberate on Public Issues Rubric. It is used to score student work produced when deliberating on public issues. Used with the permission of Eugene School District 4J, Eugene, Oregon.

provides an example of an analytical trait rubric used to score student work when deliberating on public issues. Its scale is designed to be more longitudinal than relative.

Historically, rubrics were red annotations used in Roman Catholic Church missals. These rubrics gave cues to priests and congregants on how to behave during worship. In the same way, teachers use them today to cue students on how to behave—that is, how to successfully fulfill a performance task's requirements.

Checklists

A checklist identifies critical traits that must be present in the performance (like a rubric) and provides opportunities for students to indicate the presence of the traits by checking them off as completed or not completed. Unlike a rubric, the checklist does not offer a scoring scale or descriptors for levels of proficiency.

Here is a sample checklist we used with students for a news conference activity:

1. I have created a written draft of my presentation.

2. I have practiced giving my presentation.

3. When presenting, I speak fluently.

4. I use eye contact and gestures to keep the audience interested.

5. I have given my presentation to a group of students in this class or another class.

6. I have given my presentation to my parents.

7. In my journal I have prepared a list of possible questions that I might be asked.

8. I am prepared to answer these and other questions after my presentation.

Assessment Lists

Assessment lists, like checklists, indicate to students what essential traits of excellence must be present in the performance—but they go further. Assessment lists (officially known as a criterion-referenced grading) also provide a weighted scoring value for each trait. The teacher determines the relative importance of the traits by assigning a point value, such as 10 points, 5 points, or 2 points. Many assessment lists attempt to have a total of all the traits equal 100 points.

Assessment lists also tend to provide students with the opportunity for self-assessment in a designated column before receiving the teacher's evaluation of points earned in another column. (See Figure A.4.)

Now let's look at two additional scoring mechanisms.

Scorecard Rubric

A *scorecard rubric* contains analytical traits and a scoring scale. In addition, the scorecard rubric adds a point system that provides an overall score. This overall score can then be converted into a percentage or letter grade. An example of a scorecard rubric is the Criteria and Scoring Guide from the Lane County Project Fair found in Figure A.29.

ChecBric: A Hybrid Scoring Device

A ChecBric is a combination of a checklist and a scoring rubric where the presence or absence of a particular trait is noted in one column followed by the assessment of that trait's quality in the other column. For example, look over the ChecBric in Figure 3.6 that we designed for the Open Mind mini performance that Tom Cantwell used in his folk/fairy tale unit described in Chapter 2.

Figure 3.6	**Open Mind ChecBric**
Student Checklist	Teacher Rubric

Target 1: I Understand the Reading Assignment

____ my Open Mind comments on the author's main ideas

____ my Open Mind comments on the author's key supporting details

____ my Open Mind shows that I can "read between the lines" to make inferences

____ my Open Mind offers support by referring back to the text

Trait 1: Comprehension of the Reading

6 = exceptional comprehension; way above expectations

5 = excellent comprehension; outstanding meeting of expectations

4 = proficient comprehension; good enough to meet expectations

3 = inadequate comprehension; close, but not good enough to meet expectations

2 = limited comprehension; tried to meet expectations, but a ways to go to meet expectations

1 = missing comprehension; way off on the requirements
OR: no attempt to meet expectations

Target 2: I Make Connections Between the Assignment and Other Sources [Note: Not all are required.]

____ my Open Mind shows that I connected the reading to something that happened to me

____ my Open Mind shows that I connected the reading to something that happened to someone I know

____ my Open Mind shows that I connected the reading to something that I read

____ my Open Mind shows that I connected the reading to something that I watched on TV

____ my Open Mind shows that I connected the reading to a movie, video, or DVD I watched

____ my Open Mind shows that I connected the reading to some issue or event in my community or the world at large

Trait 2: Goes Beyond the Text

6 = exceptionally strong, deep, insightful connections; way above expectations

5 = excellent, outstanding connections; easy meeting of expectations

4 = proficient, adequate connections; some obvious, but good enough to meet expectations

3 = inadequate connections; close, but not good enough to meet expectations

2 = limited connections; quite a ways to go to meet expectations

1 = missing, absent connections; way off on the requirements
OR: no attempt to meet expectations

Student **Reflections** on this assignment

Teacher **Comments** to student

Students use the "Chec" column to self-assess, while teachers use the "Bric" column to indicate the level of the student's performance.

Why use a ChecBric? We prefer ChecBrics to traditional rubrics because we have been frustrated with students who do not appreciate them. We mean, the teacher goes through all the trouble of creating one, or gets lucky and finds a template on the Internet to use as a starting point, then makes copies, and distributes them to the students only to watch the kids tuck the rubric away in their notebooks—and never look at it again. Or worse: after the bell rings and students leave the classroom, we find 17 rubrics abandoned on the floor.

We, like many teachers, have often wondered, Why the lack of appreciation for rubrics? They make sense to us, but we think we now know the reason: most kids cannot even read some of the rubrics we create! They are, after all, written in teacher language ("educationalese"), not student language. Plus, they often crowd the page with lots of text—a major turnoff to students. The ChecBric, on the other hand, pushes the rubric to the right half of the page, freeing up room on the left for a simple checklist that is far easier for kids to use as a guide to the task, and the criteria are rewritten in student-friendly language.

Scoring the Comic Strip Task

When we first designed the comic strip, the task sheet contained a checklist of scoring criteria. After using it to score student work, we found it had some weaknesses. For example, consider the work of two 8th grade reader-cartoonists, Peter and Toby.

Peter was thrilled at the opportunity to apply his considerable illustrating skill (see Figure 3.7). On the other hand, Toby was concerned about his drawing ability (see Figure 3.8). Even though the directions clearly indicated that "drawing is not the targeted skill—reading comprehension is," he apparently felt at a disadvantage. So on his own time after school, he created his comic strip using electronic clip art in the school's computer lab.

Imagine you are the teacher/assessor of these students' work. You assigned the reading and the comic strip assessment. Which student created the better comic strip? In other words, who performed better? Peter? Toby? Or was it a toss-up—close to a tie?

Actually, the answer to this question must be postponed until a more fundamental question is answered. What are we looking for here? What exactly are we assessing? The answer is reading comprehension. The task was designed to measure the degree of understanding of the history textbook's account of the 1492 sinking of the *Santa María,* its causes and aftermath.

So the assessment question is, who revealed a higher level of reading comprehension? And equally important, how do you justify the score you assign?

To be fair, as the assessor you must read the history textbook passage (Figure 3.1) in order to know what the students were expected to comprehend. We did and identified those elements of comprehension in the La Navidad Performance Task (Figure 3.2).

Are you ready to make a fair determination now as to who performed better and why? After reading "Christmas Day, 1492," compare the comics to the criteria in Figure 3.9.

Most teachers agree that Peter's (Figure 3.7) is a stronger response because he

Figure 3.7	**Peter's Hand-Drawn Historical Comic Strip**

incorporates more of the "content requirements" from the task sheet than does Toby in Figure 3.8. Toby certainly is to be congratulated on his skill with computer clip art and drawing, but his strip lacks critical information from the text—namely, what caused the crash and what happened to the remains of the *Santa María*. These two pieces of information are very important to the textbook excerpt, and Toby did not reveal them in his strip. This is often the case; Toby is not the only student we have seen who gets carried away with the illustrative/visual assessment mode and forgets the content. That is why the ChecBric, or another scoring device, must accompany the task.

The World's First ChecBric

While the content requirements from the original task sheet seemed to be a fair set of criteria to measure student performance, Dorothy and I decided to fine-tune the scoring system. We developed a two-columned scoring guide that highlighted the essential elements in two ways. First, in the left-hand column we built in a checklist for students to check on the *presence* of required components. We recognized that our students preferred using a checklist to evaluate the status of their work because it made it easy to see which traits must be present.

On the other hand, we recognized our own need for a scoring device that moved

| Figure 3.8 | **Toby's Computer-Designed Historical Comic Strip** |

beyond the binary "yes or no" of a checklist. Therefore, we incorporated a set of multi-leveled descriptors that identified the *degree* to which students met each requirement. This allowed us, as teacher/assessors, to provide students with more feedback—informing them to what degree, or level, of proficiency they performed. So the right-hand column became a rubric. Thus, the merger of the best features of a checklist and a rubric became the world's first ChecBric. (See Figure A.5 in the Appendix.)

The Evolution of the ChecBric Scoring Device

As you will see, our first attempt, in Figure A.5, was a good try and worked fine, but it just wasn't accurate and precise enough. So, like all good teachers, we revised our work and over time, voilà! By Repairing our own First Dare, we produced the new and improved ChecBric (see Figure 3.9). It is still not perfect, though. Feel free to add your improvements and share them with us.

Figure 3.9	**Comic Strip ChecBric**
Student Checklist	Teacher Rubric

Student Checklist	Teacher Rubric
Target 1: I Understand the Reading in My Comic Strip ____ I identified the author's main ideas ____ I identified the author's significant details ____ I have the correct sequence of events • the theme ____ I "read between the lines" to make literal interpretations ____ I "read between the lines" to make inferred interpretations ____ I get the overall meaning	**Trait 1: Demonstrates Comprehension of the Reading** 6 = **exceptional** comprehending; thorough and convincing 5 = **excellent** comprehending; strong understanding 4 = **proficient** comprehending; competent, good enough 3 = **inadequate** comprehending; close, but inconsistent, incomplete 2 = **limited** comprehending; confused or inaccurate 1 = **missing** comprehending; virtually NO understanding; NO attempt to meet expectations
Target 2: I Go Beyond the Reading in My Comic Strip **Note:** You do not need to do all of these, but you must explain why you are making the connection. ____ I've connected the reading to something that happened to me ____ I've connected the reading to something that happened to someone I know ____ I've connected the reading to something that I read ____ I've connected the reading to something that I watched on TV ____ I've connected the reading to a movie, videotape, or DVD I watched ____ I've connected the reading to some issue or event in my community or the world at large	**Trait 2 : Extends Understanding Beyond the Reading** 6 = **exceptional** connecting; thorough and complex 5 = **excellent** connecting; outstanding and strong 4 = **proficient** connecting; competent, good enough 3 = **inadequate** connecting; scant or inconsistent; fails to explain why and how the source connects to the story 2 = **limited** connecting; superficial or flawed; no explanation 1 = **missing** connecting; NO attempt to meet expectations, OR does NOT show any connection

Target 3: I Create an Effective Comic Strip
 	
____ I use cartoonists' tools
    • talking & thinking bubbles
    • narrator's boxes
    • panels
____ I have been neat
____ I present my ideas in a visually pleasing way with good lay-out design
____ I was careful controlling the rules of language
    • capital letters
    • punctuation
    • spelling
	Trait 3: Communicates Ideas Visually
	
	6 = **exceptional** visual appeal; absolutely delightful; few or no convention errors
	5 = **excellent** visual appeal; very strong; few or no convention errors
	4 = **proficient** visual appeal; pleasing; few convention errors, but no real damage
	3 = **inadequate** visual appeal; some difficulties with neatness, lay-out, and /or conventions
	2 = **limited** visual appeal; messy and/or too many conventional errors
	1 = **missing** visual appeal OR NO attempt to meet expectations

Holistic vs. Analytical Scoring

We presented a ChecBric in Chapter 2 (Figure 2.4), but it is *holistic;* that is, the teacher/assessor awards the student/performer one overall score for the whole task, namely a 4, 3, 2, or 1.

This Comic Strip ChecBric, on the other hand, is *analytical* in that the student earns separate, individual scores for each of these traits. The obvious advantage to the analytical over the holistic is that the student gets more specific feedback on his or her performance; this makes future growth easier because the student knows which areas were accomplished well, and which areas are in need of improvement. But the downside of analytical scoring, of course, is that it takes more of the teacher's time to score.

So which is the better way to go: analytical or holistic? We believe it depends on the amount of feedback you need to give your students. If you decide that they need a quick sense of their performance, then scoring holistically is fine. If you determine that they really need more detailed understanding of your evaluation of their work, then go with analytical.

You might assign a mini task and accompany it with a holistic scoring device, or a midi task with an analytical device with two to four traits. But when scoring a maxi task with lots of requirements, create an analytical rubric (or ChecBric or assessment list) with as many as five to eight traits. If you are teaching students to work with a new rubric—especially your official state scoring guides—you will want to focus on the analytical traits but only emphasize scoring one trait at a time so that students get the hang of it.

Because the comic strip is a midi task, taking two to three class periods, we decided to go with analytical scoring when we created the ChecBric. First, we needed to determine the essential traits we were targeting. We revisited the original content requirements of the task (see Figure 3.2) to attempt to shake out reading content comprehension from the comic strip form—two very different traits. We then asked ourselves, besides these two traits or dimensions, what others traits would an outstanding historical comic strip have, regardless of the specific historical event? After discussion, we decided to add a third trait: "extends beyond the text," because our state's reading scoring guide now includes that criterion.

So to reveal the students' comprehension of an account of an historical event in a comic strip format, we deemed that they should

- understand and interpret historical events in the passage,
- extend understanding beyond the text, and
- control the form of cartooning for greatest visual impact.

From Other Classrooms: The Comic Strip Goes to 5th and 11th Grade

The comic strip proved to be a popular Info Out form with students. We used it the following year to assess other key events in U.S. history.

We wondered whether this performance task would also work with younger students. The comic strip task idea attracted the interest of 5th grade teacher Susie Fuller at Arthur Elementary School in Sullivan, Illinois. Her class was also studying U.S. history, so she decided to use it to measure her students' comprehension of the same 1492 event.

Her goal was for her students to put their new knowledge to use by showing the historical characters' emotional responses to the burning of the Spanish settlement,

| Figure 3.10 | **Business Communication Comic Strips** |

Source: Joanne Williams, business marketing teacher, Northwest High School, High Ridge, Missouri.

La Navidad. An additional trait to assess was their ability to accurately sequence the events. She provided her 5th graders with a list of required items (traits) and told them they were free to show more.

She decided to improve Larry's 1492 comic strip task by providing students with a Plan/Prepare worksheet divided into six panels to help them decide in advance what to include. Also, she modeled and had them practice drawing a talking bubble, a key cartoonist's tool.

Likewise, Joanne Williams, a business marketing teacher at Northwest High School in Cedar Hill, Missouri, decided to use a comic strip task to assess her students' understanding of the basic modes of communication taught in the unit. She recognized that the juniors and seniors "liked the whole comic strip idea; they all really do like to draw and color." In her classes, she encourages much use of color and pictures "so they are used to that kind of thing with me. I have large buckets of markers, crayons and colored pencils, so I get to see some nice stuff."

For her game plan, she decided that the communication concepts were simple enough that three panels seemed plenty for students to fill to identify the three key concepts (see Figure 3.10). She told them they had the one class hour to complete the assignment, so they worked hard trying to get it done. At the end of the time, after seeing how well they worked, she extended the time, allowing them to finish it and add color the next day. So it took two days, a nice midi task.

Joanne liked the results so much that later in the unit she assigned students the task of creating a comic strip for good listening techniques as well. Her students now do two comic strips during the unit.

Downshifting from Midi to Mini Task: Let SnapShots Replace Comic Strips

Because comic strips require a considerable amount of class time (probably three periods) to permit students to achieve successful results, they often are viewed as "yeah, but" assessments. Given the crowded curriculum and time constraints teachers face, we understand why you might decide to pass on comic strips.

We suggest you consider a modified version of comics that we introduced in Chapter 2, SnapShots. Instead of the full-blown comic strip production, SnapShots can be pulled off in a single period, making them a mini task. Students are instructed to draw a quick representation of what they are seeing—in their "mind's eye"—as they read. This is basically the same task as a comic, but it is streamlined by removing the more formal formatting requirements of the comic strip. It still works as an assessment of student reading comprehension, and we even provided you with our favorite scoring mechanism, a ChecBric. (See Figure 2.4 back on page 21.)

Flashback to 1492: Processing the Historical Content with Info In

Let's flash back in time to see what we did instructionally in the classroom before administering the comic strip performance assessment task. In order for students to have a fair chance at performing at a high level on this reading comprehension comic strip task, each student needed solid instruction in how to understand the content that would soon be assessed. Just as a coach offers guided practice to athletes in preparation for a big game, so must teacher-coaches help their students gain higher and higher degrees of proficiency in the targeted areas, in this case, reading to comprehend historical text.

We call this process Info In—how learners process new content information. As explained in Chapter 2, learners at all grade levels need instruction not only in content (knowledge) but also in process (know-how). Remember, it is not safe to assume, for example, that all learners in any given classroom are proficient in the various Info In processes: reading, listening, manipulating, and viewing. Too many students in our schools do not have a sufficient degree of skill in using these critical processes. So before attempting to assess their comprehension of the content, we must address their processing of that content.

In order for our 8th graders to be prepared for the 1492 comic strip performance task, we needed to coach them to use reading comprehension strategies. We structured our coaching on the reading comprehension process by teaching students the generic four-step process approach: Prepare, First Dare, Repair, and Share (explained in Chapter 2).

Let's explore this process further. Good readers are skilled at preparing to read. By this, we don't mean merely the physical preparation of finding comfortable seating, limiting environmental distractions, or getting a water bottle filled. We mean the more fundamental get-ready-to-read strategies of

- tapping prior knowledge on the reading topic;
- setting motivating purposes for reading;
- predicting what the author may say;
- generating some key questions to ask about the topic; and
- scanning the text to recognize the writing structure (organizational pattern) the author chose (novel, short story, poem, text-book chapter, professional article, etc.).

To teach middle graders the critical first strategy of tapping prior knowledge and the question-asking strategy, we sometimes use the now classic KWL activity (Ogle, 1986). Many teachers know about this three-columned device, the forerunner of many other reading strategy activities. Column 1 is a place for students to think about what they already **K**now about the topic to be read, practicing the key Prepare strategy of tapping prior knowledge. In Column 2, What I **W**ant to Know, students generate questions about the topic, which helps them better tackle the text because they now have a stronger purpose for reading—to find answers to their own questions. (For a detailed explanation on how to teach student readers to generate questions at increasingly complex levels, see Larry's book *Teaching Comprehension with Questioning Strategies*, 2009.) Finally, the third column of the KWL is a place for readers to record their notes while reading. Answers to questions in Column 2 belong in the "L" column: What I have **L**earned about the topic. Additionally, other information can be recorded here.

The KWL gave birth to another Info In activity: the Folded File Folder (FFF) described in Chapter 2 (Figure A.1). By using either the KWL or the FFF, teacher-coaches are instructing their students in successful reading comprehension prepare strategies. And it is the use of strategies such as these that helps readers maximize their understanding of assigned readings. Later, when asked to reveal their understanding of what they read—via a comic strip task, a quiz, or any other assessment option—students will be better able to perform at a higher level if they are practiced performers.

Graphic Organizers

We've looked at the historical comic strip, aka the "business/marketing comic strip," the "science comic strip," "literary comic strip," and so forth. The second visual representation performance task we'll examine is the graphic organizer. As many teachers do, I (Larry) assigned my 6th grade language arts class to read a paperback novel. During our study of the theme of change as it relates to migration and immigration, we read Patricia Beatty's excellent novel *Lupita Mañana* (1981). In it, a 12-year-old Mexican girl crosses the U.S. border with her older brother in search of work to help their fatherless family. Like many other teachers, I wanted to uncover the extent to which each student was comprehending the book. By the fourth chapter, readers had been introduced to quite a number of characters, and I wanted to be sure my class understood who they were and their relationships to one another.

Instead of using a selected-response chapter test or check quiz, as I had used to measure comprehension of the previous three chapters, I opted for a constructed-response type of assessment device—the web.

The web is another type of visual representation. It goes by many different names: webs, clusters, maps. We choose to call them *graphic organizers*. Over the years, all of us have assigned our students to construct graphic organizers to share their understandings of content information because graphic organizers allow students to indicate not only their understanding of the content information but also the relationships within that content.

Examine Theresa's web of main character Lupita and her relationships with the other characters in the book (Figure 3.11). Theresa indicates the untimely death of Lupita's father with an "X" across Papa. The web also shows Lupita's mother's need to establish new relationships with the money lender and a widow in the neighborhood, while maintaining her established relationships.

As a teacher assigning this task, consider the key traits of a powerful graphic organizer. Ask yourself, what would I as a teacher expect to see in a high-quality response?

I asked myself the same question, but I had help. At a middle school conference, I had attended a presentation by 6th grade teacher Beth Larkins, who shared with her audience a Performance Task Assessment List for an Idea Web/Organizer (Figure A.6). She and her colleagues in Connecticut's Region 15 (Educators in Connecticut's Pomperaug Regional School District 15, 1996) have identified 10 elements/traits, including using geometric figures and shapes, identifying a clear main idea with supporting details, and making sure the information is accurate.

An assessment list—described earlier as a checklist with assigned point values for each trait—identifies the critical components (traits) that must be present in a strong performance. Using such a list, students may self-assess their efforts, for example, in one column—before their teacher does in a second column—and make any corrections, adjustments, or improvements as needed. Additionally, an assessment list, sometimes called a "product guide," reveals to students the relative importance of each trait by providing them, in a third column titled "Possible Points," the weight their teacher has assigned for each trait's value. Having 10 or 100 total points makes an easy conversion into a percentage for grading purposes.

Figure 3.11	**Theresa's Graphic Organizer for the Novel *Lupita Manaña***

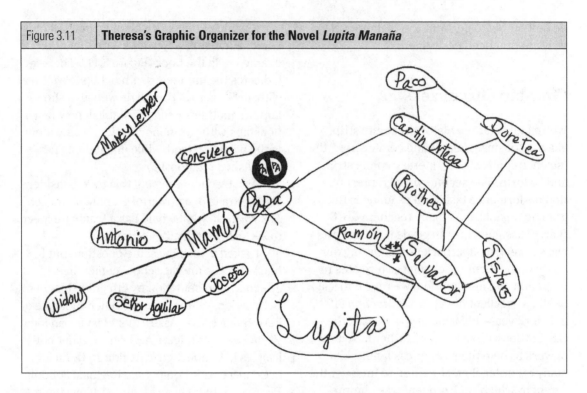

Taking a Step with a Computer Technology

While my students appreciated the opportunity to construct webs (far more than taking a test or a quiz, they assured me), I decided to increase their motivation to perform at a high level by assigning a second graphic organizer—this one to be constructed in the school's computer lab.

As the novel *Lupita Mañana* unfolds, the author describes a number of problems faced by the two protagonists (Lupita and her older brother Salvador) and how they respond to each challenge with a solution. Because many of these characters' solutions lead, in turn, to new problems, the web seemed like a useful device to show plot development: the connection between problems and solutions in literature. So I assigned a second graphic organizer: An Electronic Web on the Problems and Solutions in the Novel.

I cannot take credit for the electronic version of this task. Justin, one of my 6th graders, got behind on his web assignment, so he finished it at home electronically on his computer using a simple drawing program.

Not only was Justin's web clear and easy to understand, but also he told me that doing the web on his computer was "a heck of a lot more fun than doing homework." Good news for any teacher. When I asked him how long it took to construct an electronic web, he told me, "Not too long; about an hour."

I immediately recognized both the advantages and disadvantages of his electronic approach. First, the increased motivation and clearer presentation of the computer-generated web surely were of great value. But the hour it took Justin seemed too long to be realistic, considering how much more quickly kids can draw webs using paper and pencil. Fortunately, a colleague offered me a brilliant solution. Vicky Ayers, our district's former technology trainer, showed me a set of computer-generated graphic organizers constructed by special education high school history students using a software program called Inspiration. She told me how easily this software had allowed them to make pleasing electronic graphic organizers she calls I-Maps (*Inspiration*-Maps).

Electronic webs offer students a heightened graphic capability by providing them with hundreds of different shapes for web elements, automatic arrow-connectors between elements, swift and clean relocation of elements if needed, and, of course, the thrill of living color. After acquiring a site license for my school's computer lab and installing the software, I assigned my 6th grade literature students an I-Map on the Problems and Solutions in the Novel.

The electronic graphic organizer program created a more visually pleasing product as it also increased both student enjoyment and motivation for the task. But what about the more important consideration: students' comprehension of the problems and solutions in the novel they were reading? It's one thing to look good; it's quite another to reveal deep and clear understanding of the content information.

As classroom assessors, we must constantly ask ourselves:

• Does this task actually measure what it's intended to measure?

Putting it another way:

• Does this task really make students reveal to us what we are teaching?

In other words:

• Does this task clearly and accurately demonstrate student proficiency in the targeted outcome(s)?

Specifically:

• Is the construction of a graphic organizer a fair and thorough means for students to present to a teacher/assessor their comprehension of plot—that is, the problems and solutions faced by characters in literature?

And:

• If not, why not? What adjustments need to be made?

Or maybe:

• What is a better way to assess what we are teaching them?

If creating an electronic graphic organizer presents a problem for you (a lack of funds to purchase the software, limited accessibility to computers, or simply not enough time for this task), then you may wish to use an alternative task. Students can fill in a teacher-created graphic organizer.

The World's Second ChecBric

Teachers must not only invent classroom-based tasks to measure our students' proficiency, but we must also assess the students' performance on those tasks. So along with the graphic organizer task came the need for a ChecBric.

Building on the Assessment List idea of my colleagues in Connecticut, I devised the world's second ChecBric based on three key traits of a successful graphic organizer, either traditionally made with paper and pencil or technology assisted on a computer:

1. Information is accurate and complete to reveal content understanding.

2. Relationships among key information are clearly and accurately portrayed.

3. Visual appeal is apparent.

I kept the traits general so that I could use this performance task and its ChecBric with other reading assignments, not just with this particular novel. How nice it is to have generic tasks with accompanying scoring guides waiting patiently in one's file cabinet for repeated uses. (See Figure A.7 in the appendix.)

Please keep in mind that ChecBrics can have more than three targets/traits and that they often need revision. In fact, this one has been revised three times to make it a better and better tool for assessment. If you would like to see a more detailed ChecBric for this task, visit www.larrylewin.com/books/GreatPerformances.html and click on "Online supplements for this book." And, if you discover ways to improve upon it, please share your modifications by sending it to us.

Flashback: Teaching How to Create Graphic Organizers

Just as musical directors train their musicians with thorough practice to ensure a flawless performance at showtime, I assisted my students in preparing for their graphic organizers.

For a Prepare activity, I led my class through the creation of a problem/solution wall chart on butcher paper. Then I added a cooperative learning activity. Working in teams, the students reviewed a designated chapter of the novel to remember problems facing Lupita and her brother and their solutions. I then called upon each team to add problems and solutions from their review of the chapter to the class wall chart. This "reading-review-repair" activity served to remind everyone that good readers often *reread* to master content information in the book.

Next, I showed the class an Inspiration-Map that I had constructed on a different topic for another class. I demonstrated how the software allowed me to show both the key elements of the content and also the relationships among those elements by using selected shapes, colors, and arrows.

During my demonstration, I used the "think-aloud" teaching technique: talking about the decisions to be made while performing the assignment. This revealing of the teacher's thoughts-in-action serves as a mental role model for kids who shortly will be completing the same assignment.

Finally, I retraced the steps for using the software. As my students watched, I directed them to make notes at each step so that they would know how to do the steps independently in the computer lab the next day. In fact, their note sheet would serve as a "ticket in the door" to the lab. Without it, a student could not begin the assignment. No ticket, no computer. The next day, two forgetful kids quickly tired of trying to argue with me and sat down to copy the steps from a friendly classmate. I was strict about this because I know from prior experiences the headache of trying to assist 30 or more kids in the computer lab—it's impossible to reach them all quickly. The required note taking increased their independence and proficiency with the new software.

Not only does this modeling/preview activity help the teacher with student management, but it also teaches the students how to use the required form of the task: if a graphic organizer is the selected mode/form, students deserve instruction in how to use that form effectively—whether it's in the traditional paper-and-pencil form or the technological computer software form.

From Another Classroom: Yours

Consider the potential of the graphic organizer task (either the traditional paper-and-pencil one or the electronic version) and the comic strip task (historical, literary, scientific, and so on) for your own use. Take a moment to critique each:

- What do you like about it?
- With what content can you envision using it?
- What problems, pitfalls, or possible difficulties do you predict might arise?
- What adaptations, adjustments, or alterations might make it a better fit in your classroom?

Two More Visual Representations: Electronic Time Lines and Digital Presentations

We've discussed comic strips and graphic organizers. The last two visual representations we'll look at briefly are the electronic time line and the electronic slide show. Mary Kay McCann of West Chester, Pennsylvania, has shared with us a different performance task in the visual representation mode. Her class of 7th graders studied space flight, and to assess their understanding of the sequence of events, she designed the electronic time line performance task.

She gave each student a set of three resources on the history of space flight from its beginning to the space shuttle program. To facilitate their Info In reading, she instructed students to use highlighting pens to mark the key dates and to jot significant notes in the margins.

The midi performance task was to take the learned information and plot it along a time line using the computer software program Timeliner® by Tom Snyder Productions, Inc. The new version, Timeliner XE, is described by the developer as "the powerful and intuitive software program students use to organize data—anything from historical events, to scientific processes, to story arcs—to see the connections, and transform a world of information into real knowledge" (http://www.tomsnyder.com/timelinerxe).

To ensure student success using software for this Info Out, Mary Kay structured the task using the four-step process approach; she instructed her students in how to Prepare, First Dare, Repair, and Share their knowledge of the history of space flight by displaying completed time lines in the school's hallways. They enjoyed the process and gained proficiency in note taking and paraphrasing, as well as computer technology skills.

Presentation Software

Many teachers are now assigning another visual representation task: digital slide shows and movies. Software programs with the slide show capability are available, including the sophisticated Microsoft PowerPoint and Apple's Keynote. If you're not a confident computer user, don't feel intimidated. These programs are all designed to guide you step-by-step through creating a slide show.

For digital moviemaking, there are the two predominant platforms in schools: Microsoft's Photo Story and Apple's iMovie. In 2006, Microsoft released its Photo Story 3. Photo Story 3 allows you to create slideshows using your digital photos. You can add special effects, soundtracks, and narration.

Photo Story is a free software package included on the Windows XP install CD, or you can download it from Microsoft. But Instructional Technology Coordinator David Jakes at Community High School District 99 in Downers Grove, Illinois, informs us that Microsoft will not continue to develop Photo Story (which is a shame) as it feels that Microsoft 7 has enough capacity on board to create video without having a separate product. David has created a very nice PDF 11-page tutorial for you and your students: http://www.jakesonline.org/photostory3.pdf.

Also on the PC side is Movie Maker 2.1. Movie Maker has the advantage of being able to include video in your composition because Photostory can only take still-frame images.

On the Mac side is the popular iMovie. Apple describes this software on its website: "Plug in virtually any digital camcorder and iMovie starts importing your video. Then iMovie helps you organize your video just as you organize photos: by putting everything in one central location and grouping video clips according to the date they were taken. So it's easy to find the clips you're looking for—whether to watch or to edit. Don't have a camcorder? You can still use iMovie: It displays video you captured on your still camera and imported into iPhoto" (http://www.apple.com/ilife/imovie).

Of course students are thrilled to be allowed to use computers to create slide shows and digital movies. The technology really levels the playing field to allow all kids the chance to create powerful presentations. But as inspiring as digital slide shows and movies can be, they take lots of time to make. We teachers cannot assume that our students can accomplish this in a class period or two. Rather, they typically require several periods at the computers, which makes them maxi tasks, or in some cases, maxi-to-the-max tasks. And another heads-up: be sure to have your scoring device ready in advance of turning students loose on the computer.

A Snapshot of Chapter 3

In Chapter 2, we focused on how students use the key processes of reading, listening, viewing, and hands-on manipulating to take in core knowledge content. In this chapter, we concentrated on how students show what they have learned/what they know through our first Info Out mode: *visual representations.* Visual representations are tasks that rely more on the visual factor than either written or spoken words. The four tasks we described are

- comic strips;
- graphic organizers (webs, clusters, maps), both traditionally drawn and with computers;
- electronic time lines; and
- digital slide shows and movies.

Visual representation tasks, like other tasks, need some revision to fine-tune them. We also shared with you the world's first ChecBric, a new scoring mechanism that combines the best features of a checklist and a rubric.

Here are some questions to reflect on:

- What activities using visual representations suggested here might you use in your classroom?
- Do you currently assess student progress before, during, and after instruction?
- What do you think of the ChecBric?

Classroom-based performance assessments increase the teacher's capacity to measure which students are learning what is being taught, and to what degree they're learning it. Visual representations contribute strongly to increasing teachers' confidence in assessments. Using any of these tasks, we gain important insights into our students' learning.

And, as a bonus, kids love creating visual representations. Susie Fuller, 5th grade teacher, surely was pleased with the results:

My students need variety in the way they are assessed. They got excited when I told them we wouldn't have a written test over the Taino/Columbus unit. When they found out about the historical comic strip task, I actually received applause!

Imagine that.

chapter 4

Info Out: Assessing Students' Understanding Using the Written Mode

Larry's Happy Story

We had just completed an in-depth study of the historical relationships between the Spanish newcomers under the command of Christopher Columbus and the Taino tribe, the Native Americans of the Caribbean. I congratulated my 8th graders on how well they had learned new information about this important historical content:

> You have succeeded at gaining new content expertise about the 1492 period—a subject that you initially thought would be boring and redundant because of your 5th grade study of the European explorers. I am proud of how much you've learned and how well you used key strategies to acquire that knowledge.

I continued by expressing hope that my next year's class would be as successful. I offered them an opportunity to assist me in making that happen: "Next fall, I'd really prefer to sit at my desk and read the daily newspaper instead of teaching. How about if you take over and teach the new kids?"

This prospect got their undivided attention. "How might we do that?" they asked.

I suggested that they write a "technical training manual," with each student contributing a chapter to a class-authored "complete-how-to-do-it-guide" for the unit (see Figure 4.1). I figured that by tapping into my students' expertise on how to succeed at the unit, I would accomplish four important objectives:

- Find out what they had learned and remembered from the unit (Info In).
- Teach them how to compose technical writing—a challenging, important, and often neglected written mode (Info Out).
- Motivate them to share this information by appealing to their natural desire to play the role of expert to an audience of younger students.
- Meet my state's writing standard of "using a variety of written forms—including journals, essays, short stories, poems, research reports, research papers, business

| Figure 4.1 | **Performance Task: Writing the 1492 Unit Technical Training Manual** |

Task: Write a chapter for our booklet on how to succeed in the 1492 Unit on Relationships.

Writing Mode: Expository (Technical)

Purpose: To help your teacher do a better job next year: Share your wisdom, knowledge, and experience with students who will be assigned the same unit activities as you were. Teach them how to succeed at producing high-quality work.

Procedure:

1. Select a chapter topic that you particularly enjoyed and that you were particularly successful at:

- Chapter 1: Construction of Caribbean Island
- Chapter 2: Construction of Taino character
- Chapter 3: Construction of Spanish sailor face
- Chapter 4: How to read historical fiction novels
- Chapter 5: How to write an original historical fiction story

2. Review your working folder for work samples related to your topic.

3. Write a First Dare chapter with tips on how to do well, steps to follow, and advice on how to avoid problems. Save and print.

4. Meet with another student who has written a draft on the same chapter that you have. Coedit each other's chapters by combining them into a single outstanding chapter. Save and print.

5. Conduct three rounds of Repair: Auto-edit your coauthored chapter, ask another student to read and Repair, and find a kindhearted adult to do the same. Remember to use different colored pencils for each round.

Assessment:

Your chapter will be scored on the following traits of excellence:

- **Accurate** description of the project, not incorrect information
- **Elaborate** information, plenty of detail
- Proper **sequence**: a clear order of how to do it
- **Format** easy to follow; correct paragraphs, punctuation, and spelling

and technical writing" (Oregon Department of Education, 1998–2010).

Using Writing to "Show What You Know"

As teachers, we surely know the value of using the written mode to find out what our students have learned. Too often, however, we have used writing in the form of Stiggins's (1997) assessment type one, the selected response (paper-and-pencil tests/quizzes), and for older learners, its lengthier cousin, assessment type two, the essay. While using the mode of writing in these two ways is perfectly acceptable, Betty and I explored ways to move beyond the traditional use of the written mode to the more open-ended performance task assessment option. Our goal in this chapter is to help you expand your repertoire of written assessment tasks beyond the traditionally popular ones and to get you to consider some newer, fresher ones that can increase motivation and energy for your students.

We will present a variety of tasks using the written mode to assess students' acquisition of content knowledge. We will explore various forms of writing (training manuals, RAFT, reports, stories, magazine articles), share model "performance task sheets," and demonstrate how to score student writing.

Among the countless opportunities for revealing content understanding through written work, we will focus on our favorite performance tasks that can be administered at the beginning, in the middle, and at the end of a unit or course.

We will illustrate how to design these written performance tasks, how they mesh with the teaching of key content, and how they are assessed. We will begin with

end-of-unit written tasks. We'll look at four different types:

- A student-authored technical training manual (or "user's guide"/how-to-do-it guide)
  - A parent advisory brochure
  - A historical RAFT
  - A magazine or newspaper article

Using Writing to Assess Students' Understanding After Instruction

Let's start with the technical training manual (an end-of-unit maxi task) and work backward.

The 1492 Unit's Technical Training Manual

To Prepare for this written end-of-unit performance task, I asked my students to recall the various major activities that had been assigned during our in-depth study of 1492 historical relationships. Our list included the following:

- We studied the climate of the Caribbean Islands, including the flora and fauna. Students used construction paper to make mammals, insects, birds, plants, and physical features to add to a class-built island replica on a large bulletin board.
- We studied the lives of Taino Indians living on the Caribbean Islands and created a historically accurate Indian character to be a motivating entrée to the unit by providing that character's perspective. (We used the Scottish Storyline Method for this activity. See www.storyline.org for more information.)
- We studied the lives of Spanish sailors aboard the *Niña, Pinta,* and *Santa María* and

created a historically accurate sailor character for an alternative point of view.

- We read two historical fiction novels set in 1492, one from the Taino point of view, *Morning Girl* (Dorris, 1992), and one from a sailor's perspective, *Pedro's Journal* (Conrad, 1991).
- We created a historical comic strip about the sinking of the *Santa María* (described in Chapter 3).
- We wrote an original historical fiction story set in 1492 starring our two historical characters.

After some discussion, we decided to exclude tips on the comic strip as a topic for the manual, but we agreed to use the remaining five topics as chapters.

Each student then selected one of the five topics and wrote a First Dare (rough draft) of a chapter for the training manual. After reading some of their drafts, I realized that my students had no clue about how to produce high-quality technical writing. I needed to back up and teach technical writing. What do you think of the following list of critical traits that I generated?

Good technical writing

- provides a strong statement of purpose;
- has a clear sequence of steps without missing any key steps;
- has diagrams and illustrations to support the text (if necessary); and
- uses language that is simple and understandable to the reader.

The next day, I gave my students photocopied pages from the owner's manual to my DVR. We read the directions together and critiqued the effectiveness of the technical writing using the four traits. This sample provided them with examples of both good writing and poor writing. Next time, I plan to provide a variety of sample technical user's guides. Examining several models helps students "anchor" the expectations more clearly.

Next, I assigned writers who had drafted the same topic to work together to synthesize the "best parts from each First Dare into a top-notch chapter using what you've learned about technical writing." Candace and Stephanie cowrote the 4th chapter (see Figure 4.2).

Figure 4.2	**Advice from Two 8th Graders: How to Read Historical Fiction Novels**

1. To prepare for reading, look on the back cover of the novel. There will be a little paragraph; read it because it should tell you about the novel. It will give you an idea of what the book will be about.

2. When you are given a limited amount of days to read this novel, make a plan of how many pages (or chapters) to read each day or night. The teacher should offer you a blank calendar page to help you stay on target. You shouldn't fall behind in your reading.

3. While reading a chapter, if you don't understand something, reread a sentence slowly. If you can't see the sentence, maybe the print is too small and you should consider a different book with larger print. (Bigger print won't take as long to read!!)

Bonus Tip: Of the two novels offered in this unit, *Morning Girl* is probably harder to follow than *Pedro's Journal* because it changes narrators in chapters. *Pedro* is written like a journal, in one point of view.

The Missing ChecBric

Of course, the partners needed to know the parameters of this writing task in order to be successful, so they needed an advance look at the scoring device. However, due to circumstances beyond my control (bus duty that whole week or some such thing), I had no time to produce an assessment scoring device. Naturally, I had wanted to provide the students with a ChecBric to guide their written performance. (I have to remember that it takes time to build high-quality classroom assessment tasks with an accurate scoring tool. "Next time I will make it better" has become my mantra, and I find myself chanting it repeatedly with devotional fervor.)

The next semester *was* better. I tried the technical training manual again, this time with my 6th grade language arts class. I built in the time to create a ChecBric (see Figure A.8 in the Appendix), using some of the traits identified to assess their "How to Succeed in 6th Grade" manuals written for the next year's incoming class.

Back to the Writing Process

After the students complete their First Dares (rough drafts), we typically go to the next stage of the writing process, Repair (rewriting/revising/editing). I say "typically" because it is not automatic that all writing goes beyond the drafting stage. In some instances the writing does need to advance from Prepare, First Dare, and Repair to Share with your audience, but not always. For example, some teachers feel that writing a rough draft of a writing assignment is sufficient because the assessment will be only on content understanding and not writing ability. And in some cases, the full writing process is intended, but unforeseen circumstances (assembly, fire drill, flu epidemic) interrupt it, and it gets cut short.

For this 1492 Unit Tech Manual, the full process was needed because the students were sharing their work with my future classes, requiring them to produce high-quality work in the four areas identified in the "good technical writing" list. So class time was needed for students to examine their drafts to see how closely they came to meeting these identified traits. This was accomplished through self-evaluation, working with a peer editor, and critiquing a few samples displayed on the overhead.

Possible Adaptations to the Technical Training Manual Task

The Differentiated Study Guide: Tiered CliffsNotes

Dorothy Syfert, my longtime friend and former teaching colleague, invited me to join her 8th grade American history class last year to help teach her students how to write a CliffsNotes study guide for the Civil War historical fiction novel *Soldier's Heart* by the great young-adult author Gary Paulsen (1998). Based on the life of a real 15-year-old boy, *Soldier's Heart* is the story about the horrors of war turning a boy into a man.

CliffsNotes are well-known to most secondary students, and despite some differing of opinion on students' using them, this task turns the tables on the students and asks them not to *read* a CliffsNotes, but rather to *write* their own for the assigned novel. This writing task is in the expository mode because students have to inform their readers of the key elements of the book.

After reviewing with the class what CliffsNotes are, why they are published, and addressing the students' reference to the similar online resource SparkNotes.com, Dorothy distributed an eight-page booklet template that I created for her class using Microsoft Word. Figure 4.3 shows page 2, the table of contents, with the required targets for each page of this two-period midi task, plus the design of a symbol or icon for each of the six universal literary conflicts, which will be used throughout the study guide.

As you can see, the required elements are quite basic in that they seek student understanding mainly of literal-level comprehension—summaries, illustrations, and conflict types. However, the page 7 requirement, "Analysis of Charley Before and After," expects more from the reader in the form of a character analysis over the time of the novel—it is more interpretative in nature. Dorothy was well aware of the range of performers in her class, and she wanted to differentiate the instruction for them to better meet their needs.

So, to assist some 8th graders, Dorothy provided the prompt in Figure 4.4. This highly structured prompt was designed to assist her students in showing the evolution of the character over time. Because not all learners in

the class needed this much scaffolding, she designed a second version of the study guide with this more open-ended prompt:

> Like many characters in historical fiction, Charley underwent big changes in the novel. Using pictures, words, or both, describe how he changed from a 15-year-old boy into a 21-year-old man.

Likewise, Dorothy differentiated the back cover, page 8. Version one's assignment was to write a short bio about the author Gary Paulsen to get the students to think about the person behind the book. For version two, however, the assignment was "Make a Connection." The directions were "Compare this book to any other book, story, movie, or TV show you have read, seen, or heard this year that has the same theme or themes. Explain what it has in common with *Soldier's Heart*."

The versions are similar, but the second is more demanding because it provides less structure on page 7 and requires a deeper analysis on page 8. This is an example of a

Figure 4.3	**CliffsNotes Table of Contents**		
Chapter 1 Summary		p. 3	[worth 8 pts.]
Chapter [Your Choice] Illustration of Key Event		p. 4	[worth 3 pts.]
Chapter [Your Choice] Summary		p. 5	[worth 8 pts.]
Chapter [Your Choice] Illustration of Key Event		p. 6	[worth 8 pts.]
Analysis of Charley (protagonist) Before and After		p. 7	[worth 4 pts.]
Back Cover		p. 8	[worth 8 pts.]

Icon Key to the Universal Conflicts [worth 6 pts.]

human vs. human	☐	human vs. nature	☐	human vs. higher power	☐
human vs. society	☐	human vs. technology	☐	human vs. self	☐

Figure 4.4	**CliffsNotes page 7 Prompt**

In the first box, use pictures and words or just words to show Charley at the beginning of the book, at age 15.

In the second box, use pictures and words or just words to show Charley at the end of the book, at age 21.

---

tiered assignment: it varies the degree of complexity to better match students' current ability levels. Because Dorothy knew her students quite well at this point in the semester, she could decide which version (tier) each student would be assigned. To avoid any resentment or possible embarrassment, she could have prefaced the distribution with a comment on what tiers are and why she occasionally uses them. She could then underscore that the purpose of tiers is to ensure all students have success learning in her class. But since these two particular tiers were so similar, she merely handed them out to students based on her perception of which one would be best for each kid. Turns out, only one or two students noticed that their neighbors' version was different, so she explained her reasoning on a need-to-know basis.

As with all tiered assignments, the goal is not only to increase the chances for all students to succeed, but also to use this success to bolster competence and confidence to eventually move all students to the highest tier.

To give feedback to her students on this writing midi task, Dorothy could have considered using, or modifying, the same ChecBric for a Technical Training Manual in Figure A.8. But she opted to use a different device, the assessment list introduced in Chapter 3.

Dorothy decided that each page of the booklet was worth a certain number of points, and she delineated those values on the table of contents page for everyone to see. (The total number of points equaled 45, so after she scored the value of each page, she added up the student's totals and divided by 45 to compute a percentage, which she then converted into a letter grade.)

A Second Adaptation: *The Cold War for Dummies*

The CliffsNotes metaphor is very helpful in establishing the purpose of the study guide writing task, but other commercially published series can accomplish the same thing. History teacher Tad Shannon, formerly at North Eugene High School in Eugene, Oregon, employed the "for dummies" metaphor in an AP American history course unit on the Cold War. However, instead of assigning *The Cold War for Dummies* task to his whole class, Tad opted to use it as a backup, early-finisher assignment for students who accomplished the regular assignment quite easily.

This is another way to differentiate instruction. It is known as a *sidebar activity* (sometimes known as an orbital study in TAG circles) because it provides an enrichment activity that moves the go-getters *sideways* in the curriculum instead of letting them venture forward. As a classroom management decision, some teachers are more comfortable with the sidebar because it provides meaningful work for the advanced students while allowing the other class members to catch up before everyone proceeds to the next stage of the unit.

How much time a teacher allots for a sidebar activity depends on how much time the other students need to complete the regular assignment. It could take a single class period or maybe two periods—a midi. And since it was used as an activity and not as an actual assessment task, the scoring could be quickly done by merely assigning some points to it. If some students object that it is unfair for only some to earn the extra points, the teacher can easily offer the sidebar as an optional homework assignment for anyone who wants to earn the extra points.

In addition to CliffsNotes and For Dummies, some teachers prefer using the *Complete Idiot* series for the study guide task. Both are well-known to many students, and both have the playful I-am-the-expert point of view that kids like. However, if either feels too negative to you, opt for the CliffsNotes title.

Even More Adaptation Ideas

Of course, other technical writing tasks abound in other classrooms: how to succeed at a unit on the Middle Ages, how to write an effective short story, how to conduct a successful science lab experiment, how to survive immigration to the United States (written by ESL students at a local community college to share with other newcomers), or how to successfully survive Ms. Abraham's Biology II class. The possibilities are endless.

The various technical training manual tasks described above stress procedural knowledge (how-to), but they also reveal content knowledge. While detailing how to do something, students simultaneously express their understanding of the topic.

Another Writing Task: High Schoolers Produce the Parent Advisory Brochure

Another Info Out written performance task—one that merges expository with persuasive writing—that can be used effectively with older students is the advisory brochure. Seniors in Linda Christensen's English class at Jefferson High School in Portland, Oregon, studied children's fairy tales. But instead of the typical literary analysis of characters, setting, and plot, the class evaluated these traditional stories from a social perspective: how do fairy tales portray females, minorities, and working people? The discoveries were eye-opening, to say the least. Imagine revisiting your childhood favorites, this time armed with a critical eye on the subtle (or not-so-subtle) effects they have on young readers' attitudes toward certain groups of people.

Linda took this social analysis further. Her students were to apply their analytical skills to contemporary fiction: Saturday morning cartoon shows. Their findings were as powerful as those relating to the fairy tales. They were so powerful, in fact, that the students were bound and determined to share their findings with an audience who would care. Some elected to write articles for women's magazines, the local newspaper, *Rethinking Schools* (a national teacher journal), and church bulletins. One group decided to produce and distribute a parent advisory brochure, which they titled "What's the Grade, Doc?" Here are two excerpts from it:

> *Duck Tales:* At first glance, the precocious ducks are cute, but look closer and see that the whole show is based on money. All their adventures revolve around finding money. Uncle Scrooge and the gang teach children that money is the only important thing in life. **C–**

> *Teenage Mutant Ninja Turtles:* Pizza-eating Ninja Turtles. What's the point? There isn't any. The show is based on fighting the "bad guy," Shredder. Demonstrating no concern for the townspeople, they battle and fight, but never get hurt. This cartoon teaches a false sense of violence to kids: fight and you don't get hurt and solve problems through fists and swords instead of guns. **D** (Christensen, 1991)

On the back of the pamphlet, students listed some tips for parents to guide them in wise cartoon selection.

From Another Classroom: Yours

Perhaps you've hatched an idea of your own for adapting the technical training manual, study guide, or advisory brochure. Here are some questions to consider:

- In what topic or unit do your students have expertise (content knowledge)?
- In what procedure or process can your students share wisdom with next year's class (process knowledge)?
- What might the possible chapter titles/brochure sections be?
- Could you use or adapt the ChecBric (Figure A.8) to assess the finished student work?

Another End-of-Unit Writing Task: The Historical RAFT

While studying the history of the European–Native American encounter of 1492, 8th graders in my (Larry's) U.S. history/language arts block class were expected to analyze the events from both the Taino Indian tribe's point of view and from the Spanish sailors' perspectives.

Specifically, I wanted these 13- and 14-year-olds to wrestle with the challenging notion that history is often open to interpretation. That is, the events of the past can be described, analyzed, and explained in various ways, and the reader of history must sort through these acounts to construct an understanding of what happened. In fact, this goal of recognizing differing points of view is a required learning standard in Oregon. Teachers are expected to teach, and students are expected to be able to

SS.08.HS.01.02 Compare and contrast historical interpretations.

SS.08.SA.03 Examine a controversial event, issue, or problem from more than one perspective.

(See www.ode.state.or.us/teachlearn/real/documents/ss.pdf for the full learning standards.)

Additionally, my state expects students to be able to write to communicate ideas in a variety of writing modes: "Write narrative, expository, and persuasive texts . . . to express ideas appropriate to audience and purpose across the subject areas." (See www .ode.state.or.us/teachlearn/subjects/elarts/ curriculum/comparison1996to2003standards. pdf for the full standard.)

So, as their teacher, I was determined to assess both their understanding of historical events through multiple perspectives (content) and their ability to write informatively (process).

By knowing what the standards are, I know what I am to teach. But *how* I teach is my choice and responsibility. And I also have some flexibility in the assessment measures I use in my classroom.

I opted for a popular written mini task, the RAFT. Created in 1988 by Dr. Carol M. Santa, this is a wonderful, short, nonintimidating writing-across-the-curriculum task. RAFT stands for

- Role—who/what you are pretending to be
- Audience—who/what you are communicating to
- Format—the form of your writing (e.g. notice, letter, obituary, personal ad)
- Topic—what you are writing about

You can see the five RAFT choices I offered my students in Figure 4.5.

The beauty of RAFT writing is that it requires content understanding of the topic in Column 4; students must know about the topic of study in order to write a RAFT. It's a fun task, it develops point of view, and it offers choices of formats in which to write. But the best feature of RAFTing is that students *must* Info In before they can Info Out. Teachers like this, don't we?

The RAFT can be accomplished in one period, or even a bit less, so it falls into the category of mini tasks. However, if the teacher decides that a rough draft RAFT is not sufficient, and some editing is expected, then students would need additional time to make their repairs, changing the task into a midi—requiring two, or even three, class periods.

To add even more enthusiasm to the RAFT task, I told my students that they would be sharing their work with their classmates and with students taking this course in another period. Kids seem to like the idea of having

Figure 4.5	**1492 RAFT Choices**		
Role	**Audience**	**Format**	**Topic**
Sailor aboard the *Santa María*	Captain Christopher Columbus	Anonymous note at his quarters	Mutiny brewing
Sailor left to guard Fort La Navidad	Captain Columbus back in Spain	Letter in a bottle	Meanwhile, back at the fort
Taino Indian in the Caribbean	The cacique (chief)	FYI memo	Hospitality/hostility to newcomers?
Columbus	Spanish monarchs	Formal letter	Update on their investment
Cabin boy	Ship's helmsman	Urgent message	How do I steer this thing?

peers as an audience, and I have found that they kick up their effort a few notches. Plus, with students writing five different RAFTs, we experienced the different historical perspectives as required by my state standards.

RAFTing in Science

High school teacher Jud Landis also uses RAFTs—in science! He likes how they provide a way for those less-than-enthusiastic students to get energized about the topics he is teaching. They also provide him with a way of assessing students' understanding in an alternative format to the standard quiz. And finally, he gets major kudos from his colleagues in the English department for incorporating writing into his curriculum. It's a win-win-win.

Figure 4.6 shows some of the RAFT choices Jud offered his 9th grade physical science students during a unit on genetics.

Now, because the RAFT is not being used as an activity, but rather as a performance assessment task, it must meet the five characteristics we posited in Chapter 1. The RAFT task

1. Offers students a choice among a set of RAFTS to select.
2. Requires both content understanding of science (or history, literature, math, whatever) and the use of the writing process.
3. Has an explicit scoring system—Oops, not yet, but hang on a second.
4. Is designed for an audience beyond the teacher (the classmates).
5. Is carefully crafted to measure content understanding.

Assessing the RAFT Results

For scoring a RAFT, we have designed a ChecBric—a 4-point holistic model. You will recall from Chapter 3 that holistic scoring

Figure 4.6	**Genetics RAFT Choices**		
Mendel's assistant	Mendel	E-mail to boss	Boss, allow me to **explain** how the pea experiment is going.
Mendel	Science society	Article for their journal	I will gladly **indicate** what I have discovered about genetics.
Pea	Mendel and his assistants	Angry letter	Hey, Buddy, I'll **reveal** to you what's happening. . . . Now quit messing with me!!
Parent plant	Offspring plant	A private talk about "the birds and bees"	I must **tell** you about sexual reproduction, cross pollination, dominant/recessive traits.
Reginald Punnett, a British geneticist	Upper-and lowercase letters	Set of directions	OK, guys, I will **list** for you the rules of my brilliant Punnett square.
Coin	Biology student	Text message	I will **recall** for you why the principles of probability that predict outcomes of coin flips can be used to predict outcomes of genetic crosses.
Cross-pollinated plant	True-breeding plant	Online chat	I will put **into plain words** the difference between us.

Source: Jud Landis, Sheldon High School, Eugene, Oregon.

devices provide the student with one overall score on the task instead of multiple scores for multiple traits with an analytical device. (See Figure A.9.)

You will notice right away that our ChecBric will not be very useful for either the 1492 historical or the genetics science RAFTs because the indicators were chosen for a literature RAFT.

So a science or history teacher could adapt our Fiction RAFT ChecBric into one that matches the content they are teaching. If you would like to save some typing time and receive this ChecBric as a download in Word, visit www.larrylewin.com/books/GreatPerformances.html and click on "Online Supplements."

Or, perhaps you would prefer to use a shorter Holistic Scorecard Rubric like the one in Figure A.10.

Possible Adaptations to the RAFT Task: Lit and Math RAFTs

As mentioned previously, RAFT writing works across the curriculum. Here is an example of RAFT choices from Tom Cantwell's 6th grade literature course for a Vietnamese fairy tale called *The Story of Tam and Cam* (McDougal Littell, 2001) (see Figure A.11). Since these RAFTs are about literature, all the roles and audiences are characters in the fairy tale. All the topics, of course, relate to the plot, and the formats allow for creativity.

Likewise, math teacher Holly Walsh at Narragansett Pier Middle School, Rhode Island, generated five RAFT choices to assess her students' understanding of linear equations. (See Figure A.12.)

We want to make two last points about using RAFTs as an assessment tool. First, they can just as easily be employed in the middle of a unit as at the end of a unit. In fact, given the short nature of RAFT writing, some teachers find that they are too mini or midi for a final assessment, and therefore are better used *during* instruction.

Second, RAFTs were originally designed to be written, but they could be used as oral presentations (with an accompanying visual aid if desired). Students could get up and speak their RAFTs to the class (or to a small group in the class) instead of submitting them in writing. This would move RAFTs from the written mode to the oral mode—which is what the next chapter is about.

Now let's look at a set of writing tasks that were designed to assess student understanding during instruction.

Using Writing to Assess Students' Understanding During Instruction

The Historical Persuasive Letter

I assigned my 8th graders the technical training manual as the end-of-the-1492-unit performance task, but I still needed to assess their understanding of the unit's content *during* learning. So, near the middle of the unit, I checked in with my students to see what understandings they were mentally constructing.

Rather than rely on a pencil-and-paper test or a written essay exam, I selected persuasive writing as the Info Out mode. Because persuasive is often the most challenging writing mode for many students, it makes sense to offer our students multiple opportunities to write persuasive letters to fine-tune their performance throughout the year.

And, as always, I considered ways to gain my students' interest and to motivate them to perform at the highest possible level.

I accomplished this by reconsidering the traditional audience and purpose for writing. Instead of assigning them to write to me (teacher as the typical audience), I told them to write a letter to Columbus's bosses: King Ferdinand and Queen Isabella. This got their attention. They were excited about the task. Imagine: they would rather write a letter to two people who have been dead for nearly 500 years than to write to their dear teacher. I took no offense at this; kids crave a variety of audiences and purposes for writing.

The Performance Task Sheet instructed them to write the Spanish monarchs a persuasive letter from the point of view of an eyewitness to the historical events of this time period. The aim of the persuasive writing mode, as noted on my students' worksheet, was "to persuade, to convince, to argue effectively for your point of view." Their purpose? "To persuade the monarchs to agree with your point of view about Columbus's voyages."

The task sheet told them to address three key focus questions about the historical content in their persuasive letters:

1. To introduce your letter, which *one key word* best summarizes your point of view of what happened during this critical historical period?

- discovery
- visit
- arrival
- exchange
- intrusion
- invasion
- conquest
- genocide
- other

2. What actual *historical evidence* can you provide to support your point of view?

3. What *opposing point of view* can you predict would be presented to the king and queen by someone else, and how do you respond to it?

A Standard, All-Purpose Writing Rubric

In addition to giving the students a task sheet, I presented them with a scoring instrument. Wouldn't it be nice to have a scoring device delivered to your classroom, so you wouldn't have to design your own? Betty and I have such a tool, compliments of the Oregon Department of Education. It is a multitrait rubric that analyzes student writing using a 6-point scale. Traits include ideas and content, organization, voice, sentence fluency, word choice, conventions, and citation of sources. Not to brag, but Oregon was the first state to develop and disseminate the "6 Traits" model (now 6+1 Traits). You can access it in a PDF file at www.ode.state.or.us/wma/teachlearn/testing/scoring/guides/2009-10/asmtwriscorguide0910eng.pdf.

Try it out by using it to score the following sample, Roberto's "Dear Monarchs" letter, for Trait 1, ideas and content.

My Dear King and Queen:

I consider the Columbus story to be a discovery.

It is true that the Tainos were there first, but it was Señor Columbus who united the worled (admittedly, he thought he was in Asia).

There was an "arrival," but that was only part of the discovery. There was an "invasion and conquest," but these events have been keeped mainly by word of mouth, and as history clearly states to us, when things are kept by word, tens become hundereds, hundereds become thousands, plagues become massekurs, and fights become wars.

I am not accusing the Indians of lying, only of exaggerating to get a verry important point across.

But 500 years of exagerating can create (through fault of no one) mistakes or even fiction.

Of course, Roberto's score for Trait 1 will be higher than his Trait 6 score (conventions), and he needs specific feedback on the strengths and weaknesses of his writing. Over time, with repeated use of the rubric, students will internalize "what good writing looks like."

An important note: we do not expect teachers to religiously assess all student writing for all seven analytical traits. Due to obvious time limitations, teaching to, and assessing for, selected traits (two to four) is certainly a sane approach.

From Another Classroom: 3rd Graders Read Fairy Tales and Write Dear Character Letters

Not only do Linda Christensen's 12th graders read fairy tales, but so do many 2nd, 3rd, and 4th graders. The study of fairy tales from around the world is a popular literature unit in many elementary classrooms, including Linda Barber's 3rd grade class at Guy Lee Elementary School in Springfield, Oregon.

During this unit on fairy tales, Linda wanted to check on her students' Info In processing. She knew that by selecting a motivating performance task, she would increase the accuracy of the assessment because her students would work to perform at their highest level. Rather than waiting until the end of the unit, she wanted to check in the middle of the unit on two targeted standards.

She chose a Dear Character letter in which a protagonist from a fairy tale the class had read writes a letter to a protagonist (or antagonist) from a different fairy tale. In the letters, students were expected to reveal their understanding of target one: the structure of fairy tales through retelling the main story elements: characters, setting, and plot.

The kids were given practice time prior to performance time (letter writing). Just as a director of a play would never expect a cast to perform on opening night without benefit of rehearsal, so too should we give our students opportunities to practice before show time. Early in the unit Linda modeled how to compare two fairy tales' structures using a two-columned worksheet:

Title		
Setting		
Protagonist and two characteristics	Name: 1. 2.	Name: 1. 2.
Antagonist and two characteristics	Name: 1. 2.	Name: 1. 2.
Problem		
Ending		

The second major target of the unit was the concept of literary point of view. To teach this critical standard, the class read a number of fairy tales from the *Point of View* series (Granowsky, 1993). These paperback books contain two opposing versions of the same fairy tale narrated by a different character; for example, Cinderella tells her story followed by a stepsister's version. Naturally, the two versions differ dramatically and humorously, so the students quickly and easily understood how a story can be told from differing points of view.

Another clever book that teaches an alternative perspective to a fairy tale is Jon Scieszka's *The True Story of the Three Little Pigs,* narrated by A. Wolfe (Scieszka, 1989). In a very funny rendition of the classic story, the wolf puts an entirely different spin to it. For example, he swears that all the "huffing and puffing" was due to an unfortunate head cold, and that the trouble with the pigs ("those little porkers") was caused by their lack of neighborly courtesy.

Next, Linda instructed her 3rd graders to select a favorite protagonist (e.g., Papa Bear or Goldilocks) and write a Dear Character letter from that perspective to another protagonist/antagonist from a different fairy tale. To give her students the best possible chance for performing well, Linda provided them with two items: (1) a sample letter (written by her) to critique and (2) a scoring rubric with two traits drawn from the Oregon Analytical Trait Writing Scoring Guide. (See above.) The state expects all 4th graders to meet the standard in all the traits, and because the teacher has the option of deciding how to teach them, Linda only focused on two of the traits on this assignment. Naturally, the other traits would be addressed at another time(s) during the year. (See http://www.ode.state.or.us/teachlearn/testing/dev/testspecs/asmtwrtestspecsover.pdf.)

Here is Linda's sample letter:

Dear Goldi,

Guess what! I made a bad mistake last week. Do you remember that my grandma was sick? Well, mom sent me to her house with a basket of bread, cheese, and wine to make her feel better. She told me not to talk to anyone and to go straight there, but here's where I blew it.

While I was walking through the woods I met a very nice (I thought) wolf who I stopped to chat with. I told him about Grams, and he told me where I could get some very nice flowers. I know mom said go straight there, but I thought some flowers would make Grams feel better, so I took a bit of a detour to pick some for her. I thought I was doing a good thing.

—Little Red Riding Hood

Figure A.13 shows a rubric for scoring the Dear Character letter. After reading his teacher's sample letter, young Jacob opted to be Jack (of beanstalk fame) and write to a famous antagonist, the Big Bad Wolf (costar of "Little Red Riding Hood"). Notice that he circles spelling uncertainties in his First Dare for correcting later in the Repair stage (Figure 4.7).

Possible Adaptations to the Dear Character Letter

Older students could write the Dear Character letter from the point of view of a minor character to the fairy tale's author, expressing reasons to reconsider the traditional plot and increase the minor character's role. Both point of view and story elements would still be the targets. Likewise, one could write from the antagonist's point of view rather than the more typical perspective of the protagonist.

Of course, fairy tales are not the only genre of literature that lend themselves to character letters. Teachers routinely find opportunities to assess their students' understandings of literature through the mode of writing. For example, they can ask students to write letters to a character in which they express approval or disapproval of the character's actions, offer advice on changing an attitude, or reveal some key information that the character doesn't yet know.

Older students could be expected to go beyond character and plot description to a deeper analysis of the folk tale's theme/moral, or to a comparison of the tale to another piece of fiction. The scoring rubric would be altered accordingly.

| Figure 4.7 | **3rd Grader's Dear Character Letter** |

the Jack   10-14-96

Dear Big bad Wolf,
I'm Jack. I have stolen from the rich and got the gold eggs including the harp and the gabbery, it first started when I bought this seed. They weren't just seeds. They were magic seeds but mom threw them out of the window. At night they grew higher and higher to the clouds. Then I climbed up the bean stalk. I saw a castle and a big giant's wife. I went into the castle. I chopped the beenstalk and the giant fell down and me and my mom lived happily ever after, and then we were rich because we got the money from the giant.

your friend,
jack

The Historical Fiction Story

Many teachers employ narrative story writing in addition to letter writing to assess students' understandings of new content. Beginning in the primary grades, students can write stories based on Info In content knowledge. Stories about whales and dinosaurs, Native American legends and Greek myths, tornadoes and life cycles, all are possible assignments.

In the above examples, the narrative mode is actually merged with the expository mode, so that students are explaining and informing (expository) through a story format (narrative). Even older students can benefit from this merger. At the risk of overdoing the

1492 unit, please read one 8th grader's combined expository and narrative:

> Oh, it was not a pleasant journey! I was 34 and had lived in Spain. I was an able-seaman and got paid $7 a month to sail on the *Santa María*, while the captain, Señor Columbus, got paid zillions. We ate hard biscuits and dried peas and salted meat for two meals a day. We had to eat with hands out of one wooden bowl between us all.

Teachers will recognize this type of writing as first-person historical fiction. The student shares her content understanding (of life aboard Columbus's ship in 1492) by way of story writing. She weaves the true historical facts she learned into an invented account of a fictitious character. James Michener himself would have been proud.

Now, let's consider using writing to assess very young students: Betty's 1st and 2nd graders during a health unit.

Assessing Primary Graders' Health Knowledge with the Informative News Article

During a unit on germ transmission, "How to Catch a Cold," my (Betty's) 1st and 2nd graders became Disease Detectives and conducted controlled experiments to Info In. To assess their understanding of the unit's important concepts, I chose the Info Out mode of writing: the students were to write humorous pop-up books. The next year, I changed the assignment: my new class was to write informational articles about germs and colds for our classroom newspaper. In expository writing, I told the kids, the writer explains or informs the audience about a topic.

To guide them to success on this performance task, I referred them back to the key focus questions we had addressed in the unit:

1. What is your hypothesis about the relationship of germs to catching a cold?
2. What experiments did you conduct?
3. What variables did you consider?
4. What are the results of your experiments?

And I added a fifth question:

5. What advice can you share with a reader?

Their assignment was to write an article with information containing answers to the above key questions. I reminded them that the best articles would not only answer the questions for a reader (content) but also meet the standards of good writing (process). To score the work, we selected three traits from the Oregon Analytical Trait Writing Scoring Guide (ideas/content, organization, and conventions). (See Figure 4.8.)

Using Reflective Writing Tasks

Reflective writing involves thinking about one's learning, both the content and process. Many teachers use "reflective journals" to teach students how to keep track of their learning. Successful forms of journal writing include a literature journal, a writer's diary, and a math log. Students record their thoughts about the literature they're reading, about struggles and successes with a writing assignment, or about how they attack math problems.

Tim Whitley, a science teacher in Eugene, Oregon, uses a reflective log writing performance task with his 9th and 10th grade biology students. To assess his students' understanding of ecosystems, Tim required every student to record thoughts, ideas, perceptions, illustrations, and/or facts in a spiral-bound mini-log. Throughout the unit, he reminded his students to make entries in whatever form(s) worked for them.

Figure 4.8	**Primary News Article ChecBric**
Trait	**Score**
1. I provided the reader with a lot of information. —— My hypothesis is stated. —— My experiment is described. —— I identified the variables. —— The results of my experiment are clear. —— I give advice to the reader.	**1 2 3 4 5 6** Comments:
2. My writing is organized. —— I have a catchy beginning. —— I have a "meaty" middle. —— I have a clear ending.	**1 2 3 4 5 6** Comments:
3. I checked my work and corrected it. —— I corrected all spelling errors. —— I fixed all punctuation mistakes. —— I wrote a neat final copy.	**1 2 3 4 5 6** Comments:

A score of **6** means that my work is really great.

A score of **5** means that my work is strong.

A score of **4** means that my work is OK and I am getting better all the time.

A score of **3** means that my work is weak but getting better.

A score of **2** means that my work is like that of a beginner.

A score of **1** means that I did not do this.

Angela wrote a poem about life cycles (Figure 4.9).

Nathan used annotated sketches to "show what he knows" about producers, consumers, and decomposers in nature (Figure 4.10).

To assess their understanding, the teacher responded to the students' recorded observations by writing comments, questions, and suggestions on yellow Post-it notes and attaching them throughout the biology journals. This method seems very appropriate to us. Assessing students' reflective writing differs from assessing the other writing modes because the purpose and audience are different. They are intended to help students be personally thoughtful about the content being studied or about the learning process being employed. The audience, of course, is oneself. Therefore, teacher assessment can be gently probing and supportive rather than coldly objective, as with a rubric or ChecBric.

Figure 4.9	**Angela's Reflective Biology Log Entry**

LIFE'S SECRET

A quick glance at nature,
and life stands still.
But peeking closer,
life reveals . . . ,

An endless cycle,
A busy chain
Mysterious wonders,
An intricate game.

The rules are a secret,
hidden behind an invisable [*sic*] muzzle
for who could ever decode,
life's magnificent puzzle.

Historical Reflective Writing

Of course, the more objective approach is valid, too. Cathy Bechen, a teacher from Shasta Middle School in Oregon's School District 52, assigned her 8th graders to keep a journal as a member of Lewis and Clark's historic expedition across the West to the Pacific Ocean. The content knowledge she was assessing is different from Tim Whitley's biology content, but the Info Out mode is the same: reflective writing.

Cathy set up the writing task by distributing a task assignment sheet with four steps for each team of student adventurers to follow. After making sure everyone understood the instructions, she gave each student a Lewis and Clark Simulation Task Sheet, which split the task into three subtasks: a chart, a map, and the journal (see Figure A.14).

Notice that the three subtasks are weighted in importance—the journal being the most important Info Out component, valued at 50 points. Here is one journal entry written by teammates Angela, Garrett, Darcy, Danielle, and Joe. Read to see how they revealed their understanding of this historical event by writing reflectively about it as if they were experiencing it firsthand through the eyes of a historical character:

May 16, 1804

Dear Journal,

Today we encountered a Shoshone Indian woman along the way. We decided to bring her with us, for an interpreter.

Figure 4.10	**Nathan's Reflective Biology Log Entry**

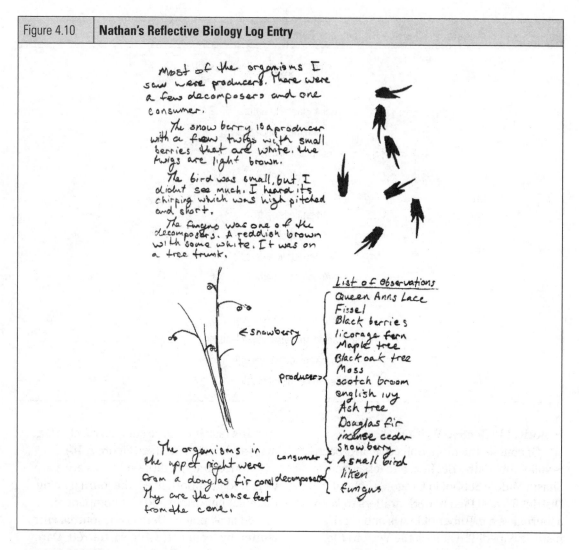

Most of the organisms I saw were producers. There were a few decomposers and one consumer.

The snow berry is a producer with a few twigs with small berries that are white. The twigs are light brown.

The bird was small, but I didn't see much. I heard its chirping which was high pitched and short.

The fungus was one of the decomposers. A reddish brown with some white. It was on a tree trunk.

← snowberry

The organisms in the upper right were from a douglas fir cone. They are the mouse feet from the cone.

producers {

consumer {

decomposers {

List of observations

Queen Anns Lace
Fissel
Black berries
licorage fern
Maple tree
Black oak tree
Moss
scotch broom
english ivy
Ash tree
Douglas fir
incense cedar
snow berry
A small bird
liken
fungus

Many of our men are sick with dysentery and boils. I believe that the dysentery came from drinking the river water, which was very rich in sediment.

The boils are the men working too hard and sweating which resulted in extreme exhaustion.

Earlier today I went down to the river and discovered a fish that I've never seen before. . . .

The team cowrote 10 pages of journal entries, complete with drawings of their observations, a map of the expeditions, and a chart showing the supplies taken and the money spent.

To assess her students, Cathy scored their reflective writing using the assessment list embedded in the Lewis and Clark Simulation Task Sheet (Figure A.14). She reports that there were no arguments or disagreements over the earned scores because everyone knew beforehand how they were going to be graded. Fairness and consistency are critical to successful performance assessment.

Additionally, Cathy avoided group scoring dissatisfaction by using a Group/Self-Assessment Chart (Figure A.15) for the Lewis and Clark Simulation. This assessment instrument asks for student input on how to evaluate individual learners' contributions to a group task. The groups decide who earns what.

We are excited about this student self-scoring instrument for cooperative effort. It offers great potential for us to solve the persistent problem of laggards in student groups.

Using Writing to Assess Students' Understanding Before Instruction

Although teachers typically use writing tasks as end-of-unit assessments or during-unit assessments, teachers may use them to assess student understandings *before* instruction begins. Just as visual representations—such as the Folded File Folder or concept maps (see Chapter 3)—are effective pre-assessments, so too can writing reveal to teachers what our students know in advance of instruction. Let's look at three useful mini tasks.

The Picture Postcard

At the beginning of a unit or topic of study, teachers can "peek" into their students' existing knowledge base by asking them to jot ideas on a 5- by 8-inch index card. Students write what they already know or think they know about the topic. On the front side of the "postcard," students draw a picture of the topic.

When assessing student understandings at this early stage, teachers have a different objective than they do during or after instruction. This objective is to complete a preteaching diagnosis that determines the general level of content understanding and any consistent misconceptions. The purpose is to inform the upcoming instruction rather than to scrutinize each student's level of understanding. Therefore, creating a rubric, ChecBric, or checklist seems unnecessary to us. However, a teacher may want to consider using a Concept Acquisition Development Continuum (see Figure A.26).

The Dear Teacher Letter

To check students' Info In knowledge before instruction, teachers may also use another writing task: the Dear Teacher letter. Students compose a short, friendly letter to their teacher announcing what they already know about the topic. To indicate their uncertainty about the accuracy of any of their content knowledge, they add a question mark (?). Likewise, students can mark certain preknowledge with an asterisk (*) to indicate what they think is especially important. Finally, in a P.S. to the letter, students inform their teacher what they hope will be covered in the unit, perhaps including a question or two they hope will be answered.

"Who's on First?"

A third assessment mini task that occurs before instruction is "Who's on First?" This task, a combination of the written and visual modes, plays off a baseball metaphor. At four different times during a unit (the four bases), students reveal their current content understanding. The first time (first base) occurs before instruction. For example, at the start of a literature unit on the theme of survival, students fill out the worksheet shown in Figure 4.11.

Figure 4.11	**"Who's on First?" Pre-assessment for Reading a Novel**

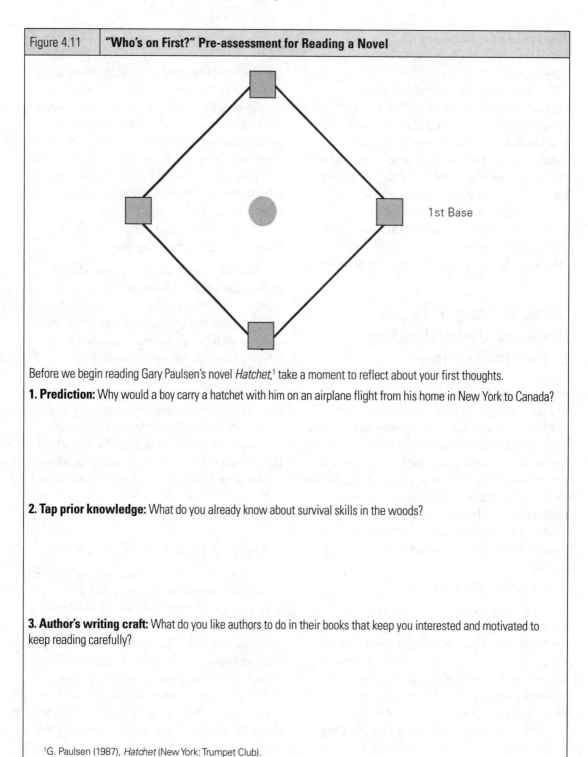

1st Base

Before we begin reading Gary Paulsen's novel *Hatchet*,[1] take a moment to reflect about your first thoughts.

1. Prediction: Why would a boy carry a hatchet with him on an airplane flight from his home in New York to Canada?

2. Tap prior knowledge: What do you already know about survival skills in the woods?

3. Author's writing craft: What do you like authors to do in their books that keep you interested and motivated to keep reading carefully?

[1]G. Paulsen (1987), *Hatchet* (New York: Trumpet Club).

A "Maxi-to-the-Max" Writing Task: The Civil War Magazine

What about expanding the news article, a midi task, into a maxi? Cathy Bechen, the middle school teacher referred to earlier, uses the desktop-published magazine performance task to measure her students' understanding of the Civil War. She also provides her students with a pre-task list of the five required ingredients: factual articles, interviews, letters to the editor, advertisements, and an illustrated cover.

Read this student-written article, set in 1860, about white Americans who fought against slavery and ask yourself, Does this student understand abolitionism?

> The first thing you think about when reading the words "slave uprising" might be, "O.K., what Negro started it this time?" Actually, we do remember Nat Turner's famous revolt that claimed 57 lives, and the proud black American named Denmark Vessy, and other rebellious slaves.
>
> But what about white Americans who took a stand, and decided to fight for the freedom of slaves? There were different kinds of fighting, though. William Lloyd Garrison fought with his anti-slavery newspaper, *The Liberator*. He tried to make the Southern plantation owners realize that this was against God's ways. In his newspaper, he "demanded to be heard." Garrison was considered very radical.
>
> Angelina Grimke Weld published a pamphlet called, "Appeal to Christian Women of the South." She was also considered a radical.
>
> Another way to fight was John Brown's way. He led an attack with 18 fugitive slaves on Harper's Ferry. Before he could go through with an ambush, he was caught, tried, and convicted for treason. John Brown was hung.
>
> These are acts of bravery. We should be grateful to them, and what they have done for us. —*Garrett*

The question of whether Garrett understands abolitionism actually needs to be restated: to what *degree* does he understand abolitionism? And because he is using the Info Out mode of writing, we must ask, To what degree does he understand abolitionism, *and* how well does he write about it?

Consider Timothy's writing ability to hook readers' attention in this introduction to his factual article on Sojourner Truth:

> Ms. Truth, like most black women of our time [mid-1800s], started with humble, if not horrible, beginnings.

Cathy decided to assess their writing using an adaptation of Oregon's Analytical Writing Traits Assessment. She opted to score for the original six writing traits, but to shorten the rubric into one page using "kid-friendly" language. She used the 6-point scoring scale shown in Figure A.16. This modified rubric is designed to assess students' use of the writing process. The fourth trait, ideas, may need to be reworked to add more content specificity. Cathy assigned each student in a group to write all four of the required pieces and to sign them, so she could assess each writer independently from his or her teammates.

Cathy has also assigned the magazine writing task to assess her students on the topic of westward expansion. And, of course, magazines can be handwritten instead of computer printed, and topics certainly are not restricted to U.S. history.

A Snapshot of Chapter 4

For centuries, teachers have used writing to measure their students' understanding of what has been taught. Now, with performance assessment, we can fine-tune writing assignments and convert them into writing tasks that more accurately assess students' content knowledge.

In this chapter, we have described the use of writing as an Info Out mode to assess student understanding. Writing performance tasks

- may be assigned before, during, and after instruction;
- have a variety of purposes: to persuade, to explain/inform, to narrate a story, or to reflect on one's learning of content and/or process;
- should offer a variety of audences instead of the traditional teacher-as-sole-reader;
- may be scored using a variety of devices, including a premade, generic rubric, such as the Oregon Department of Education's Analytical Traits (1996, 2009);
- are strengthened and student performance improved when teachers provide students with task assignment sheets that preview the procedure, share the scoring device up front, and provide sample papers that model a range of performances.

By attending to these factors, teachers can serve as coaches who guide their charges to higher and higher levels of performance.

In the next chapter, we consider using oral presentations in the same way.

chapter 5

Info Out: Assessing Students' Understanding Through Oral Presentations

Betty's Story

Gilian, one of my 4th grade students, gave a speech to the class about library systems. She spoke articulately and precisely about the alphabetical system, the circulation system, and in particular, the Dewey Decimal System. After her presentation, I asked her how she knew so much about the Dewey Decimal System. "I found it in the encyclopedia and copied it down," she said, "Then I memorized it and told it to the class." Hmmm . . . .

When we began to work on this second edition of *Great Performances,* we asked numbers of teachers about their experiences in having students speak in front of the class. We heard several stories that were funny, some that were enlightening, and many that were agonizing. What made these anecdotes agonizing? Most characterized the terror that students feel when they must speak in front of a group and the effects on the individual student—all the way from hiccups and giggling to freezing up, vomiting, fainting, and

losing bladder control—all reported as true by teachers.

Our goal for including this chapter on oral presentations is not to emphasize the challenge; rather, it is to help you get your students comfortable in front of a group. Nor is our goal to give you specific strategies that you can use with students to develop and deliver effective speeches. Our goal is to help you remember that, for most students, speaking is their first way of communicating their thinking about how to make sense of the world. Regardless of the content of the curriculum, *sharing understanding* is the essential ingredient in the teaching-learning equation. As teachers, we must maximize our use of speaking as a means for ascertaining a student's conceptual understanding of what it is we have been teaching.

In this chapter we intend to convince you both that speaking is important and that traditional oral reports are not an adequate means of assessing content knowledge; rather, if we are to fairly assess students' content acquisition, discourse—verbal *exchanges* between the student and others—must occur. We will describe four contexts in which these verbal exchanges are fostered:

1. Argumentation in the classroom
2. Formal speeches in front of the class followed by questions and answers
3. Rotating mini-speeches to small groups
4. Substantive dialogue between a student and the teacher

Students can use each setting to share the extent of their content knowledge with you. Additionally, we will

- share some scoring mechanisms for assessing these verbal exchanges,
- talk about the critical role questioning plays in prompting this dialogue, and
- describe how these exchanges involve the use of key thinking strategies.

What Do We Mean When We Say "Speaking"?

Let's be clear. Children use oral language as their primary vehicle for asserting, clarifying, and changing their perceptions and beliefs. Oral expression is "the core process in formulating and sharing human experience" (Marzano et al., 1988). As Marzano and his colleagues state:

> It is a key pedagogical method because students who make meaning by stating academic knowledge in their own words demonstrate a depth of understanding well beyond what is reflected in recitation or in the recognition-testing of many paper-and-pencil tests. (p. 64)

In its simplest form, speaking can be defined as using words to say what one is thinking. However, when using speaking as a tool for assessment, most teachers prefer the more narrow definition of *public speaking*—that is, making a speech before an audience. Using this more narrow definition, assessment of speaking has tended to focus on the mechanics of giving the speech (delivery, organization, audience, etc.). For our purposes, we want to broaden the definition of "speaking" to encompass the larger concept of oral discourse. Oral discourse is verbal interaction at length about some subject—that is, the content we are teaching.

As noted, we'll look at four contexts in which speaking exchanges are fostered.

Argumentation in the Classroom

Have you ever noticed that some students will not share a word with their classmates even when you nudge and nurture them to express their opinions? And yet at other times, you cannot get these same students to stop talking, chill out, calm down, when confronted with a school-, classroom-, or community-based issue unrelated to your curriculum. Why does this happen? Frankly, it has been our experience that these students do not speak up in a convincing and effective way because they simply perceive that the content under discussion has little or no meaning or value to them.

So we propose the following notion. Start with relevant, contemporary issues that arise at school, in the classroom or school community. Teach students about debate and one of its components—argumentation—and then expect them to make effective arguments in favor of their position about the issue.

When we think of debate, we often think of a formal method of interaction based on argumentation between two teams or individuals in a contest. We will highlight here the model used by the Middle School Public Debate Program (MSPDP) centered at

Claremont McKenna College. The program uses three speakers on each of two teams and has the following debate format:

First Proposition: The first proposition speaker makes a case for the motion for debate. That is, she provides assertions, reasoning, and evidence in support of the motion. She may offer a specific interpretation of the motion.

First Opposition: The first opposition speaker presents arguments against the case presented by the other team. He uses direct and indirect refutation to undermine the case and show why the other side's position is wrong and ill advised.

Second Proposition: The second proposition speaker supports the case presented by the first proposition speaker. He answers all arguments made by the previous speaker and brings in new ideas to bolster his side's position.

Second Opposition: The second opposition speaker extends upon her partner's arguments against the case. She continues to refute proposition's arguments and brings in new ideas to bolster their side's position.

Opposition Rebuttal: The third opposition speaker continues to refute proposition's major points. She should explain how, given the arguments advanced in the debate, the opposition wins the debate.

Proposition Rebuttal: The third proposition speaker refutes the arguments advanced and extended by the opposition side. He then extends his partners' arguments. He ends by showing how, given the arguments advanced in the debate, the proposition wins the debate.

Most debate follows this format. But for our purposes here, we want to zero in on the notion of "argumentation." Effective speakers must know how to make an argument—they must share proofs that support their claims or position. This is one major difference between everyday conversation and formal speaking or debating.

In their book, *Speak Out! Debate and Public Speaking in the Middle Grades,* Kate Shuster, program director for the Middle School Public Debate Program, and her colleague, John Meany, Director of Forensics at Claremont McKenna College (Shuster & Meany, 2005), teach students a simple yet effective approach to argumentation: the ARE method. ARE stands for (1) making an Assertion, (2) providing your Reasoning, and (3) providing Evidence in support of your assertion. An assertion is a statement that says something is so. Reasoning is the "because" part of an argument, and evidence is the "for example" part that supports or validates the reasoning.

So, we propose here to refocus the issues that spontaneously come up in class and use them for their potential speaking advantage. You don't need to set up a formal debate every time (although you can and should do that at times). Have students speak either in support of a position or in opposition to assertions based on these issues. Argumentation then can become a midi or maxi task, depending on the day, the time, and the intensity of the issue (and your sanity!).

Let's flesh out a middle school example here. Let's say that some students come to you and state, "We want to skateboard to school. Why can't we skateboard on school grounds?" You, in turn, seize this teachable moment and propose that students make a case either for or against skateboarding on campus. You employ the ARE method to teach students how to make an effective argument.

The following two examples share an assertion in support of or against skateboarding at school. See how all three elements of the argument (ARE) are present.

Assertion: Students should be allowed to skateboard on school grounds.

Reasoning: In a time when many teens are overweight and out of shape, skateboarding is great exercise, AND it encourages you to practice tricks until you get them right. It increases your confidence and your balance. And I don't need to tell YOU how much people think teenagers can't concentrate or commit these days!

Evidence: In a recent survey in the United States, skateboarding was found to be the third most popular sport with teenagers, coming in just under football and basketball. Currently, 103 students skateboard to this school each day. Why can't they skate on school grounds when bicycles can be ridden on school grounds? Is this fair?

Assertion: Students should not be allowed to skateboard at school.

Reasoning: Skateboarding is an activity in which you move quickly over hard surfaces. It can lead to injuries that range from minor cuts and bruises to catastrophic brain injury. Mostly boys skateboard, and they cut in front of girls to get their attention and the girls end up hurt.

Evidence: Online we found that each year in the United States, skateboarding injuries cause about 50,000 visits to emergency departments and 1,500 children and adolescents to be hospitalized. Sixty percent of skateboard injuries involve children under age 15; most of those injured are boys, according to the American Academy of Orthopedic Surgeons. I have observed skaters

spitting on the sidewalk. Do we really want spitting on campus, too?

What are some other possible issues that might create opportunities for argumentation? We have addressed the following in our teaching:

• A change in Oregon law states that a teen receiving a driver's license for the first time cannot have other teens ride with him or her for the period of one year unless an adult is also present in the car.

• Teachers report that text messaging in class among secondary students is increasingly distracting, yet many students don't find it inappropriate. We propose that cell phone use be outlawed from class.

• During recess, why are students not allowed to bring out a book, sit on the bench, and read it? We propose that students be allowed to sit and read during recess.

• The removal of soft drink machines from all middle schools is unfair and unreasonable. (This issue was raised when the school board decided to remove all soft drinks machines for all schools in our district.)

• What justifies the removal of all locker bays at a high school? (A high school removed the locker bays to control substance abuse and other illegal activities on campus.)

• Freshmen and sophomores will not be allowed to park on campus because of overcrowding in the parking lots.

In addition to those items listed above, we have dealt with the residue from transitions to and from the playground at the elementary level (soccer field, sharing equipment, taunting, etc.) and passing times at the middle and high school levels (fighting with friends in the hallway, competing for the opposite gender's attention, teasing, etc.).

Can you score these arguments? Yes, you can. We suggest that you use a simple checklist like the one in Figure 5.1 to help students attend to the three elements of argument (Assertion, Reasoning, and Evidence) and not focus on the delivery of the speech. For practice, you can ask a student volunteer to give a speech in front of the class and inform the student that you will interrupt the presentation on occasion to practice scoring. You can project the checklist on an overhead or a document camera and have students discuss the oral arguments as the student presents arguments. This can be done using a video clip as well. You might invite some students to work with you on developing a practice set of video clips for this purpose.

If you want, you can ask the class to rate the reasoning and evidence with a score of 1 to 4 or 1 to 6 after the presentation. This can be done by having students discuss and evaluate the impact of the reasoning and evidence on them as an audience. This is a great time to use those classroom electronic response systems we call "clickers." Having students score the reasoning and evidence using the clickers is efficient as well as visual. And it's fun. (You can do a web search using "classroom response systems" and find numerous websites that sell such products.)

We hesitate to take precious time to deal with these in- and out-of-class issues, but many times you have no choice. They won't go away—you are going to end up having to deal with them, so you might as well turn them into teachable moments. We have found that at times, there is a palpable mood in class when something happened outside of class that simply prohibits you from moving forward with your lesson until you address the issue.

Our point here is that when students have a vested interest in the topic, they are more motivated to gather evidence that supports their position and are more willing to spend time to make sure that their position is well received through effective communication. Using the ARE method above will lead to more and better formal speaking later, when assigned topics are of less interest to students.

Let's now move on to more formal speaking at the end of a unit or course.

At the End of the Unit or Course: Speaking in Front of the Class

Most of us at some time or other have asked students to get up in front of the class and give an oral report on some subject. When scoring these presentations, most of us have focused on the features of the delivery of the speech and done little to score the content. How might a simple oral report assignment become a vehicle for students to demonstrate their content understanding? Here is how Betty adapted a traditional 2nd and 3rd grade oral report on animals to increase her ability to assess her students' acquisition of core knowledge content.

Speaking in Betty's Classroom at the Primary Level

Each year, I assigned my young students a simple research project to gather information in the library on an animal of their choosing. I instructed each student to keep note cards on basic information about the animal and prepare a three- to four-minute speech to present in front of the class. The main emphasis of my instruction was on how to stand in front of the group, maintain eye contact, and project one's voice. Even though I gave students a short list of questions to answer, I did not focus on the content of the speech. I *did* focus on delivery and organization—making sure

Figure 5.1	**ARE Argumentation Checklist**

Name _____ Date _____ Period _____

All good arguments follow this format:

1. An argument starts with an **assertion**—a statement that claims something is true or takes a position about something. "This school should guarantee that winter break is at least two weeks long."

2. The next part of an argument is to provide a **reason** (or an explanation) for why the audience should believe the claim you are making.

3. The third part of an argument is the **evidence** you give to support your assertion or its reasoning, or both.

To make a complete argument, you must always include all three parts.

Complete the checklist below:

1. Put your initials in column one as you complete that element of the ARE.

2. In column two, circle all the bullets that apply to your argument.

3. In column three, record your own assertion, reasoning, and evidence.

I did this.		
	1. I make an assertion. • I claim something is true. • I take a position for or against something.	My assertion is:
	2. I share my reasoning. • I state that my assertion is true because . . . . • My reasons are clear.	My reasoning is:
	3. I provide evidence in support of my assertion in one or more of the following four ways. • I provide illustrations. • I give examples—either personal examples or historical examples. • I use an analogy; that is, I use what was true in one situation to convince the audience that it would be true in this situation. • I use statistical data; that is, I share the results from studies, surveys, and opinion polls.	The evidence I provide to support my assertion is:

Adapted from a model developed by Kate Shuster at the Middle School Program, Claremont College.

that my kids knew that a good speech had a beginning, a middle, and an end.

What were the results? I could not tell whether each student's content knowledge reflected simple memorization and regurgitation or actual concept development. In fact, as I listened to their animal speeches, I increasingly suspected they were reciting paragraphs directly out of the *World Book Encyclopedia.*

In the meantime, the Oregon State Content Standards were published. As I looked over the science section of the document, I noticed that, by the end of grade 3, my students would be expected to

- identify examples of change over time;
- classify organisms based on a variety of characteristics;
- describe a habitat and the organisms that live there;
- identify daily and seasonal weather changes.

I began to explore ways to adapt the oral report into a strong performance task that I could use to assess the above standards. Here is a synopsis of the task I created (see Figure 5.2). In the first assignment, I had included a list of questions for students to answer. However, in revising the task to better match the standards, I modified the questions. I also adapted the task and the scoring guide (Figure A.17) to emphasize core content knowledge.

Speaking Assessment at the High School Level: The Debate

Another example of using speaking to assess core knowledge content comes from our colleague, Lilly Edwards, business systems teacher at Willamette High School in Eugene, Oregon. We have taken her basic idea and modified it slightly to enhance the scoring mechanisms. She uses this task with 11th graders in a business systems course. Part of their study includes social and environmental responsibility in business. This project, which includes a written paper and a debate, comes at the end of the business ethics study. In groups of four or five, students research a company that Lilly selects (see Figure A.18). She typically chooses companies that market high-interest products such as soft drinks and sports equipment. In the assignment for the oral presentation, two groups studying the same company argue in support of or in opposition to a company's environmental and social record.

As explained at the bottom of Figure A.18, students assess their own work using the ChecBric (Figure A.19), classmates assess their work also using the ChecBric, and each team conferences with the teacher to come up with a grade for the project. Lilly uses a unique system to determine the scores for all members of each group. This system, the Peer Evaluation Scoring Guide, is shown in Figure A.20.

Of course, we have chosen to detail the oral component here—the debate rated in the last column (p.175). However, remember that we mentioned earlier that students, as a part of the whole culminating project, were expected to discuss/brainstorm, conduct research, produce a work plan, and write a report in preparation for the debate.

One last point: we don't do full-blown oral presentations all the time. Realistically, we try to incorporate only a couple of these more formal oral presentations throughout the year because of obvious time constraints.

Round-Robin Mini-Speeches in Larry's Middle School Class

During a study of U.S. history in the 1800s, I (Larry) offered my students a menu of topics

Figure 5.2	**Primary-Level Animal Oral Report Task Sheet**

Name _____ Date _____

Here is your task:

A. Select an animal from the following list. You should select an animal that you find interesting and that you would like to learn more about.

B. Find out as much as you can about the animal you have selected. Get information from at least three different books, magazines, or people. Our media specialist will also help us learn how to use the World Wide Web to get more information.

C. You will receive four note cards. On each note card, copy these focus questions:

As you find out more about your animal, write notes about what you learned on the note cards.

D. Prepare a speech about your animal. The speech should be about 3–4 minutes long. Use the information on your note cards to create your speech. Your speech will be scored on three parts:

Figure 5.2	**Primary-Level Animal Oral Report Task Sheet** (*continued*)

E. When you make your speech, it is OK to use props to help you. You may want to show a picture of your animal that you found or drew. You may also refer to your note cards to remind yourself of what you want to say. But you should not read your speech.

F. You will need help. What kind of help is OK? It is OK to have someone help you read and discuss what you read. It is OK for someone to listen to you practice your speech and give you feedback on how to improve it. You should take your own notes.

G. Your speech needs to be completed and ready to give by _____. I will check in with you on the following days to see if you are getting parts of your work completed. These dates are important:

Date: _____	You have selected an animal to study.
	You have copied the questions on the note cards.
Date: _____	You have gathered information and recorded it on the note cards.
Date: _____	You have a speech prepared and are practicing giving it.
Date: _____	You give your speech in front of the class.

Take this sheet home, and read over it with your parents. Complete the bottom of the form, tear it off, and bring it back to school tomorrow.

· ·

Name _____

I have selected this animal to study for my

oral report: _____

Student Signature

Parent Signature

_____   _____

Check any of the following supplies you may want to get from school:

_____ large sheet of butcher paper   _____ scissors

_____ a set of felt-tip pens   _____ tape

_____ a set of colored pencils   _____ books, magazines

to choose from for a research project. Realizing that we didn't have time for an in-depth study of all the topics of this historical period, I opted for the "divide and conquer" approach. Each kid would become a mini-expert on a topic and then teach classmates what he or she had learned.

After my students indicated their first, second, and third topic choices, I paired them to learn about the topic using resources such as their history textbook, a supplemental text, and the Internet. Before the pairs began their research (Info In), I told them what the Info Out was going to be. Each team would create a visual representation of newly learned content information in the form of a graphic organizer on 11- by 17-inch paper (see Chapter 3.) This graphic organizer would then serve as a prompt for a five-minute mini-speech to a small group of classmates who would rely on them for learning about the topic.

When the class found out that the Info Out was an oral presentation, they displayed what could be described as major signs of displeasure. But their concerns were largely mitigated upon learning that the oral presentation would be made to a small group and that everyone would be working with a partner.

I also told them that they would repeat their mini-speech to four small groups that would rotate from team presentation to team presentation. This repetition would help them become increasingly comfortable presenting in front of a group. To clarify what I meant, I drew a picture of how the classroom would be set up to accommodate this round-robin oral performance task.

I was pleasantly surprised at how well they accomplished the rotations. As I circulated around the room, sitting in on all four groups, three things impressed me. First, I liked how each pair of speakers used their graphic organizer as a cue card for the mini-speech. I was also pleased with the partners' ability to share the speaking load. (I had told them that they had better both contribute.) Third, I was thrilled at the small-group audiences' behavior. They were attentive, polite, and seemingly interested in the content material.

Of course, I was wise enough to coach the audiences in how to listen properly. I had distributed small booklets of blank paper for required note taking at each rotation. The kids were to begin each booklet page with the title of the topic and the two speakers' names. Then, as the mini-speeches progressed, they jotted down notes, wrote questions, or drew quick illustrations to facilitate their Info In from their classmates.

Day 2 also went very well. Four new pairs of students were stationed at the four presenter tables, armed with their graphic organizers. I split the remaining students into four rotating audiences that spent five to seven minutes with each pair of presenters, taking notes and asking follow-up questions. I, too, circulated during all four presentations so that I could assess the oral Info Outs. At the end of Day 2, eight presentations had been completed (with two kids on each team), so we were halfway home.

Day 3 didn't go as well. Perhaps I should have given the class a break from the activity, or maybe it was the bad luck of the draw that two of the four presenter pairs were jokers—and irreverent jokers at that! For example, the students presenting on Lewis and Clark were less than inspiring: they failed to mention the reason for the expedition, its main effect on the development of the United States, and even the role of Sacajawea (Sacagawea). They did, however, reveal to their antsy audience that "Lewis and Clark were cool dudes who kicked b_ _ _ when faced with danger." Good to know.

Possible Pitfalls

As with any assessment task, pitfalls loom before us. The above description of the Lewis and Clark fiasco discloses the most dangerous potential problem: lack of content expertise. If students are supposed to reveal their understanding of new content information (Info Out), then they had better do a good job of learning it (Info In). The graphic organizer mini task worked for most teams, but obviously not all.

Next time I will work with several teams—ones I suspect might need it—for a quick assessment of their graphic organizer before they make their oral presentation. This added step should improve quality control. And quality is essential not only for the two presenters, who need to learn about their topic, but also for the audiences, who count on them for quality teaching.

Another pitfall I quickly identified was how rushed I was in moving among and scoring four presentations (times two presenters) during each 50-minute class period. If the task's scoring device has more than just a few traits to assess, then it's doubtful that it can be done. I suggest that if you use this round-robin approach, you score just two traits:

- *Delivery:* oral communication ability to have an impact on your audience
- *Content:* shared expertise of key points of your topic

Of course, you could give each audience member a copy of the scoring device (like one created from the above two traits, or the ones Lilly and Betty used earlier) for peer evaluation. The problem becomes what to do with the peer data. On the "outside" chance that you receive some inappropriate or useless comments, simply scan the stack before handing the feedback over to the presenter. Some teachers aggregate the peer review scores and incorporate them into the overall grade. We have, on occasion, asked other adults (university student volunteers or trained community members, for example) to give feedback, which we have incorporated into the grade. However, we don't make it a practice to incorporate student feedback as a part of the overall grade. If you have had experience in this area and would be interested in sharing it with us, please give us your thoughts.

With students listening to four oral presentations each day, a third pitfall involves the danger of their losing track of all this new content information. Although the note-taking requirement in the booklets was a stroke of genius for focusing students' intake of information, too much content was being shared for significant processing and remembering to occur.

To assist in the latter, I altered the presentation schedule by beginning each class period with a review session. I asked the kids to open their note-taking booklets to a particular topic from the day before and highlight with a colored pen or pencil the two to three facts they believed were "important enough to remember into adulthood." I then led a class discussion on their highlighted notes to gain consensus on the key points.

This exercise improved my students' Info In by giving them a chance to Repair their initial note taking. Some kids had missed key points; others had tried to record everything the presenters had stated. I suspect that this Repair activity improved their note-taking skills. Having a daily review slowed down the schedule, but it was well worth it.

Naturally, I collected all note-taking booklets to assess the audience's listening and processing ability. I did not have a scoring device for this assessment, so I merely assigned points. Next, time I intend to use Tim Whitley's "Post-it" technique. (See Chapter 4, page 75.)

Speaking During a Unit or Course

We want to suggest a few possibilities for using speaking as an assessment during a unit or course. One easy way to assess content knowledge acquisition during instruction is for students to share a two- to three-minute extemporaneous speech on the subject at hand. This activity will quickly give you a picture of each student's current thinking. Ask students to respond to one or two questions. To do so, list each student's name on a 3- by 5-inch index card, and randomly draw out two or three names to present on the topic when you lack time to listen to everyone. For some reason, we have noticed that students tend to be more attentive when they know that the teacher is making an effort to check in with everyone randomly.

Another of Betty's favorite during-unit oral assessments used to be the *Home Improvement* Triangle. When we first published *Great Performances,* most students were familiar with the popular television series *Home Improvement.* Students were asked to assume the role of one of these three characters and speak to the topic at hand from that person's point of view. These days, most students are unfamiliar with the show. However, you can still assign students to represent three different roles: the person who doesn't get it at all or is mixed up on several key points (Tim), the person who gets it but just the basics (Al), and the person who really gets it (Mr. Wilson). The three students then work together to create a script reflecting each role and share them with the class. A friend of ours now uses Lisa, Bart, and Homer Simpson for the three points of view.

Speaking Before a Unit or Course

For us, the most effective way for students to share their content knowledge through speaking at the beginning of the course is by conducting a press conference. Work through key focus questions (see Chapter 2), and give students an opportunity to make opening remarks about their current thinking (prior knowledge) on the question. Then have the audience, as the press corps, ask follow-up questions in a popcorn fashion (popping from around the room randomly and asking questions).

Substantive Dialogue

It is important to note that, in some cases, you may not be clear about students' content understanding even after examining work produced in the activities described earlier. For all students—and *in particular* for these students—it is imperative that you engage them in "substantive dialogue," our third format for speaking. We have found this format particularly appropriate with both special education and talented/gifted students.

What we call "substantive dialogue," Fred Newmann (1991) refers to as "substantive conversation." For authentic student achievement to occur, he says, substantive conversation must be present. That is, when assessment of content acquisition is the goal, substantive conversation between the learner and some supportive resource—teacher, critic, or other knowledgeable authority—is necessary.

Working from Newmann's constructs, we suggest that substantive conversation is present when

• two or more people engage in sustained, continuous talk;
• there is considerable interaction about ideas related to the subject at hand;

• the talk is not scripted or controlled—the course of the conversation is less predictable than in conventional classroom exchanges;

• the conversation builds coherently on the student's ideas through the teacher's/expert's/critic's use of questioning prompts; and

• the student is able to deal with the knowledge hierarchically from specific facts, concepts, and generalizations to applying these concepts in other contexts.

Facilitating Substantive Dialogue

How might teachers engage students in substantive dialogue? Consider using a series of questioning prompts tied to specific thinking strategies. Students cannot show what they know about a topic without "thinking" about that topic. In particular, thinkers use

• focusing strategies;
• remembering/retrieving/summarizing strategies;
• analyzing strategies;
• generating strategies; and
• evaluating strategies;

Figure A.21 lists these strategies, their purposes, and appropriate questioning prompts (Marzano et al., 1988). Remember, when you ask salient questions about the topic, you force students to use one of these thinking strategies. So not only do you as the assessor get a better picture of what students understand, but you are giving them practice in improving their thinking!

Scoring All Four Types of Oral Presentations

We imagine that you are all sitting back thinking, "Larry and Betty, get real! No way do I, or any other teacher I know, have time to pull off the oral presentation assessments

that you are suggesting." Believe us, we understand. We have been hard-pressed to do so ourselves. We have had to make a number of time-saving adaptations in order to survive. These adaptations include the following:

1. For efficiency, scoring the task during the presentation instead of waiting for a post-presentation conference.

2. On occasion, videotaping the presentations and having students review the tape to score their own work.

3. To prevent teacher and listener burnout, having only two or three students give their presentations each day, thus extending the assessments over a couple of weeks.

4. Training a cadre of adult volunteers to help you score student oral presentations.

Betty's Core Content Cadre

So—you ask—how do you train adults to score student presentations? When I train students to use the speaking scoring guides shown earlier, I invite a corps of parents and other adult volunteers to join us for the same training. At an after-school follow-up session, I give the adults time to practice scoring as needed to increase reliability. If your district provides training in scoring for teachers, I would suggest that you invite adult volunteers to the in-service session, too.

Originally, when asking other adults to participate in substantive dialogue with students about their work, I had trouble helping them know how to score the work. So I developed a Substantive Dialogue Scoring Guide (Figure A.22). Participating adults simply select one or two prompts from each area in the left column to ask students and then record a few phrases that illustrate student responses in the second column. Next, using something like the Generic Rubric for Declarative Standards developed by Marzano,

Pickering, and McTighe (1993), they can assign an overall score.

Of course, you can customize the questions for the specific task at hand and coach your scorers, as needed, in how to use the scoring mechanism. Because we are just beginning to try out this mechanism, we haven't worked out all the bugs yet. If you try it, let us know how it works and if you needed to make any adaptations.

Yes, but . . . Significant Effects and Adaptations

When designing task assignment sheets and scoring mechanisms for speaking performances, it is important to pay attention to some significant effects and adaptations. In the way you frame the task or scoring mechanism, you can inadvertently influence the results of student responses. Here are a few to note.

Leading the Witness: When you engage in substantive dialogue with one or more students, the kinds of questions or prompts you provide will shape the responses you receive. That is, occasionally we have found ourselves prompting students in such a way that indicated not only the *type* of response we were looking for, but also the *content* of the response, as well. For example, when interviewing students, you might be tempted to ask, "What evidence can you list that clearly shows us that the XYZ Corporation is socially responsible to its subcontracted employees?" From our point of view, this type of prompt tends to push the student toward a particular point of view. Teachers must guard against "leading the witness." A better prompt would be "What evidence from your analysis supports the notion that XYZ treats its subcontracted workers fairly or unfairly?"

The Paint-by-Number Effect: When constructing a scoring mechanism for assessing content knowledge, it is very easy to make the question prompts and scoring guide traits so explicit that you get what we call paint-by-number responses. It is obvious that formula questions often lead to formula responses, and most of us know how "artistically moving" paint-by-number is!

The Broadside-of-the-Barn Effect: On the other hand, when working with younger students, we feel justified in making the target easier to hit so that they can learn how to successfully respond to these kinds of assessments. In other words, we design the scoring guide for younger students so that their target *is* the "broadside of the barn." We want the target to be "unmissable" at first so that students experience success from the get-go. As they mature, you can make the targets ever smaller and more focused. This may also apply to some of your special needs students.

Regurgitation—Confusing Reading or Memorization/Recitation for Speaking: Some folks would hold that students must write out their oral presentations word for word before presenting them to the group. In our experience, many students resort to writing the report and then reading it. Reading is *not* speaking. Students need to be able to understand the difference between reading canned scripts and speaking. Also, some students use props as a distraction to conceal the fact that they are speaking from rote memorization. We want to know how well a student can talk on his or her feet about the subject—not memorize and regurgitate canned knowledge.

A Snapshot of Chapter 5

In this chapter, we introduced you to our third Info Out mode—oral presentations. Simply speaking in front of a class, we emphasized, is not an adequate means to assess core content knowledge acquisition. We discussed the importance of oral discourse as your main vehicle for doing so.

We then introduced you to several possibilities for assimilating oral discourse/substantive dialogue after, during, and before unit assessments. They included argumentation using classroom- or school-based issues, formal debates, round-robin mini-speeches, and press conferences.

We also suggested that you increase the amount of substantive dialogue that occurs in your classroom by training your own personal CCC—Core Content Cadre—who, working from a Substantive Dialogue Scoring Guide, engage all students in substantive oral discourse.

chapter 6

Info Out: Assessing Students' Understanding Through Large-Scale Projects or Performances

Betty's Story

I watched as the judges made their way to my spot at the 7th grade science fair. I anxiously stood to the side of my home-made telegraph machine. The first judge approached me and said, "Tell me about your telegraph. How does it work?" I stuttered and finally uttered something like, "Well, my dad helped me make it, and I think he said it works like this. . . ." Even though I had actually done most of the construction myself (with elaborate coaching from my dad), I had absolutely no idea how it worked. But it sure looked great! And I am proud to announce that I turned it in on time. But unfortunately, I did not have a clue about the basic concepts involved in telegraphy.

Another Betty Story

A few years ago I was packing for a speaking engagement. It was about 11 p.m., and I was preparing to fly out the next morning. As I rushed around the house gathering materials and organizing my overhead transparencies, my 9th grade son approached me saying, "Hey, Mom! You remember that big science project I need to do?" I asked, "You mean the one where you run a classic scientific investigation, track your data, and write up the results?" "Yeah, that's the one. Well, I need to get started because it's due tomorrow. I need your help." Enough said.

Why Some Large-Scale Projects Fall Short

So what do these stories have to do with performance tasks? These kinds of performances—science fairs, exhibitions, and other elaborate productions—have been around for years. Many schools have long histories of incorporating culminating projects at the end of substantive courses of study. However, these types of projects have been known to generate a number of negative phenomena including the following:

- *The Razzle Dazzle:* The performance has a lot of flash but no substance.

- *The Parasite:* The parents pick the topic. The student may do the work but has no interest or ownership in the project. Moms or dads, however, get to live out their dreams/interests/fantasies through their child's pseudo-performance.

- *The Surrogate:* The student picks a project of personal interest but may not do any of the actual work. It is difficult to determine how much scaffolding (shoring up) by others (usually parents) occurred.

- *The Fizzle:* Not enough guidance or direction is provided. The task is assigned, and students are expected to miraculously produce a fantastic project in six weeks. They rarely do.

- *The Celebration:* This category results from an erroneous belief that performances should be showcases—festivals, parties, or other gala events—without evaluation. Everyone should be honored, no matter the quality of the work.

- *The Uneven Playing Field:* Some students draw from many resources (e.g., parents, computers, libraries, and art supplies) in creating their projects, while other students draw from few or no resources.

- *The Near-Death Experience:* Teachers, near exhaustion, walk around school with glazed-over eyes mumbling, "Why did I do this to myself? What was I thinking?"

Given the negative effects associated with these types of tasks, can the construction of large-scale projects or performances serve as an effective Info Out mode? We hold that they can and should be one critical form of evaluation—a form in which students "pull it all together." As teachers, then, how do we frame the production of models, displays, projects, or other elaborate performances to minimize the above-mentioned effects and, at the same time, maximize the opportunities for students to explicitly reveal their understanding of core knowledge? And how might we evaluate the quality of these performances?

We call these large-scale tasks substantive synthesis projects and define them as maxi tasks in which students use a *combination* of key Info Out processes (writing, speaking, hands-on manipulation, and graphic representations) to synthesize and extend their learning through producing or constructing a large-scale project.

In this chapter, we will show you how traditional large-scale projects can be converted into Great Performance tasks. We will also describe how to create an audience for the task and how we host such events in the classroom, at the school or district level, and in the community. To do this, we will use several examples.

Developing Great Large-Scale Projects and Performances

Our goal is to construct an end-of-unit substantive project or performance that incorporates our definition of a Great Performance task plus a few other traits critical to the success of substantive projects. Figure 6.1 provides a description of these traits.

Because teachers appreciate a step-by-step approach in developing a task, we want to familiarize you with the 10-step task design process we use. We used it in developing the examples in previous chapters.

1. Be clear about your targets: the skills and knowledge students must demonstrate and the standards that they will be expected to meet. (Use district and state documents to assist you.) Consider the following:

Figure 6.1	**Key Elements of Large-Scale Great Performance Tasks**
Content Standards	The task targets a combination of process and core knowledge content standards.
Elaboration of Core Knowledge Content	The task facilitates the development of expertise through the synthesis and application of core knowledge content.
Application of Key Processes (Graphic Representations, Writing, Speaking, and Constructions)	The task uses key Info Out processes in combination to get students to reveal their current construction of content knowledge.
Explicit Scoring System	The task is evaluated with an overt scoring system shared with students up front.
Audience Larger Than Just the Teacher	An engaging and authentic context is created for the task in which someone would be interested in the work besides the teacher or parent.
Student Choice	The task allows for student preferences to a greater extent than other types of tasks previously described.
Contract	Students and parents sign a contract specifying that the project reflects the work of the student.
Work Plan	The teacher provides students with a step-by-step plan for accomplishing the task within given time periods.
Student Self-Reflection	Students are required to produce a reflective journal and "processfolio." The processfolio is a collection of all of their work—the final product, drafts, sketches, revisions, and so on.

• Most performance tasks will include a process standard (such as speaking, writing, or composing) and a core content knowledge standard (such as the concept of separation of powers in a democracy or the concept of form in the arts).

• You may work from your state department of education's content and performance standards, your district standards, or various national standards projects to identify specific standards to target.

• It is possible to connect a few targets, but don't try to make it the "mother of all tasks" in which students are held responsible for too many targets at one time.

• When eliciting performances of key processes (speaking, writing, problem solving, etc.), examine the scoring guide to familiarize yourself with the critical traits that must be present in a performance. Work from existing scoring guides or construct one unique to this task. There are many examples posted online that you can use or adapt.

• When eliciting performances of core knowledge concepts, develop a set of key questions, the answers to which will elucidate key conceptual understandings. Answer the questions yourself to identify the key points students will need to make later when they answer the questions.

2. Create and describe a context in the task that will make it meaningful and engaging. Be creative about the audience and purpose.

- The context must be of interest to students.
- The context must clearly elicit performances related to the targets.
- The context can be an important issue, situation, question, or integrating theme that will engage students' interest.
- The task must be authentic (replicate as nearly as possible what a real-world performance would entail). To be authentic, tasks need not always be set in the real world, but they should involve students in experiences and processes that simulate those of practitioners in the field.
- The performance should have a wider audience than just the teacher; that is, the work is shared with someone outside class who would find the work worthwhile and meaningful.

3. Write a short description of the task.

- Incorporate the key questions into the task statement as appropriate.
- Include critical traits from the scoring guide as appropriate.

4. Rewrite the task in a clear and concise manner, so students have unambiguous marching orders of what it is they are expected to do. Use language that will clearly specify the various ways that students might communicate about or exhibit their conclusions. Also, be as specific as possible about the parameters in which students must complete the task. List any criteria related to the following:

- Information sources (required number, notes, bibliography, use of particular references, etc.)
- Time elements (date final project is due, date individual components are due, etc.)
- Collaboration/assistance (guidelines for working alone/with others, how many, reporting individual contributions, parental/other adult involvement, etc.)
- The presentation of the project (specifications for size of display area, whether an oral presentation is required, appropriate labeling, written description, etc.)

5. Develop a (or borrow an already developed) scoring device, making sure it hits (assesses) the targets/traits identified in #1 above.

- We tend to use the official state scoring guides (rubrics) whenever possible, as this gives students more practice working from the performance criteria that our state will hold them accountable to.
- If an official state rubric is too formal for use with students, you can work with the class to create a more student-friendly one. We find that students sometimes set quite high standards for themselves!
- You may want to consider reformatting the official scoring rubric into a ChecBric, which is a much more user-friendly scoring mechanism.
- Decide how much feedback you need to provide in this task (along with how much time and energy you have), and design or borrow the scoring mechanism accordingly.

6. Develop a step-by-step work plan for the class to follow.

- The work plan should provide students with guidance and assistance in completing the project.

- Break the task into parts, and delineate the sequence in which various parts are to be completed.
- You may want to have students keep a "processfolio." A processfolio is a collection of all of their work—notes, drafts, final products, and so forth.
- If necessary, specify what kinds of help parents and other adults can or cannot give.

7. Introduce the task to students.

- Share and discuss the scoring guides for the standards you are going to assess.
- Discuss the task in class, and answer any questions.
- Distribute a task description sheet and work plan with due dates to students. Post copies of the task sheet, the scoring guide, and work plan in the classroom.

8. To show students what "good" and "not so good" (both strong and weak) look like, provide models of work from other classes or past years.

- Strive for excellence.
- Show a range of samples of weak to excellent work as models.
- Reinforce with students the developmental process of creating multiple drafts/trials/attempts ("repairs"), with each subsequent draft representing work of higher quality.
- Throughout the process, give students opportunities to reflect on their work and how to improve it.

9. Provide instruction.

- Offer instruction that supports the development of necessary knowledge and skills, and coach students toward effective performances.

- Throughout the completion of the task, conduct formative evaluations of students' progress through observation, examination of documents, and student self-assessment. Use this information to give students feedback on how to improve their performance before the due date.

10. Score the task and make necessary revisions.

- Use the scoring guides to give students feedback on how their overall performance on the task reflects mastery of the content standard benchmarks.
- If possible, join with other teachers to score a number of the tasks together. Doing so will allow all of you to calibrate your scoring with one another and to clear up any questions that may arise from the responses.
- It may be helpful to create a common form on which to record your feedback. In some cases, the scoring guide itself provides room for comments. For example, note the "teacher comments" section at the bottom of our ChecBrics.
- To be efficient, some teachers make initial judgments about the performance as students present their work in class, followed by a short teacher-student conference.
- Take the time to identify the rubs in the task, and note any changes that need to be made for next time. If you wait until later, you will forget.

An In-Class Large-Scale Performance: The Homelessness Task

Let's walk through these 10 steps creating a sample substantive synthesis project, a large-scale maxi task for 7th and 8th graders that could be adopted to use at the high school level. We'll have students produce a traditional research report and oral presentation assignment within the context of this maxi performance task. The issue will be the growing homeless population in Eugene, Oregon.

We should note that, historically, teachers in our district have not been assigned particular topics to teach in a specified time frame, but rather are given major conceptual themes to develop within particular courses. Each teacher then has some flexibility in selecting topics as vehicles to develop particular concepts. Teachers are able to tap into lively, contemporary community issues if desired. You may not have that much flexibility. As we work through this task, examine how you might adapt the idea to your own setting.

1. Be clear about your targets: the skills and knowledge students must demonstrate and the standards that they will be expected to meet. (Use district or state documents to assist you.)

Our local newspaper had been carrying a series of articles on homelessness. Some folks had suggested that the city and county should work cooperatively to find a location for a "car camp," an area where the homeless could camp in their automobiles throughout the winter. One suggested location was a parking lot next to a community science and technology museum frequented by school children. A number of citizens, assuming that the homeless were dangerous, objected to this location. Of course, this objection led to heated debate about the characteristics of homeless people. The letters to the editor of the local paper were full of stereotypical depictions of the homeless.

At the same time, we were exploring ways that we could teach to the state content standards in the social science analysis. The 8th grade targets (benchmarks) are

SS.08.SA.01 Clarify key aspects of an event, issue, or problem through inquiry and research.

SS.08.SA.02 Gather, interpret, use, and document information from multiple sources, distinguishing facts from opinions and recognizing points of view.

SS.08.SA.03 Examine a controversial event, issue, or problem from more than one perspective.

SS.08.SA.04 Examine the various characteristics, causes, and effects of an event, issue, or problem.

SS.08.SA.05 Consider two or more outcomes, responses, or solutions; identify their strengths and weaknesses; then conclude and justify which is the best.

The Oregon State Content Standards are coded SS for social sciences followed by the grade level (08 for grade eight) and then the area of the social sciences (SA for social science analysis) and ending with the number of the standard (01, 02, 03, and so forth). (See www.ode.state.or.us/teachlearn/real/standards/ for the full standards.)

We knew students had had opportunities to demonstrate their understanding of these concepts in relation to historical events such as the Civil War and the development of industrial America. We wondered whether we might use the homelessness issue to bring the concepts to life in the present. Could the topic incorporate the depressed timber economy in the Northwest and its impact on maintaining housing for unemployed families?

In addition, we identified 8th grade benchmark content standards in writing and speaking. You could identify similar standards from your own state and district curriculum frameworks or from national curriculum standards. We set about examining our state rubrics (called "scoring guides" in Oregon) in writing, speaking, and social science analysis to be clear about what traits to teach and assess in each performance. As referenced in Chapter 4, in Oregon we work with an analytical trait assessment scoring guide for writing that includes the following traits:

• *Ideas/Content.* The paper shows clarity, focus, and control. Key ideas stand out and are supported by details.

• *Organization.* The paper shows effective sequencing. The order and structure of the text move the reader through it.

• *Sentence Fluency.* The sentences enhance the meaning, and the writing has a flow and rhythm to it.

• *Conventions.* The writing reflects the control of standard writing conventions such as grammar, paragraphing, punctuation, and capitalization.

• *Voice.* The writing is expressive, engaging, and sincere. It reflects an awareness of the audience.

• *Word Choice.* The words convey the intended message and a rich, broad range of words are used.

• *Citations:* References to sources are noted in the text. If appropriate, a bibliography is attached.

Our speaking scoring guide includes the following traits:

• *Ideas/Content.* The communication is clear and focused. The speaker has a clear purpose in speaking, and the main ideas stand out.

• *Organization.* The speaker uses effective sequencing suited to the purpose. The speech has an effective beginning, body, and ending.

The Official Social Science Analysis Scoring Guide for grades 6, 7, and 8 in Oregon includes the four following traits:

• *Frame the Event, Issue, or Problem.* Defining and clarifying an issue so that its features are well understood—Question.

• *Research.* Using and evaluating researched information to support analysis and conclusion(s)—Collect and Compare.

• *Examine.* Identifying and analyzing characteristics, causes, and consequences of an event, issue, or problem—Analyze.

• *Conclude.* Presenting reasoned conclusions or resolutions, acknowledging and evaluating alternative interpretations, using supporting data and defensible criteria—Justify.

We could have searched our state content standards and probably identified a number of other targets to incorporate into this task. But we realized that we had too many already. We have found that students cannot attend to a lot of traits *and* do a credible job. And teachers lose their sanity in trying to teach to and assess each trait! The list above (social science, writing, and speaking) has worked for us because we have a long history of working with the analytical trait assessment in writing and speaking. Students at this level come to us with some familiarity with the traits. You may need to zero in on a smaller combination of social science core knowledge content and writing or speaking—or focus on just one area as you get started.

2. Create and describe a context in the task that will make it meaningful and engaging. Be creative about the audience and purpose.

To help students examine the relevant facts, concepts, and generalizations related to the topic, we generated some key focus questions to be addressed in the task (as introduced in Chapter 4). There is no magical number of questions, and both you and your students can generate them. Here is a list of questions around the concepts of cause and effect, change, and continuity using the content topic of homelessness.

• How has homelessness changed over time in Eugene?

• What are the causes of homelessness?

• What effects does homelessness have on the individual, the environment, and the community?

• What are the characteristics of life for homeless teens?

• Who are the interested parties in this situation, and what are their points of view on a solution?

• What are the strengths and weaknesses of each of these proposed solutions?

• To address this issue, what solution do you propose? Why did you select this solution?

3. Write a short description of the task.

We like to begin by identifying an important issue or situation within the school, community, or national context—as a possible starting point for producing a performance. For example, students might explore:

• Is the playground equipment inadequate?

• Should popular à la carte menus be changed in middle school cafeterias to incorporate more nutritious foods?

• Is homelessness a problem in our community?

At this stage you as the teacher/assessor make a first attempt to put your main ideas on paper. Your description needn't be elaborate. Here is our First Dare:

Is homelessness a problem in Eugene? Some people are telling the city council that it is becoming a large problem. The council has asked you to investigate this issue. You will work in small collaborative work groups to study homelessness in Eugene, Oregon. Your group will need to write a technical report and make a speech about this important issue.

4. Rewrite the task in a clear and concise manner, so students have unambiguous marching orders of what it is they are expected to do. Use language that clearly specifies the various ways that a student might communicate about or exhibit his or her conclusions. Be sure to include any parameters you want included in the performance. Here is our Repair/revised task:

Homelessness Task

Some people are telling the city council that homelessness is becoming a large problem in Eugene. The council has asked you to investigate this issue. You will be working together on a team with three other students. You will need to apply the problem-solving/decision-making process and the writing process to formulate a systemic citywide proposal/plan to address this issue.

On _(date)_ representatives of the city council and the city staff will give you an opportunity to share your proposal. You will have 20 minutes to present your proposal orally, followed by 15 minutes in which you will be expected to respond to questions.

Your proposal may take any format that you decide is appropriate. You will also submit your proposal in writing and provide copies for all representatives. Make sure you answer the following key questions in your written work and presentation:

• How has homelessness changed over time in Eugene?

• What are the causes of homelessness?

• What effects does homelessness have on the individual, the environment, and the community?

• What are the characteristics of life for homeless teens?

• Who are the interested parties in this situation, and what are their perspectives on a solution?

• What are the strengths and weaknesses of each of these proposed solutions?

• What solution do you propose to address this issue, and what is the reasoning in support of your proposed solution?

Be sure to include a "Works Cited" list that identifies your information sources. Attach a one-page description of your collaboration that describes how you accomplished this task and how you worked together to complete it. Also, as individuals, complete the attached scoring guide. When you complete the project, score your work. I will then conference with you and score your work also.

5. Develop a (or borrow an already developed) scoring device, making sure it hits (assesses) the targets/traits identified in #1 above. Figure A.25 shows the rubric we constructed for this homelessness task. Of course, we drew from the existing state scoring guides but adapted it with student-friendly language.

In this and previous chapters, we have described a number of useful scoring devices. We summarize them in Figure A.31. Select, adapt, or develop a device to use for this task.

6. Develop a step-by-step work plan for the class to follow.

Our repeated experiences with students who are unable to manage a large-scale project to meet deadlines have convinced us that a work plan is *absolutely* necessary. We sense that many of you are nodding in agreement. A work plan provides the needed structure for the work to be accomplished and gives the teacher planned opportunities to assess student work throughout the process. And when you break the larger task down into its component parts, with each part being due on individual dates, more students complete the task and the quality of the work improves. Believe us—we learned the hard way to do this. For the homelessness task team work plan, see Figure 6.2.

7. Introduce the task to students.

As with every task, we give students a copy of the task assignment and scoring guides at the beginning. We review the task as a class and post it somewhere in the room. At the start of each subsequent class period, we discuss class and individual progress and provide tips to those who need to get to work. Students are constantly directed to the team work plan checklist presented in Figure 6.2 to monitor their progress. Each student is given a copy to incorporate into their "binder reminder" (listing assignments and due dates).

8. To show students what "good" and "not so good" (both strong and weak) look like, provide models of work from other classes or past years.

We use student work from year to year as models with our current classes. These examples help students to visualize what a strong

Figure 6.2	**A Team Work Plan**

Names of Group Members _____

_____

_____

_____

Please work from this worksheet as you complete the homelessness project. On the following dates, you will be expected to conference with the teacher and review your work. When you have completed a task, all group members should place their initials in the second column. In the third column, assign your group a score from 1 to 6. Assigning yourselves a score of 1 means that you think your work in this area is very poor. Assigning yourselves a score of 6 means that you, as a group, agree that your work in this area is excellent.

Date Due	Initial When Complete	Score	Tasks to Be Completed
			Group Work Plan • Describe how you have assigned jobs. • Share the agreements that you have made about the storage of materials and supplies. • Describe the decision-making process your group will be using to complete the work.
			Information Gathering/Group Process Check-in • Turn in a rough draft of the answers to the questions. • Provide an oral status report on your group work. • Brainstorm a format for your oral presentation.
			Next-to-Final Draft • Turn in your next-to-final draft of the written proposal. • Turn in an outline of your oral presentation. • Provide an oral status report on group work.
			Final Presentation • Make your oral presentation and present your written proposal. • Turn in the written description of your group collaboration. • Turn in your processfolio and individually completed scoring guide.

performance might look like. Additionally, we provide examples of less-than-excellent work for students to critique. When no student samples are available, we create samples ourselves. If we are pressed for time and can't create our own, we scan the local news sources for examples. We collect editorials and letters to the editors from our local paper, and we occasionally video- or audiotape debates, forums, and other performances from the nonprint media (like YouTube and TeacherTube). These examples show students what works and what doesn't work.

9. Provide instruction.

Let's walk through two instructional methods that could be used to teach (and informally assess) "before, during, and after" acquisition of core knowledge concepts (cause and effect, change and continuity) using the topic of homelessness.

Consensus Definition

One method that we have used successfully, the Consensus Definition, is from our friend Nancy McCullum, a gifted teacher, principal, and administrative mentor. Students write a short definition of the concept being explored, in this case, homelessness. Then they pair with one or two others and construct a group definition.

This is a great time for you to stroll around the room collecting anecdotal records on students' initial perceptions. Judi Johnson—our friend and an extraordinary teacher in Sun River, Oregon—suggests photocopying sheets of address labels with a different student's name on each label. Attach the sheet to a clipboard, and carry it around with you as you observe. Jot notes onto each individual's label and date them. After class, you can affix these note labels to wherever

you keep anecdotal records. This system also enables you to notice which students you need to observe/interact with. As you remove labels, you will consciously attend to those students whose labels are left on the sheet.

When creating a Consensus Definition, we instruct students that our goal is a two- or three-sentence statement that defines the concept. As a class, all small groups share their definitions, and the class comes to agreement on one definition. Posted in the classroom, this definition becomes the working definition for the study. Throughout the unit, students can suggest modifications and revisions.

UmbrellaTella

From that definition, we can begin to explore the related concepts through a method we call UmbrellaTella. Using UmbrellaTella is a way to graphically represent the relationship of larger "meta" concepts to their related subconcepts and topics.

When using the UmbrellaTella with younger students, we bring an umbrella into the classroom, record the concept name and definition on strips of paper, and attach them to the main fabric of the umbrella with safety pins. It works better if the umbrella is large and has a number of metal spokes. Our goal is to hang several related subconcepts and facts to each of the metal tips around the umbrella's edge. We do this by

• giving students a copy of an umbrella on a sheet of paper;

• asking them to examine each key question and jot down quick answers to each question on the strips hanging from the umbrella;

• partnering students with one or two others who then create group answers to each key question and record them on larger card-stock sentence strips;

- sharing each group's sentence-strip answers with the whole class (at this point, no judgments are made about the accuracy or quality of the responses); and
- clustering similar sentence strips and attaching them all to the UmbrellaTella near the metal tips. Older students may work from the paper diagram of the umbrella rather than a real one.

Throughout the unit, as students acquire new content understanding through Info In methods of reading, listening, viewing, or manipulating (see Chapter 2), allow them to remove, revise, and re-create sentence strips for the UmbrellaTella. Figures A.23 and A.24 show how an 8th grader completed an UmbrellaTella before unit instruction about watersheds and later during instruction. At the end of the unit, each student can complete an UmbrellaTella to summarize what he or she has learned.

10. Score the task and make necessary revisions.

Figure A.25 shows the rubric we constructed for this homelessness task. After the task is scored is an ideal time—while the problems with the task are fresh in your mind—for making any necessary revisions. While scoring the tasks, you may want to ask yourself:

- Did the students' performances reveal what they were intended to reveal?
- Did the scoring device accurately measure student performance?
- Did the task sheet and the work plan adequately prepare the students for the performance?
- What improvements could be made? What revisions (repairs) are necessary?

Concept Development à la Development Continuum

The more we work with assessing concept development, the more intrigued we become with the notion of creating a developmental continuum to assess content acquisition. This continuum tracks a student's development of conceptual understanding from *novice*—with no conceptual understanding—to *expert*—able to present a superior degree of breadth and depth of information on the subject. In creating this continuum, we crafted language based on our own experience as well as Bloom's Taxonomy of Cognitive Objectives (Bloom, 1956). (See Figure A.26.)

You may ask students to rate themselves using the continuum. You may also want to use this continuum as the "ideas and content trait" on a rubric with other traits. Or you might monitor each student's concept development progress over time as students move through a number of units.

Your Turn: What Do You Think?

In summary, the homelessness task incorporates the following assessments:

- For core knowledge concepts

Before and During: Anecdotal records and informal interviews related to student work using the Consensus Definition and UmbrellaTella methods.

After: The content of the position paper using the Concept Acquisition Development Continuum.

- For the writing process

Before, During, and After: Analytical trait assessment using the Homelessness Project Rubric.

- For the speaking process

During and After: Analytical trait assessment using the Homelessness Project Rubric.

- For social science analysis

After: Analytical trait assessment using the Homelessness Project Rubric.

From your point of view, does the homelessness task measure the intended core knowledge outcomes of cause and effect, change and continuity, and the process standards in writing, speaking, and social science analysis? In what ways could you adapt this task for use in your classroom? Did you find anything particularly intriguing about the task or scoring mechanisms?

A County-Level Maxi Task: The Student Achievement Convention

We designed the homelessness task as one form of large-scale culminating performances to share in class with invited guests. Our next example is a model for a maxi *out-of-class* exhibition for use with K–12 students at the school level, at the district level, and in this case, at the county level. The Student Achievement Convention idea was developed by Marilyn Olson and Kermit Horn, formerly at our countywide Lane Education Service District. Sadly, the project fair is not currently offered in our county because of the severe budget crisis in Oregon Public Schools. However, we wanted to continue to address it in this chapter as it is such a fine example of sharing large-scale projects with an audience larger than the teacher. In past years, the convention offered students from Lane County schools an opportunity to provide evidence of academic achievement in three areas:

- The *Project Fair* includes presentations of the processes and products of in-depth learning experiences.
- The *Portfolio Exhibition* contains collections and reflective evaluations of selected works that show individual achievement and progress toward specific goals and standards.
- The *Video Festival* features original video productions.

How the Convention Works

From January through April each year, teachers introduce the convention events to students, students select topics, and then they develop projects, videos, and/or portfolios. Each Lane County school is assigned a number of spaces (one space per 100 students enrolled). By the first of April, schools are expected to submit an "intent to participate" form. If a school chooses not to participate, other schools are assigned their spaces.

By May 1, schools must also submit a list of judges—one judge for each one or two projects. Judges can be teachers, parents, community members, or administrators. The first day of the convention, judges receive instruction in using the scoring rubrics and conducting interviews with students. It is interesting to note that, year after year, a number of retired folks return to judge at the convention along with teachers and parents. What a great way to help inform our retired community about what is going on in schools!

The three-day convention is held at our county fairgrounds exhibit hall the third week of May. The first day, Tuesday, students set up their projects in the morning. Each project, portfolio, and video is judged in the afternoon by at least two judges, and major scoring discrepancies are settled by a third party.

Schoolchildren from around the county are scheduled to visit the convention on Wednesday and Thursday. In addition to viewing their fellow students' projects, portfolios, and videos, these children may enroll in other special events such as a science celebration, Starlab, and young writers' workshops offered simultaneously in other areas of the fairgrounds. Let's examine the Project Fair portion of the convention in more detail.

Creating and Evaluating Project Fair Entries

The Project Fair gives students an opportunity to exhibit a major learning experience that combines content knowledge with process skills to produce a product, a portfolio, or a video that demonstrates their learning—what we call a large-scale maxi performance task. Each project is evaluated by two judges who look for and score three specific traits described on the scoring guide:

1. Topic and treatment
2. Learning development and process
3. Presentation/communication

Each participant is expected to complete an exhibit with an accompanying project notebook, as well as participate in an information presentation and interview. Figures A.27 and A.28 show, respectively, the Project Fair Guidelines/Participation Checklist and the Registration Form. Judges score students' work using the Project Criteria and Scoring Guide (an example of a scorecard rubric) shown in Figure A.29.

A sampling of projects previously submitted for the Project Fair have included these:

• Nitrate Contamination of Groundwater from Fertilizers (grade 10)
• How Hiccups Happen (grade 3)
• Dams: Pros and Cons (grade 7)
• Hidden Lessons: A Study of Gender Bias in Our Schools (grade 10)
• What Attracts Bees? (grade 5)

What kind of scoring mechanism is the Project Criteria and Scoring Guide? We refer to it as a "scorecard rubric." The scorecard rubric has a number of attributes of a rubric (analytical traits, descriptors, and scoring scale), but it adds an additional feature, a total overall score—a feature that middle and high school teachers particularly like. This total score enables them to convert the scores into percentages for calculating letter grades.

A Community-Based Substantive Synthesis Performance Task: From a Drop of Rain—A Tale of Two Rivers

Let us shift our attention to an extensive, elaborate, large-scale project where the audience is the whole community—"From a Drop of Rain: A Tale of Two Rivers." The project culmination was a six-month-long museum exhibit April through September at the University of Oregon Museum of Natural History. We share this maxi-to-the-max task as another example of a large-scale performance task that is suitable for grades 6 through 12. We don't want to scare you off with the magnitude of the project. You can, of course, make modifications, adjustments, and reductions as you choose.

A Tale of Two Rivers is a hands-on, field-based project in which secondary students from three school districts studied watershed ecosystems, stewardship, and natural resource management. The project is centered within the Willamette Valley of central Oregon on the main stem of the Willamette River and one of its major tributaries, the McKenzie River. Students are conducting field studies at diverse sites within this watershed region.

Students, teachers, and administrators from six middle schools and two high schools participated. Each school has a core team of three to five teachers, two parents, and five students to steer the project. In the first year, each of the eight schools selected a site to explore and study within the McKenzie and Willamette river systems. Together, these sites represented the richness of the watershed as a whole. For example, they included

- the oldest state-owned fish hatchery in Oregon;
- the largest complex of native prairie remaining in western Oregon;
- the largest population of western pond turtles;
- several water resource management projects;
- the settlement of the Willamette Valley's earliest human residents, the Calapooia peoples;
- high-use recreation areas;
- sites requiring restoration because they play a critical role in providing basic community needs (i.e., electricity and water);
- sites that provide enjoyment to a vast number of residents and visitors, and are greatly valued by local communities.

Targeting 6th through 12th grade students, the project has been a springboard for school districts to develop career paths for students interested in careers in natural resource management. One of its great strengths is the active participation by more than 20 community agencies and organizations that provided technical expertise and advice via e-mail and in the field.

A major goal of the project is to apply concepts in natural resources settings and create products that benefited the community, such as nature trails, interpretive guides, or research findings.

A Dream Becomes Reality

As teachers and agency folks brainstormed possibilities, several potential studies emerged. The eight participating schools framed their work as follows:

1. Each school would identify one particular site for a long-term study.
2. Core team members would begin to explore one topic for in-depth study at that site (e.g., salmon migration, western pond turtles, prairie wetlands, or early human inhabitants).
3. All students at each site would begin their study with the hydrologic cycle—in particular, how water is captured, stored, and released in the Willamette Watershed.
4. Following a study of the water cycle, students would then map their site in detail and identify the specific elements of the site including soil, vegetation, wildlife, climate, and water quality.
5. The focus of the study would then shift to uses of the watershed: agriculture, forestry, recreation, and urban uses (water systems and electricity).
6. In-depth studies unique to each particular site would be completed throughout the project.
7. The studies would end by exploring natural resources management and public policy planning.
8. The results of the project would be exhibited at the Museum of Natural History as a way to showcase student studies to an authentic community audience interested in the topics.

"From a Drop of Rain" Emerges as the Theme of the Exhibit

In our second year, we soon discovered that constructing a culminating, interactive exhibit at the museum wouldn't happen without a lot of planning. We had to address a number of key elements unique to museum exhibitions with teachers and students. To do this, we designed a course of study for a core team of teachers and selected students who then returned to their home schools and trained others. The course, incorporating five full days over four months, covered numerous topics that prepared them for their Info Out sharing in the exhibit:

• **Day One:** *What is a museum? What makes a good exhibit?* Core teams visited three local museums and identified aspects of effective museum exhibits.

• **Day Two:** *How do we develop a story line?* A consultant from an exhibition design company worked with the core teams in developing the story line "From the watersheds of the McKenzie and Willamette rivers, a story emerges of life cycles and human impact." See Figure A.30 for the story line used in the prototype development.

• **Day Three:** *What is the history of local native peoples?* A professor of anthropology from the University of Oregon spoke with team members about the 9,000-year history of native peoples in the Willamette Valley of Oregon. He also shared how this information has been translated into museum exhibitions.

What technologies might we use in our exhibit? Again, team members, working in three groups, rotated from station to station to learn about digital cameras and computers, mature photography basics, and use of manipulatives in museum exhibits.

• **Day Four:** *How might we keep accurate and informative field data to incorporate into our exhibit?* Presenters shared examples of and techniques for creating historical journals and nature field journals (see Chapter 4 for some high school biology examples).

Focus topics included creative writing, nature collages, and Xerox transfer techniques.

How will our individual ideas come together in the total exhibit? Participants helped generate an overall outline of various museum modules as they related to the theme. See Figure A.30 for a story line of the exhibit modules.

• **Day Five:** Each participating school shared its prototype module and received feedback on how to improve it. The group explored how to evaluate the quality of the prototypes and the actual museum exhibit when it was completed.

Whoa! How Might We Evaluate a Maxi Task Like This?

Betty worked with a small group of teachers to begin exploring ways to evaluate the museum project. She shared a process for creating a scoring guide from scratch. Our goal was to create a scoring mechanism that could be used in a number of different settings. Our process had four steps:

1. Identify the Critical Traits of a Strong Performance

First, we set about to specify the essential traits of a strong performance—in our case, of a strong museum exhibit. The program staff from the museum, Patty Krier and Cindy Gabai, were invaluable in helping us identify the following three traits of a strong museum exhibit: story line, objects, and interactives. While the end product—the exhibit modules —were important to assess, teachers were also committed to assessing the *process* that small groups of students used to develop them. (Remember the coin model used in Chapter 1 to distinguish between content and process.) Therefore, we added the following process-oriented traits to the list: work plan and time lines, collaboration, and prototype development. We also generated a list of key questions to accompany each exhibit trait.

2. Explore Scoring Devices and Select Assessment List

Next, we examined scoring devices that could be used singly or in combination with others, and we selected an assessment list. We have described each of these devices in previous chapters. Our choices are reviewed in Figure A.31.

We agreed to construct a checklist for students to use throughout the process based on the six traits and the key questions we had generated and then to create a weighted assessment list to score the project as a whole.

3. Construct a Draft of the Scoring Device

Our next step was to create a draft of the scoring device, including students in the process when appropriate. As part of the five-day museum class we offered, participating staff and students visited several area museums and practiced using the above criteria in order to internalize what "good exhibits" looked like. At the end of the visits, the whole group reviewed each element and commented about what made some exhibits superior to others. After the class, a small group developed the Museum Exhibit Assessment List of Traits and Key Questions shown in Figure A.32. We hope that educators in many different schools who use exhibits as culminating tasks will try this list. If you use it and like it, let us know.

4. Use the Scoring Device with a Project and Revise It

Finally, teachers used the scoring device with a project and revised it as needed. We anticipated that, in most cases, students would be more than eager to help improve it. We wanted to ask them to identify language that was ambiguous or confusing. We also wanted them to argue the merits of the weighted scoring. However, the attention that the exhibit drew from the community was so exciting for students that we were unable to get them to focus on revising the guide at the end of the school year. When the governor came to visit, the revisions were set "on the back burner."

We have shared with you how to create a performance task from scratch. We also shared with you three large-scale tasks that you may be able to use or adapt in your setting: the in-class homelessness task, the countywide Project Fair, and the community-based museum exhibit. These types of large-scale assessments require creativity, inventiveness, and energy, but they're worth it! Just think back to your own K–12 schooling experiences. We will bet that these types of projects come to mind as the most memorable and meaningful of your learning career.

A Snapshot of Chapter 6

In this chapter, we have

• described performance tasks that incorporate many Info Out modes in a large-scale substantive synthesis project;

• described three types of large-scale maxi tasks: in-class, countywide, and community based;

• given you a step-by-step approach for developing a good task;

• shared two new scoring devices, the Concept Acquisition Developmental Continuum (Figure A.26) and the Scorecard Rubric (or Project Criteria and Scoring Guide [Figure A.29]); and

• shared a process for creating your own scoring devices.

Update: The A Tale of Two Rivers project ended after the museum display was removed. Students from the three districts continue to study the two rivers through various projects, from salmon monitoring (hatching, releasing, tagging, tracking, and counting them) to monitoring river water levels and water quality, among others. The museum exhibit was loaned out to regional museums and is now housed at the Eugene Water and Electric Board offices in Eugene, Oregon.

chapter 7

A Scenic Tour of Reading Assessment

Betty's Assessment Story

Several years ago, I was privileged to have a young girl who was born and spent her early years in Thailand join my 3rd grade class. The previous summer she and her family had moved to our community. She spoke very little English when she arrived at the door of Room 6 in early September. Even though Areva was very shy and quiet in class, I soon discovered how bright she was.

In the spring, as was our practice in our school district at that time, we administered a standardized norm-referenced achievement test to all of our students.

In order to assure reliability in administration, the district's assessment specialist set two requirements. First, he required all teachers to attend training sessions to learn the precise administration protocols. Second, the district required each teacher to be joined by another staff member in the classroom to assist in maintaining the integrity of administration.

As students were completing the reading portion of the test, Areva raised her hand. I made my way to her desk. She looked puzzled and said, "I don't get this." I responded, with "You understand that I can't help you?" She nodded. I then suggested she read the item again and make a good guess. She very quietly read the following statement perfectly. I overheard her then try out each of the four choices provided.

He taught _____ to play an instrument.
a. herself   b. themselves   c. himself   d. itself

She turned to me, looking puzzled and said, "They probably want you to pick 'himself.' " She repeated the whole sentence using "himself" as her choice: "He taught *himself* to play an instrument." Again she gave me an anxious, perplexed look: "That sounds right but it doesn't make sense. How could he teach himself to play an instrument if he doesn't know how to play it?" I can't remember which choice she marked.

When I got the results back for my class, as I remember, Areva scored in about the 20th percentile, indicating that she was at risk of reading failure. However, once she learned her second language, English, she proved to be a very adequate reader and an astute thinker!

So I knew when I saw the results of that test that it would not help me to identify Areva's reading strengths and weaknesses in order for me to refine my instruction with her.

Why This New Chapter on Reading?

Assessments have come a long way since that day in the classroom when Areva's reading test was made up of a number of items like the one described above. First, reading researchers have identified a number of factors that contribute to reading success and have worked with teachers to develop several classroom- and curriculum-based measures to assess these factors (National Institute of Child Health and Human Development, 2000). Second, in the context of No Child Left Behind, there has been increasing pressure from the federal government for schools to identify students at risk of reading failure early in their school careers. Third, the debate over the process used to identify students as learning disabled (LD) and in need of special education under the Individuals with Disabilities Education Act (IDEA) has gained considerable momentum during the last several years. This has led to the development of a new option for LD identification called Response to Intervention, or RTI. The U.S. Department of Education National Research Center on Learning Disabilities (NRCLD) is now conducting a major study of the effectiveness of RTI as an alternative method for LD identification.

We have added this chapter to help you sort through RTI as it relates to classroom-based assessments, and we explore several published reading assessments commonly called "curriculum-based measures" (CBM). First, we will provide you with a brief description of RTI and its built-in need for progress-monitoring assessments. Then we will provide some *brief* information about recent developments in classroom- and/or curriculum-based assessment in reading (both at the elementary level and the secondary level) as well as our perspectives on the use of these measures in your classroom. It would be impossible in this format to include information about every published reading assessment currently being published and evaluate each in its entirety. But we do want to share with you some general impressions we have.

Response to Intervention

Candace Cortiella, writing for the Charles and Helen Schwab Foundation (Cortiella, 2009) in *Response-to-Intervention: An Emerging Method for LD Identification,* states:

> There is currently no formal definition of RTI, nor is there an RTI model that is well established and widely endorsed by researchers and educators. However, the following could serve as a description of the essential elements: RTI is an individualized, comprehensive assessment and intervention process, utilizing a problem-solving framework to identify and address student academic difficulties using effective, efficient, research-based instruction.

The RTI Action Network defines RTI as "a multi-tiered approach to help struggling learners. Students' progress is closely monitored at each stage of intervention to determine the need for further research-based instruction and/or intervention in general education, in special education, or both" (RTI Action Network, n.d.).

According to the National Research Center on Learning Disabilities (2007), there are eight core features of strong RTI. The following four features are among them:

- *Classroom performance.* General education instructors and staff assume an active role in students' assessment in the general education curriculum. This feature emphasizes the important role of the classroom staff in designing and completing student assessments rather than relying on externally developed tests (e.g., state- or nationally developed tests).

- *Universal screening.* School staff conducts universal screening of academics and behavior with a focus on specific criteria for judging the learning and achievement of all students, not only in academics but also in related behaviors (e.g., class attendance, tardiness, truancy, suspensions, and disciplinary actions). Teacher teams apply those criteria in determining which students need closer monitoring or an intervention.

- *Continuous progress monitoring.* In RTI models, one expects students' classroom progress to be monitored continuously. In this way, staff can readily identify those learners who are not meeting the benchmarks or other expected standards. Various curriculum-based assessment models are useful in this role.

- *Progress monitoring during interventions.* School staff members use progress monitoring data to determine interventions' effectiveness and to make any modifications, as needed. Carefully defined data are collected, perhaps daily, to provide a cumulative record of the learner's response to the intervention.

The underlying notion here is that prevention of reading difficulties begins with universal literacy screenings to identify students who could be at risk. It should be noted that currently, any state receiving Reading First monies must have identified a literacy screening for use in grades K–3. Classroom personnel screen all students on basic literacy skills approximately three times per year and provide support to students not meeting benchmarks.

The need for easily administered, effective, valid, and reliable measures for use across classrooms to support the RTI model leads us to an examination of classroom- and curriculum-based measures.

Curriculum-Based Measures (CBMs)

The literature on reading is rife with references to various forms of classroom- and/or curriculum-based measures. Many authors use terms so similar to each other that readers may be confused. We like to work from a definition by Gerald Tindal and his colleagues, Leanne Ketterlin-Geller and Julie Alonzo (Florian, 2007). They suggest that curriculum-based measurement can be distinguished from other types of measures along a number of dimensions, including the following:

- The assessments generate data over time to reflect improvement using frequent comparable measures.

- The designers of these curriculum-based measures do not tie them to specific curriculum but rather to universal representations of the general curriculum. This means that CBMs are designed to assess reading skills in general and are not tied to a specific textbook or classroom lesson.

- CBMs provide three kinds of measurement: *norms* (demonstrating how a student's performance compares with that of other students), *criteria* (identifying each student's specific skills and deficits), and *progress* (comparing the student's improvement to his or her previous performance).

There are numerous classroom- and curriculum-based literacy screeners being marketed nationally. They include, among others, Dynamic Indicators of Basic Early Literacy Skills (DIBELS; Good & Kaminski, 2002), Phonological Awareness Literacy Screening (PALS; Invernizzi, Juel, Swank, & Meier, 2005), the Texas Primary Reading Inventory (TPRI; Texas Education Agency & University of Texas System, 2006), the Illinois Snapshots of Early Literacy (ISEL; Illinois State Board of Education, 2004), and easyCBM (Tindal et al., 2008). Let's take a closer look at three of these reading assessments.

Measures for Younger Students

The Phonological Awareness Literacy Screening (PALS)

Researchers at the University of Virginia developed an assessment system for young students titled "The Phonological Awareness Literacy Screening." The PALS website shares the following about the system: "The Phonological Awareness Literacy Screening (PALS) provides a comprehensive assessment of young children's knowledge of the important literacy fundamentals that are predictive of future reading success." PALS consists of three instruments: PALS-PreK (for preschool students), PALS-K (for kindergartners), and PALS 1–3 (for students in grades 1–3). Figure 7.1 summarizes the PALS subtests.

Dynamic Indicators of Basic Early Literacy Skills (DIBELS)

Research units at the University of Oregon have developed two assessment systems. Drs. Roland H. Good III, Ruth Kaminski, and colleagues in the Institute for the Development of Educational Achievement (IDEA) developed Dynamic Indicators of Basic Early Literacy Skills (DIBELS). As these researchers state on the DIBELS website:

The Dynamic Indicators of Basic Early Literacy Skills (DIBELS) are a set of procedures and measures for assessing the

Figure 7.1	**The Phonological Awareness Literacy Screening (PALS)**	
PALS-PreK	PALS-K	PALS 1–3
Name Writing	Rhyme Awareness	Spelling
Alphabet Knowledge	Beginning Sound Awareness	Word Recognition in Isolation
Beginning Sound Awareness	Alphabet Knowledge	Alphabet Recognition Letter Sounds
Print and Word Awareness	Letter Sounds	Concept of Word
Rhyme Awareness	Spelling	Passage Reading
Nursery Rhyme Awareness	Concept of Word	Timed Passage Reading (reading rate)
	Word Recognition in Isolation	Comprehension
		Fluency (phrasing and expression)
		Blending
		Sound to Letter (segmentation and letter sounds)

Note: PALS assessments are also being developed to assess a student's literacy strengths in his or her native Spanish language.

acquisition of early literacy skills from kindergarten through 6th grade. They are designed to be short (one minute) fluency measures used to regularly monitor the development of early literacy and early reading skills.

DIBELS were developed to measure recognized skills related to reading outcomes. They include the following measures:

- ISF: Initial Sounds Fluency: Assesses a child's skill at identifying and producing the initial sound of a given word.
- PSF: Phoneme Segmentation Fluency: Assesses a child's skill at producing the individual sounds within a given word.
- NWF: Nonsense Word Fluency: Assesses a child's knowledge of letter-sound correspondences as well their ability to blend letters together to form unfamiliar "nonsense" (e.g., ut, fik, lig, etc.) words.
- ORF: DIBELS Oral Reading Fluency: Assesses a child's skill at reading connected text in grade-level materials.
- (ORF) Oral Reading Fluency and (RTF) Retell Fluency: Assesses a child's understanding of verbally read connected text.
- WUF: Word Use Fluency: Assesses a child's ability to accurately use a provided word in the context of a sentence.

In the past, DIBELS also offered an additional subtest, LNF: Letter Naming Fluency, in which students were asked to state the name of the letter in a one-minute timing.

Easy Curriculum-Based Measures (EasyCBM)

Dr. Gerald Tindal and colleagues at the University of Oregon's Behavioral Research and Teaching (BRT) Center, in collaboration with area schools and Eugene Public Schools in particular, also developed an assessment system. Both Larry and Betty worked for the Eugene Schools, and it is important to note here that Betty played a role in the early development of a previous district-level assessment system that influenced the development of easyCBM. This early assessment system was designed for use by general education, Title One, and special education teachers in grades K–9 to assist them in the diagnosis of students' reading performance.

In designing this assessment system, Betty, then a curriculum coordinator for the district, formed a test development group she nicknamed "the Fishbones." The group agreed from the start on certain criteria that must be present in any assessment system:

- Provide the needed materials all in one place to complete student reading assessments.
- Use authentic literature, as much as possible, as opposed to "synthetic" passages developed specifically to teach students to decode "decodable" words.
- Assess what teachers need in order to help them shape their instruction, not just items psychometricians suggest that might be easy to assess.
- However, make sure that these assessments are psychometrically sound.
- Provide assessment subtests that would be short and easy to administer.
- Build an assessment system that can serve as the Title One screener as required by administrative rules.
- Build an assessment system that can be used to show progress over time.
- Provide needed continuity around testing to assist in the development of district norms.
- Build an assessment system that will be predictive of performance on the Oregon Assessment of Knowledge and Skills (OAKS).

This early work has evolved into "easy-CBM." Currently, easyCBM.com provides teachers with a free progress-monitoring system for students through grade 8 that incorporates many different reading assessments, including,

- letter names,
- letter sounds,
- phoneme segmenting,
- passage reading fluency,
- word reading fluency, and
- multiple-choice comprehension.

It should be noted that the early editions of easyCBM did include vocabulary assessments. Staff at the BRT Center are planning to revisit the issue of vocabulary to create and add a more effective assessment in the future.

The BRT Center offers two different versions of easyCBM: one designed for school- or districtwide adoption and another designed for individual teacher use. Their District Version easyCBM System has both benchmark/screener tests and progress-monitoring measures and gives different users different levels of access to data within the system. The Teacher Version easyCBM System is limited to progress-monitoring measures (under the assumption that teachers will have access to some other form of screening information that will enable them to identify students most in need of progress monitoring).

Betty's Three Perspectives on Assessing Young Children

There are three points that I want to make here about assessing young children. First, it is inappropriate to assess kindergarten and 1st grade students who are new to any form of schooling experience in the first three or four days of school. If you assess these students who have never been in school before,

I can guarantee you that the results of the assessments that you get will be skewed, for obvious reasons. Far too often, students who score poorly are then placed in the lowest-performing instructional groups, which—due to the common pecking order of seniority—are often taught by the least trained and/or least experienced staff (new teachers and Title One instructional assistants). These students then remain in a track that slows down their instruction, labels them as failures, and predisposes teachers to see them as underachieving. Instead, let these students get used to the routine of school and see how they handle instruction (which they missed because they did not attend pre-school). Wait six weeks or two months before assessing these students. To read more about developmentally appropriate assessment with young children, check out the Early Childhood Curriculum, Assessment, and Program Evaluation Position Statement of the National Association for the Education of Young Children at www.naeyc.org/positionstatements/cape.

Second, we discourage use of early-grade-level reading assessments that ask students to read nonsense words to see if they know letter sounds and can blend sounds into simple "words." Many teachers and researchers believe that asking students to read made-up words leads to the assumption on the part of students that what they read does not need to make sense. We agree!

Patricia Cunningham (1990) developed the Names Test as a quick and easy screening tool for teachers to obtain information about a student's developing decoding skills. This assessment is a good compromise in that the words used (first and last names) do have meaning yet are probably unfamiliar to students as they decode. The test is individually administered. The student reads the names aloud, and the teacher places a check mark by each first and last name read correctly.

After analyzing the original Names Test, Duffelmeyer Kruse, Merkley, and Fyfe (1994) developed a revision that they designed to improve reliability, usability, and validity while retaining the quick scoring of the test. To increase the number of examples, they added 10 names to the original Names Test and developed a scoring sheet and comprehensive scoring matrix to increase the diagnostic information based on error patterns.

Since that time, researchers at the University of Arizona (Mather, Sammons, & Schwartz, 2006) further developed the Names Test by having a sample of students read the Duffelmeyer version and then reordering the first and last names by difficulty level based on the errors made by the students in the sample. This allows students to attempt to read easier names before attempting more difficult names and allows the teacher to

discontinue the assessment if the names become too difficult for a student to pronounce. This downward extension of the Names Test is shown in Figures 7.2 and 7.3. The directions for this revised Names Test are the following: "I want you to pretend that you are a teacher and you are calling out your students' names to take attendance. You are trying to figure out who is at school and who is not. Some of these names may be hard, but just do the best you can."

Record a 1 for a correct response and a 0 for an incorrect response. Score both the first and last names. Write incorrect responses directly above the name.

One's score on the Names Test is determined by keeping a running record of a student's responses on the initial consonant sounds, initial consonant blends, consonant digraphs, short vowels, long vowels (VC-e), vowel digraphs, and controlled vowels. In

Figure 7.2	**Proper Names Included in the Revised Early Names Test**	
Rob Hap	Kate Tide	Beck Daw
Jud Lem	Brent Lake	Dell Smush
Ray San	Flip Mar	Gus Lang
Pat Ling	Jet Mit	Lex Yub
Tim Bop	Rand Lun	Ross Quest
Brad Tash	Jen Dut	Dane Wong
Pam Rack	Jake Bin	Tom Zall
Trish Mot	Sid Gold	Gail Vog
Fred Tig	Frank Lug	Rod Blade
Bab Fum	Grace Nup	Tag Shick

Note: The work of the Arizona group found that for the 60 first and last names, the average score for the 2nd graders was 43 with a standard deviation of 12.2. To replicate the procedures of Cunningham (1990), a statistic of internal-consistency reliability (Kuder-Richardson 20) was calculated. The resultant KR-20 reliability was .93, a high reliability estimate.

Source: From "Adaptations of the Names Test: Easy-to-Use Phonics Assessments," by N. Mather, J. Sammons, and J. Schwartz, 2006. *The Reading Teacher, 60*(2), p. 117.

Figure 7.3	**Proper Names Included in the Revised Names Test**		
Dee Conway	Gus Clark	Tim Brooks
Fred Wright	Chuck Dale	Grace Wade
Jay Anderson	Kimberly Tweed	Wendy Spencer
Ron Blake	Austin Westmoreland	Neal Loomis
Ned Yale	Patrick Murphy	Chester Skidmore
Homer Sheldon	Stanley Smitherman	Flo Sherwood
Jake Pendergraph	Shane Slade	Glen Sampson
Floyd Shaw	Vance Fletcher	Cindy Preston
Ginger Quincy	Dean Shepherd	Troy Hoke
Zane Swain	Bertha Whitlock	Roberta Brewster
Thelma Mittleton	Yolanda Rinehart	Bernard Cornell
Joan Thornton	Gene Bateman	

Source: From "Adaptations of the Names Test: Easy-to-Use Phonics Assessments," by N. Mather, J. Sammons, and J. Schwartz, 2006. *The Reading Teacher, 60*(2), p. 116.

addition, in the original study, Cunningham (1990) reported that students in 2nd grade obtained an average score of 22.6 out of 50 items (or about 45 percent correct), whereas Duffelmeyer et al. (1994) found that the mean score in 2nd grade for the 70 first and last names was 63 percent correct. The mean score in grade 3 was 73 percent correct, with scores at grade 4 at 89 percent correct, and grade 5 at 91percent correct.

Our third and most important caveat when assessing young students is this: use assessments that encompass measures of *vocabulary and comprehension* and include graphics or pictures in these assessments. We are in the business of teaching students to read, with reading defined as "lifting meaning from the text." It is ludicrous to assess a young child's reading skills and not include a measure on vocabulary and comprehension. We suggest that you use two types of

questioning with young students—multiple-choice questions and open-ended questions.

If students can read the passage with fluency, they read and respond to the comprehension questions themselves. However, if a student is a nonreader or falls in the lowest quartile on the national norms for reading fluency (Hasbrouck & Tindal, 2005), then read the text to the student while having the student follow along. Follow by reading the questions to the student while pointing at a printed copy of the questions in front of the student. Give 8 to 10 multiple choice questions to children in kindergarten, 1st grades and 2nd grade. The questions in the following example were designed to address various levels of comprehension using Dr. Taffy Rafael's conception of questioning from QAR (Question, Answer, Relationship) (Raphael & Au, 2005). The test developers (the "Fishbones" group) developed "right there" questions, "think and search" questions, and "author and you" questions.

We also suggest that you give students two or three open-ended questions. Figure A.33 in the Appendix is an excerpt from a reading test from grade 3 and was created in Eugene Public Schools, Betty's old stomping grounds.

Betty wrote the story to be consistent in difficulty while also being engaging, and to have the potential to be interpreted at different levels of comprehension. When we did the pilot testing on this at randomly selected schools, the assessors reported students coming up to them afterward and asking if they had any more stories about the big fat cat!

Measures for Older Students

In addressing classroom-based measures with secondary students, we would like to share three approaches that have worked effectively for us: conducting an informal reading assessment followed by a short interview with each student, using an adapted cloze technique called a "maze" with middle and high school students, and shifting the emphasis away from phonics and onto the construction of meaning in any intervention used with secondary students.

The Personal Reading Assessment

First and foremost, we believe that it is critical to engage the adolescent reader in self-reporting what is up with his or her reading before that student is given any formal reading assessments. It is important to *listen* to what they have to say about what is causing them reading difficulties. We understand that as secondary teachers, we avoid putting students on the spot in such a way as to embarrass them and so we don't often bring reading difficulties up with classes when, in fact, students can provide us with crucial information on their own perceptions of their reading problems. So we work to create a climate in the classroom where "confusion is cool" (Betty learned this expression at a "Reading Apprenticeship" training at WestEd in San Francisco), and all students know that asking questions and raising issues about the passage being read are crucial to understanding.

It is our experience that after a "quick" informal reading assessment, these students, in most cases, can articulate quite clearly what they are having difficulty with—that is, if they are in a safe environment in which to communicate with you. Here is a tool that I (Betty) use with older students. I originally called it "What's Up, Doc?" and then somehow it evolved to "What's Up with Your Reading?" (see Figure 7.4). Here is how it works.

1. Select a reading passage from your textbook or other print media that would be typical of those used in your class. It should be about 250 words. Each student needs a copy to write on, so we suggest that you retype the passage selected using double spacing, which will give students plenty of room in which to mark responses.

2. Make a copy of the personal reading assessment "What's Up with Your Reading?" (Figure 7.4) for each student. In addition, give students a copy of the 250-word passage to be read. Review the codes with students and ask them to follow the directions. If you feel it necessary, you can make an overhead of a different passage and model the process for students.

3. Give students adequate time to read and mark up the entire passage. Have them

tally their responses and then turn in both forms.

4. Schedule a brief conference with each student to review the assessment and discuss the results. At that conference, reinforce the notion that all readers—even great readers—get confused at times and have trouble comprehending text and that one can learn strategies to overcome these times of confusion. Assure each student that you will be teaching them specific strategies that will help with this.

To be honest, sometimes I just didn't get to all students because of the time constraints. But I did, for sure, get to those students who I knew were experiencing difficulties. I didn't make a big deal out of it. I have used "What's Up with Your Reading?" with elementary students, middle school students, and high school students.

The Maze

Now let's move on to our second approach—a more formal type of classroom-based assessment called a maze. Developers of curriculum-based assessment efforts over the last two decades have primarily focused on students in grades K–3. Until recently, there has not been a lot of attention paid to secondary students and literacy. To be sure, there are a number of commercially published assessments for older students—some that have been around for a long time and some that are tied directly to commercially published reading programs. The assessments then serve as a placement test and as a progress-monitoring test for that series.

In Eugene Public Schools, we set out to develop an assessment that would better track our students' comprehension as they read. We decided to use district-created mazes as tools in 9th and 10th grades, with the intention that at some time in the future, we would expand their use into 7th, 8th, 11th, and 12th grades. The maze (a reading selection where certain words have been deleted and students are given choices of words to use in each blank) is well established as a classroom-based reading measure (Kingston & Weaver, 1970; Cranney, 1972–73; Guthrie, 1973; Fuchs, Hamlett, & Fuchs, 1990; Parker, Hasbrouck, & Tindal, 1992). It can provide reliable assessment of student improvement in reading. Mazes can be either fiction or nonfiction passages.

What is the difference between a *cloze* test and a *maze* test? A *cloze* test is usually constructed from a passage where every fifth to seventh word is blanked out. A student is asked to read the passage orally and to make a guess as to the word that goes in the blank. A *maze* test is similar to the *cloze*. However, in the case of the maze, the student is provided with a set of three to five choices from which to choose to fill in the blank.

Mazes typically contain grade-level-appropriate reading passages of 250 to 500 words. In constructing random mazes, every *n*th word is deleted—typically, every 7th word excluding articles, conjunctions, and prepositions. Each item lists three or four answer choices—oddly, called "distracters." The choices are carefully selected so that one distracter is an exact match, one distracter is close to the correct answer, and another distracter is clearly incorrect. Students read the passage silently. Then they select the alternative they deem most appropriate *in meaning and usage* for the missing term.

Figure A.34 in the Appendix is an example of a 9th grade maze. Created for use with 9th graders in Eugene Public Schools, it is drawn from the book *My Antonia* by Willa Cather. We started with a somewhat longer passage from the book and literally removed every

Figure 7.4	**Personal Reading Assessment**

What's Up with Your Reading?

You, like all readers, will have difficulty understanding some texts you are reading. This happens to everyone and happens for various reasons. Some of these reasons are:

- Now and then you *can't decode* (sound out) some words in the text.
- At other times, even when you *can decode* a word, you have *no clue* as to what that word means.
- Sometimes, even when you can decode the words, and you think you know what they mean, you still *don't get* what the author is trying to say in the passage.
- Another big issue is concentration—that is, staying focused on the text. Your *mind wanders* away even though you notice that you are decoding the words.

Let's understand what happens when you are reading. Pay attention to the kinds of problems you are having by talking back to the text. As you read, circle any word or phrase that is confusing to you. Above the word or phrase, code your problem.

If:	Write:	Number of Times You Marked Each
You *can't decode* it.	CD	
You have *no clue* what it means.	NC	
You read it but *don't get it.*	DGI	
Your *mind* is *wandering.*	MW	

After you finish, take a look at what you recorded. Add up the number of times you marked each category and record it above.

Why should you take the time to do this?

- If you are having trouble with *decoding,* you can learn strategies to help you break down these hard-to-sound-out, multisyllable words.
- If you can't figure out what a word means, you can learn strategies for figuring out the word's meaning.
- If you don't seem to be able to pull all of the information in the text together and understand what the passage is about, you can learn strategies that will help you do that.
- And if you know that your mind is wandering, you can learn strategies that you can use to help you stay focused on your reading.

7th word (excluding articles, conjunctions, and prepositions) to create 60 deletions. Following an extensive pilot test, test-builders from the University of Oregon did their "psychometric thing" by analyzing student responses to each deletion and its distracters, ending up with the best 25 items for the final version of the assessment. This reduced the number but still gave us enough information to be a valid assessment and, at the same time, made it a more manageable assessment to complete. We included no deletions in the first paragraph to give students a straight set to read before we confronted them with the maze text. We also used the rest of the chapter to create a multiple-choice assessment, giving us two data sets from which to look at a student's comprehension.

In the classroom, the assessor/teacher reads the first paragraph of instructions (in boldface) and then has the students begin. The assessment was designed to be administered in one 50-/55-minute period but was not timed. (Teachers allowed students to ask for extra time after the class period; however, we found that this rarely happened.) Teachers encouraged students to mark their responses on the actual test booklet and then transfer their answers to the scan sheet used for scoring, as it is critical to allow students to go back and change answers if they discover some new information from further reading that will change their response on previous items.

What we have found is that the maze is effective at identifying those readers who clearly stay engaged with the text by constructing meaning as they go, versus those students who are clearly not staying engaged with the text and are misconstruing the meaning. The maze also identifies students who have more depth of background knowledge to bring to their reading.

Focus on Comprehension

Our third approach is to make sure that the assessments you use and the secondary interventions you choose focus on *vocabulary and comprehension*. Reading comprehension is the heart in the act of reading. And vocabulary is the coronary artery that supplies the heart with oxygenated blood, allowing it to thrive.

We have found that the emphasis of instruction for many of our struggling teen readers has been on decoding in their elementary years. We have found this to be particularly true for students previously enrolled in Title One and special education classes. When we interview these students, many perceive reading as simply decoding—that is, sounding out the words. Somehow, along the way, they have lost the notion that the goal of reading is to lift meaning from the print, that reading must

- make sense;
- lead to understanding something; and
- be enlightening and, at best, enjoyable.

We hazard a guess that if a student has been enrolled in classes primarily focusing on decoding for four to six years and has had solid phonics instruction but has not yet mastered the phonetic code, he or she is not likely to become a good reader—meaning a person who can lift meaning from the text—in that way. As a result, we need to teach him or her alternative ways of constructing meaning.

This is not to say that phonics should never be a part of a secondary reading program. It just means that there has to be a shift away from "decoding only" programs to programs with a strong emphasis on comprehension and its related companions, background knowledge and vocabulary development.

Also, our sense is that we, as educators, often provide students with text that is either poorly written or written using concepts and vocabulary way beyond students' developmental levels. In these cases, we need to stop giving students these "inconsiderate texts" and replace them with developmentally appropriate and well-constructed texts.

It should be noted that we have also observed a pattern with many of these students in which they struggle when they arrive at middle and high schools because they have spent much of their time in elementary classrooms in which their teachers have directed nearly all of the classroom instruction and interaction. When these students arrive at a secondary school that requires them to move from setting to setting and respond to various instructional styles, they flounder because they have no experience being self-directed, have no experience reading various types of texts, and have not internalized any strategies to persevere when reading becomes difficult or confusing.

In the News: A Scenic Detour of Adolescent Reading Assessments in the Midst of Our Scenic Tour of Reading Assessments

The Carnegie Corporation of New York just released a capstone report of the Carnegie Council for Advancing Adolescent Literacy. Since 2004, under the direction of Council Chairperson Catherine Snow, professor in the Harvard Graduate School of Education, the council has gathered knowledge and ideas from experts nationwide on topics ranging from linguistics to the social science of teaching. *Time to Act* was released with five corresponding reports that delve deeper into how to advance literacy and learning for all students. In one of

these reports, *Measure for Measure: A Critical Consumer's Guide to Reading Comprehension Assessments for Adolescents* (Morsy, Kieffer, & Snow, 2010), the authors draw together evidence about nine of the most commonly used, commercially available reading comprehension assessments and provide a critical view into the strengths and weaknesses of each. They focus on the utility of each assessment for the purposes of screening groups of students to identify those who struggle and diagnosing the specific needs of those students who struggle. For those readers looking for commercially published assessments to use, we recommend you review their work.

A Snapshot of Chapter 7

States and school districts are scrambling to address calls for increasing reading achievement by identifying those students most at risk of reading failure and intervening sooner through an approach called "response to intervention." We support these concepts in general but have offered a few caveats to the reader.

In this chapter, we have suggested the following:

• For young students, we suggest that teachers of kindergarten and 1st grade students, especially those new to the school environment, delay the use of district- or state-sponsored assessments for about six weeks to give students an opportunity to acclimate and feel safe in the classroom environment.

• We also suggest the use of assessments for young students that incorporate effective and meaningful comprehension measures and that incorporate real-word reading, not nonsense-word reading.

• For secondary students, we suggest the use of three approaches:

• First, rely on secondary students to self-report on the issues they have with reading.

• For a more formal assessment, we recommend the use of the modified cloze technique called the maze.

• And lastly, we suggest the importance of a focus on vocabulary and comprehension in assessing as well as instructing those students at risk of reading failure at the secondary level.

Now let's move on to Chapter 8, where we will address many of the sparkles and blemishes we have encountered in our work with performance-based assessments in the classroom.

chapter 8

Sparkles and Blemishes

A Universal Teacher Story

A student approaches a teacher and asks a question—sometimes politely, other times more demandingly, and sometimes even suspiciously.

"What grade did you give me?"

"*Give* me. . . ." The words resonate menacingly. As if the teacher randomly tossed out grades to the students. As if all teachers merely fling out the grades—here are some *B*s, many *C*s, and pitifully too few *A*s. Too many of our students do not understand the concept of connecting grades to an *earned* academic performance. They have difficulty evaluating their own performance because they are often unclear about what is being evaluated.

So they assume their teachers *give out* grades.

And, sadly, we teachers share the responsibility for this misconception. If students are not clear about the performance expectations their teachers hold for them, then they will have little chance of recognizing how well they are doing. If students do not clearly understand "what good looks like," then they won't know if they're "doing good" and will have to rely on asking, "What grade did you give me?"

To improve students' understanding of what we expect them to do, how well they should be able to do it, and how they should go about accomplishing it is what this book on classroom-based performance assessment has been all about.

Classroom-Based Performance Assessment

As we have explained, classroom-based performance assessment is an approach to teaching and learning that stems from *our* curriculum and instruction, not from somewhere else, far away from where we teach and where our students learn.

It is this connection to the classroom that makes this assessment system work:

- It informs our students exactly what we expect them to be able to do.
- It leads them to those expectations through abundant, guided practice and reveals to them how they will be scored in advance of their performance.
- It is designed to lead to Great Performances, many of which we have proudly shared with you in the preceding chapters.

But we promised you an honest journey. Not only are there benefits and advantages to this approach, there also are difficulties with what we have advocated—difficulties that need to be wrestled with. So let's review both the sparkles and the blemishes, the strengths and the weaknesses, of classroom-based performance assessments.

Sparkles

As you know, we have found a number of solid reasons for using classroom-based performance assessment.

The Great Motivator

First, performance tasks are a turn-on for students. Good tasks motivate kids to work hard to perform at their highest possible level. Tasks that are new, different, and even fun surprise students who think they've "done it all" in school. Engaging tasks capture their interest, their energy, and their pride of ownership. This is welcome news to classroom teachers who struggle to engage disengaged learners. Additionally, we have built the element of choice into some of the tasks. Providing students with an occasional choice boosts motivation, because students definitely like having a say now and then in what goes on in their classes. Offering students a choice

once in a while is a great way to differentiate our instruction by increasing student buy-in. Third, performance tasks add value to school assignments by widening the audience. In many of the tasks we shared in this book, students are working toward an audience beyond the teacher; this allows students to function more like adults in the real world than kids stuck in a classroom. And finally, performance tasks allow students to become experts on the course content topics and showcase their knowledge and skills. School becomes a place where they can "get good" at something.

Accurate, Meaningful Indicators

Because performance tasks are aligned to the curriculum, they are accurate and meaningful indicators of "who knows what" and "who can do what." Performance tasks serve as the arrows that students aim and shoot at the targets. And when tasks are aligned to learning standards—whether the standards are national, state, or local—the performance improves. When students, their parents, and school personnel all know what the academic targets are, then everyone can get down to the business of hitting those targets. Furthermore, when those tasks are assigned during an instructional unit, we harvest the results *in-progress,* when we still have time to do something about it. This is formative assessment, and as W. James Popham (2008) explains in his book *Transformative Assessment,* we teachers use it to inform our instruction, "to improve the caliber of *still-underway* instructional activities" (p. 4; italics ours).

Teacher Confidence in Assessment

Performance task assessment increases teacher confidence in assessing student learning. The feedback we receive from assessing our students' performance using well-constructed performance tasks is solid when those tasks meet the five criteria presented in Chapter 1:

- They offer some degree of student choice.
- They require both the elaboration of content knowledge and the use of processes.
- They reveal the explicit scoring criteria in advance.
- They provide an audience beyond the teacher.
- They are accurate indicators of targeted outcomes.

In addition to receiving feedback on student learning, we also get feedback on how well we're teaching. Performance tasks inform assessment and instruction simultaneously. This information increases our confidence in knowing how effective, or ineffective, our instruction is. And given the public's great interest in how well we are doing, this information is vital.

Linking Content and Process

Performance tasks require learners to integrate content and process. Good tasks link them together—this linkage of "the what" with "the how" replicates work in the real world, as opposed to the atomistic breakdown of facts versus skills in the traditional school world. Instead of merely regurgitating content back (like on a test or quiz), students must *apply* that newly learned content in a meaningful way by using a process, such as using the writing process to write an article about the findings of a science experiment or the speaking process to create an oral presentation on a contemporary community issue.

We love how performance tasks force learners to put their knowledge to use. When

kids use a process to reveal their understanding of content knowledge, they learn more deeply. Whether the process involves constructing visual representations (Chapter 3), writing (Chapter 4), speaking (Chapter 5), constructing large-scale projects, or performing (Chapter 6), our students learn the content better, remember it longer, and are more able to perform as adults would in the real world. It is the analysis, the synthesis, the creation, and the application that move students to deeply process the content. We must not forget that in the real world, they will be expected to *do* things—to put information to *use*—not just remember things.

Info In Together with Info Out

Performance tasks merge Info In and Info Out. After students learn new content information through the Info In processes (reading, listening, viewing, and manipulating), they are expected to reveal their understanding of the new knowledge in a task that applies an Info Out process (visual representation, writing, speaking, or construction). This merger strengthens the link between student learning and teacher assessment of that learning.

Distinguishing Performance from Effort

A final sparkle relates to the burning question "What grade did you give me?" Not only do many students fail to connect their effort to earning a grade, but they also do not distinguish effort from performance. There is a huge difference between trying hard and performing well. Good effort does not guarantee a great performance. Ask any disappointed athlete, musician, actor, dancer, or artist.

Performance task assessment separates the effort from the performance, the practice from the game, the rehearsal from showtime. While it is most definitely true that good effort, like good practice, will increase the chances of a great performance, effort and performance are two different things. And while effort is a behavior we all want to instill in our students, *performance* is critical. It is the ability to do what we expect of our students—and the ability to do it well. Through classroom-based tasks, students learn how to perform in mathematics, literature, science, history, and all subjects to reveal what they know and what they can do.

Blemishes and Suggested Solutions

As we have demonstrated throughout this book, not every student performance turns out to be a "great" one. As much as we believe in performance assessment, we recognize that it has some weaknesses and challenges— or, as we call them, blemishes. Following each one we will offer some suggested solutions for "un-blemishing" them—that is, to help convert them into sparkles.

Blemish 1: The Dreaded Effort/ Performance Gap

In our first edition in 1998, we admitted, "One sparkle leads to a blemish: distinguishing between effort and performance can cause problems." Many students, and certainly many of their parents, believe that if you try hard— do your homework, have good attendance, and behave yourself—then you'll get a good grade. And for the most part, they are right! We do tend to reward effort; if you do the work, you'll accumulate enough points, or earn a high enough percentage, to earn an *A* or a *B,* at worst a *C.*

But how many of us who use letter grades for reporting student achievement have felt that awkward sensation of inaccuracy as we fill out a report card with high grades for a student who, even though he or she has earned the points, when asked to fails to clear the bar and perform? Or what about the low grades for the student who lacks consistent effort, misses too many assignments, and maybe even causes periodic disruption, but who can nail a target when the chips are down? And what about the students who come every day, work hard, and are cooperative but who have developmental issues that inhibit their ability to clear the bars set by the state?

This is the dreaded gap between effort and performance. The question is, *Can we measure the actual performance while continuing to reinforce good effort, a good attitude, and good classroom behavior?* Yes, we can.

Our Proposed Solution for the Dreaded Effort/Performance Gap: Summative Assessment

To bridge the great gap between performance and effort, we can separate our reporting of each.

For example, the Madison (Wisconsin) Metropolitan School District decided to avoid the awkwardness that accompanies this dreaded gap between effort and performance by separating the *results* of a task from the *behaviors* that affect those results—that is, disconnect the performance from the effort. Middle school teachers there use a report card that identifies cumulative scores on "Academic Power Standards" using a 4-point scale, but they also report on the important "Learning Skills," defined as "work habits and behaviors that *support the learning process.*"

The Power Standards

For Madison, the Academic Power Standards are the *prioritized* state learning standards that are derived from a systematic and balanced approach to distinguishing which standards are absolutely essential. Madison's Power Standards represent a group of standards that have many features in common. Each subject area reports on two to five Power Standards each quarter. A student's performance is assessed on a 4-point scale:

- 4=Demonstrates an *in-depth* understanding and application.
- 3=Demonstrates *full* understanding and application.
- 2=Demonstrates *partial* understanding and application.
- 1=Demonstrates *little or no* understanding.

The Learning Skills

Learning Skills, on the other hand, are the work habits and behaviors that support the learning process. Because "Learning Skills" sounds to us more like the academic skills, we prefer using "Characteristics of Your Student as a Learner and Classroom Citizen," or perhaps more simply, "Classroom Habits Conducive to Learning." You can label them as you choose.

Madison's Learning Skills include use of class time, homework completion, and cooperation with peers and adults.

A student's learning skills are assessed on a three-letter scoring scale reported in addition to the Power Standards:

- M=Most of the time
- S=Some of the time
- R=Rarely

For more information about this program, go to secedweb.madison.k12.wi.us/files/seced/7th_parent_brochure.pdf.

Our Proposed Solution for the Dreaded Effort/Performance Gap: Formative Assessment

This report card, of course, is for summative assessment. That is, it comes at the end (or the midterm/quarter) of a marking period. This is different from *formative assessment,* which reports the results of student progress *during* a semester or quarter while there is still time to adjust instruction and/or learning to enhance student improvement. Recall James Popham's definition of ongoing, in-progress formative assessment: "a planned process in which teachers or students use assessment-based evidence to adjust what they are currently doing" (2008, p. 6).

So the question becomes, can we report the results of a *formative* assessment to students in a way that also separates performance from effort? That is, how do teachers break apart effort and performance on a classroom performance task given during a unit of instruction? More specifically, the teacher asks, "How will I know how much effort you put into this work?"

To answer this critical question, we must identify the key behaviors for successful completion of a task and *separately list them* from the performance task's key traits of excellence—that is, the required content information and perhaps the appropriate process(es) needed for the task.

We have explained how to do this in previous chapters. For an example, check out the Group/Self-Assessment in Figure A. 15. Teacher Cathy Bechen provided it to her students to assess their, and their teammates', effort on writing a Civil War magazine article. But for assessing the *results* of their effort—the actual written articles—she used a separate newspaper Article Evaluation Scoring Guide (see Figure A.16).

However, if designing two separate scoring devices is too much, we can use any single scoring device to list effort characteristics along with the key content requirements for our student performers. For example, the Museum Exhibit Assessment List, Figure A.32, does this well. Items 1–4 deal with the content requirements (performance), while items 5–6 address the good work behaviors (effort) the teacher needed to target.

Or, to determine the amount of effort a student exerted while performing any task, a teacher could develop a more generic scoring device to answer the question "How will I know how much effort you put into this work?"

Well, as your teacher I can observe three possible behaviors. I can see that:

1. You completed all *required components* of the assignment, as listed in the checklist above.
2. Your *work is ready* to be turned in. It is well thought out, organized, neat—not just thrown together—showing a pride of ownership.
3. You turned in your work *on time*—both final due date and any midpoints.

OK, so you may be asking, "What should I do with a student who turns in the assigned task that fails to demonstrate one or more of the above effort criteria, but who clearly performed well—that is, he demonstrates a full understanding of the key concepts?" Like many teachers, we handle this occurrence by routinely weighing the grasp of the concepts over neatness and timeliness. That is, the value of the work exceeds the value of the effort.

However, there are some times when we insist that those very bright, but careless or sloppy, students rework the task to meet standards that they will face in the adult world. This seems to us to be a fair and reasonable balance of performance and effort.

Another Example of Scoring Effort—Using a ChecBric

Here is another example of a single-scoring device that assesses both performance and effort simultaneously. This ChecBric was designed to measure a "Student-Authored Study Guide" task for a textbook chapter that we shared earlier. (See Chapter 4.)

As you will recall from Chapter 2, a ChecBric is our two-columned hybrid scoring device: the left-hand column—in the form of a checklist—is for students to be aware of the task's requirements and to self-monitor (check off) their progress through the task; the right hand column—in the form of a rubric—is for teachers to assess the work. We have found that students are more apt to actually use a ChecBric versus a traditional rubric because (1) the checklist format is easier to use than a rubric's point scale, and (2) the language in a ChecBric is more student-friendly compared to the education jargon used in a traditional rubric.

Notice Target 3 in the student checklist of the column (see Figure 8.1) for the effort category "Being Productive," with five specific behaviors listed.

You will see that the five behaviors are generic in that they describe productivity in a way that could be applied to any performance task, not just this particular study guide task. This approach certainly has the benefit of keeping the effort indicators consistent across many different tasks throughout the school year or the semester.

Alternatively, consider using Robert Marzano and Deborah Pickering's five behaviors that assist learners in performing successfully. In their seminal book *Dimensions of Learning, Teacher's Manual,* they call them "mental habits that *exemplify self-regulated* thinking" (italics ours):

Figure 8.1	**Study Guide ChecBric**

Student-Authored Study Guide

Task Summary: Create a Study Guide Booklet for Chapter 7 in your math textbook. Your job is to teach the key information in the chapter to other students in a way that is *easier to understand* than the textbook's version. To accomplish this task, you cannot just copy some things out of the textbook (which would be plagiarism), but rather you must paraphrase, summarize, prioritize, and rewrite in your own words. Of course, you can quote some select words or phrases from the textbook if you think they are perfect. (Put quotation marks around them to show that you borrowed them.)

Assessment: See the ChecBric below to be sure you understand how you will be graded.

Student Checklist	Teacher Rubric
Target 1: Expressing My Understanding	**Trait 1: Content Understanding**
My Study Guide Booklet is helpful to readers by providing them	**6** = exceptional, compelling, thorough understanding of key points presented in summary paragraphs, plus helpful, supporting study questions and commentary
_____ the chapter section's **key points / main ideas using:**	**5** = excellent, outstanding, thorough understanding of key points presented in summary paragraphs and study questions
• short phrases or	**4** = proficient understanding: interesting and accurate key points presented in short phrases or bullets
• bulleted informal outline or	
• summary paragraphs	
_____ the chapter section's key **supporting details that are brief** but **to the point**	**3** = inadequate understanding; close, but overly broad or simplistic; not quite good enough to meet expectations
_____ a *translation* of the information into **"student-friendly"** language	**2** = limited or minimal understanding; unclear or sporadic; tried to meet expectations, but a ways to go to meet expectations
_____ **study review questions** to think about	**1** = missing, absent understanding; lacks a summary or missed the purpose; way off on the requirements OR no attempt to meet expectations
_____ my **comments** on the material	
• tips for remembering the info	
• connections to other sources, experiences	
• examples, analogies	
	Trait 2: Presentation
Target 2: Courtesy to My Readers	**6** = exceptionally strong presentation: exquisite layout and design with engaging visuals; error-free or minor, non-interruptive errors
My Study Guide Booklet is easy to use because it	
_____ has a pleasing **layout:**	**5** = excellent, outstanding presentation: pleasing layout and design with useful accompanying visuals; few errors, but cause no interference
• bullets	
• boldface and/or italics	
• boxes	**4** = proficient, adequate presentation: basic layout and design, but without visuals; some minor errors that do not cause confusion
• colors	
_____ offers **graphics** to support the words	
_____ is **neatly designed**	**3** = inadequate presentation; close, but layout or errors interrupt ideas; not good enough to meet expectations
_____ has been **checked** to **eliminate problems:**	
• **spelling** errors	**2** = limited presentation: layout confusing or inconsistent; frequent, significant errors disrupt; tried to meet expectations, but quite a ways to go to meet them
• **capitalization** errors	
• **punctuation** errors	
• **handwriting** problems	

Figure 8.1	**Study Guide ChecBric** (*continued*)
	1 = no apparent attempt at presentation: layout a mess; numerous errors cause breakdown of meaning; way off on the requirements
Target 3: Being Productive While working on my Study Guide Booklet _____ I followed the **directions** _____ I used my **time wisely** _____ **I allowed my neighbors** to work in peace _____ I stayed **at my desk** _____ I worked **independently** without talking	**Trait 3: Productivity** **6** = exceptionally productive **5** = excellent productivity **4** = decently productive ————————————————————— **3** = inadequate productivity **2** = limited productivity **1** = disruptive OR unproductive

- You monitor your own thinking.
- You plan appropriately.
- You identify and use necessary resources.
- You respond appropriately to feedback.
- You evaluate the effectiveness of your actions (Marzano et al., 1997).

We like this list and can see how easily it could be embedded into a ChecBric for the effort component. And we appreciate the descriptor "self-regulated learning" because it clearly places the responsibility on the students. Some teachers use the term "self-directed learner" to describe for students what they need to do in order to be successful in school.

Finally, instead of using broad, general terms for effort/productivity/self-directed learner behaviors, a teacher could decide to modify those terms for a specific task. For example, with the Study Guide Booklet task, consider these specific descriptors of productivity:

- I met the deadlines for this Study Guide assignment by completing the rough draft on Nov. 6 and the final copy on Nov. 9.
- I worked with my peer partner to identify any problems and to improve my Study Guide through editing.
- I double-checked my Study Guide to make sure it was up to the high standards listed in Targets 1 and 2.
- My neighbors will vouch for my quiet and supportive behavior every day I worked on my Study Guide.

Whichever option you chose, the good news is that this format separates the key learning *behaviors* in Target 3 from the key *qualities* of the product in Targets 1 and 2. The bad news, however, is that this third trait will be factored into the final overall score on the performance—a no-no for many teachers because they are uncomfortable with and/or have been directed to resist including behavior/attitude into grades. Our position on this is that although behavior cannot become the most important consideration in scoring tasks, it should be factored in because, as we all know, as adults, our behavior is factored into our compensation in the workplace. So we are comfortable including effort in letter grades, as long as it is subservient to performance.

This brings us to our next blemish: letter grades.

Blemish 2: Letter Grade/ Performance Score

In the first edition of this book, we admitted we had concerns about, and hopes for, bridging the great divide between traditional letter grade–based reporting and the newer rubric point-scale system. We wrote:

> Given the difference between two assessment systems (letter grades and rubric point-scores), can and should teachers convert performance task rubric scores into letter grades for reporting purposes? Or, can/should the report card indicate *both* letter grades and task scores?

A key factor here is that letter grades are summative evaluations, a more permanent label. They tell a student (and a parent or guardian) where he or she ended up in comparison to other students in the class and, more importantly, whether the student earned credit for the class. Performance task scores, on the other hand, are formative. They tell the learner how well he or she did on a specific task—not compared to other students, but in relationship to a standard at a particular time.

We pondered the prospect of merging the two systems in the transition from strictly letter grades to rubric reporting:

> More practically, can performance task scores be weighted, so that they can be converted into numerical values or percentages for letter grades? The gurus of performance assessment strongly advise

us not to because they are two different systems; in other words, "Thou shalt not mix apples with oranges."

Yet many classroom teachers who value performance task assessment still must fill out report cards for each grading period. This is a gigantic problem facing advocates of performance assessment. But it is not unsolvable. Assessment expert Grant Wiggins states:

> If a school's policy is to give letter grades only, what can an individual teacher do? There's nothing to prevent teachers from expanding their modes of assessment while still living in a letter-grade world. Assessment reform is about getting different and richer information about students' performance, all of which teachers can factor into a grade. It's a matter of *expanding your pile of evidence,* not necessarily changing the grading system. (Wiggins, 1995)

We agree, of course. But how are we going to merge that "expanding pile of evidence" into an overall letter grade—even though we recognize the problems in doing so?

Three Proposed Solutions for Bridging the Letter Grade/Performance Divide

Now, 12 years later, we have found several interesting answers to that question for teachers who use performance assessment and who also must fill out student report cards using letter grades. Let's see if any can "de-blemish" this concern and transform it into a "sparkle" by considering three possible options to get out of this jam.

Use a "Point and Percentage" Rubric

New Jersey teachers Mike D'Ostilio and Carrie Crispin at Gateway Regional High School District in Woodbury Heights developed a rubric that easily translates points earned on a performance assessment into percentages that convert into letter grades. They first identified the percentages for letter grades. In their school, 91–100 percent equates into an *A* grade, 83–90 percent into *B*, and so forth. Next, they connected point values to each percentage; for example, 5.1 on the rubric equals 91 percent equals *A*–. Now, for some point values, they had to repeat the percentage; for example 3.6 and 3.5 both equal 78 percent. They don't see any problem with this necessity, nor do we.

6.0 = 100	4.0 = 82	2.0 = 66
5.9 = 99	3.9 = 81	1.9 = 65
5.8 = 98	3.8 = 80	1.8 = 64
5.7 = 97	3.7 = 79	1.7 = 63
5.6 = 96	3.6 = 78	1.6 = 62
5.5 = 95	3.5 = 78	1.5 = 62
5.4 = 94	3.4 = 77	1.4 = 61
5.3 = 93	3.3 = 76	1.3 = 60
5.2 = 92	3.2 = 75	1.2 = 59
5.1 = 91	3.1 = 75	1.1 = 59
5.0 = 90	**3.0 = 74**	**1.0 = 58**
4.9 = 89	2.9 = 74	
4.8 = 88	2.8 = 73	
4.7 = 87	2.7 = 72	
4.6 = 86	2.6 = 71	
4.5 = 85	2.5 = 70	
4.4 = 85	2.4 = 70	
4.3 = 84	2.3 = 69	
4.2 = 84	2.2 = 68	
4.1 = 83	2.1 = 67	

Mike and Carrie report, "Parents and students love this because it helps them wrap their brain around where they perform. So when we get state test scores back, and they see the performance scale, they can quickly make sense of how their children did based on the traditional structure." Connecting classwork grading with state assessment reporting is very helpful to students and parents.

Additionally, on a classroom assessment task, Mike and Carrie add a comment to the student to accompany the earned scores. Here, Mike expands his feedback to a student before posting the rubric scores at the bottom. To save paper grading time, Mike merges four writing traits into two general categories, Style and Content and Formatting and Grammar:

Kyle, it was really impressive to see how well you fixed the previous errors. You did this very well and with great command. I think your analysis is good. However, I do see some of your ideas are loosely connected. It's not what you said. Rather, it's when you said it. For example, you mentioned "Weary Blues" at two different parts in the paper. I recognized that you were doing this for two different purposes, but when reading it, it became very repetitive. This paper in general was so much better than your initial drafts because you really fixed the fact that it was too biographical, and you really fixed MLA stuff. Lastly, when doing an in-text citation, the citation always comes at the end of the sentence. Formal rules don't allow for citing in the middle of sentences. I didn't tell you that, so I didn't take points off for it, but I wanted you to know for the future.

Style and Content = 4.5 = 85%

Formatting and Grammar = 5.3 = 93%

Because some teachers prefer using a 4-point rubric, Mike and Carrie have developed one. While similar to the above 6-pointer, it required them to condense the percentages. 4.0 = 100 percent; 3.0 = 85 percent; 2.0 = 70 percent; 1.0 = 55 percent. If you would like to view this 4-point version, see www.larrylewin.com/books/ GreatPerformances.html and click on "Online Supplements."

Use Robert Marzano's Holistic 4-Point Rubric

Bob Marzano's contributions to teachers' understanding of both instruction and assessment are legendary. In his book *Classroom Assessment and Grading That Work* (2006), he advocates for performance assessment as a better way of reporting student progress than exclusively using the end-of-term letter grade. He supports formative versus summative assessment by recommending that we provide our students with "dollops of feedback" (John Hattie's term in "Measuring the Effects of Schooling," *Australian Journal of Education,* 36[1], 1992).

We concur, obviously, but the problem remains: how do we report these "dollops" to students and parents who live in a percentage-based, letter grade, report card world—a world with lots of problems?

Marzano realistically appraises the drawbacks of relying on letter grades for report cards: "an overall grade is *relatively meaningless* from a measurement perspective. However, overall grades will probably be the norm in most schools for some time to come" (2006, p. 119; italics ours). Yes, we have not seen a decrease in their use since our first edition, and they no doubt will continue, but it is useful to put overall letter grades in this perspective.

Middle school teacher, presenter, and author Rick Wormeli goes further to critique letter grades:

> Grades are inferences, personal interpretations on the part of the teacher, not infallible truths about students' mastery . . . . Grades are *fragile little things* on which

to base so much. It's worth keeping them in perspective. (2006, p. 95; italics ours)

Well put.

So what's a teacher to do about all this criticism of letter grades? Marzano has developed a generic 4-point rubric named a "Simplified Scoring Scale" that not only works for all performance assessments in all subjects but also easily converts into a letter grade:

4.0 In addition to Score 3.0 performance, independently no errors or omissions with in-depth inference and applications that go beyond what was taught

3.0 Independently, no major errors or omissions regarding any of the information and/or processes that were explicitly taught

2.0 Independently, no major errors or omissions regarding the simpler details and processes but major errors and omissions regarding the more complex

1.0 [Only] with help, a partial understanding of the simpler details and processes but not the more complex

He added one more performance level to represent a 0 score (making it a 5-point scale):

0 Even with help, no understanding or skill demonstrated (Marzano, 2006, p. 45)

He has further developed his holistic rubric into ½-point values for fine-tuning assessment. We strongly recommend checking it out in his book (Marzano, 2006, pp. 40-41).

A similar, but even simpler, 4-point scoring scales was developed by the Madison Metropolitan Area School District. Its district-wide point-scale definitions are as follows:

4 = in-depth
3 = full
2 = partial
1 = little

Now, to bridge the rubric–report card gap, both Marzano and the Madison District offer scales for translating a rubric's 4-point scores into an overall summative letter grade; note the use of ½-point scores in Marzano's:

3.00–4.00 = *A*
2.5–2.99 = *B*
2.00–2.49 = *C*
1.50–1.99 = *D*
below 1.50 = *F*

Now look at the scale for Madison Metropolitan Area School District. Its slight modification to the grading scale was based on the attempt to reflect that an *A* would contain evidence beyond "meeting standards." Teachers there use a set of collected point scores—from a combination of multiple tasks—to determine a summary letter grade:

A = 3.01 and above
B = 2.5 to 3.0
C = 2.0 to 2.49
D = 1.50 to 1.99
U = 1.49 and below

(*U* means unsatisfactory and is equivalent to an *F;* they do not use that grade at the middle school level.)

Over time, teachers become familiar with these descriptors and understand their full meaning. However, it might be wise to flesh these out a little to increase the clarity of meaning of each. For example, the high 4-point descriptor "in-depth" could become "The student demonstrates a comprehensive and thorough understanding." Refer to Figure A.25 for an example of a 6-point scoring scale with fuller descriptions.

According to Lisa Wachtel, Madison's executive director of teaching and learning, the district changed their reporting system to a standards-based report card because of concerns with traditional reporting:

• Single grades hide student strengths and weaknesses.
• Single grades often combine different factors.
• Methods used to report and grade vary widely from one teacher to another, even among those who teach at the same grade level within the same school.

Madison teachers feel more confident of the grading accuracy by moving to a standards-based reporting system, in that it

• provides specific information on a student's academic achievement;
• reports student proficiency as demonstrated throughout a marking period; and
• reports elements such as use of class time, homework completion, and cooperation separately from a student's academic achievement.

For more information on their approach to grading, visit their website at http://oldweb.madison.k12.wi.us/topics/ms_report_cards/docs/issue5-reporting.pdf.

Wachtel explains that while this system merges the two separate realms of rubric scores and letter grades, the rationale behind the "hybrid" version is "to ensure our students and families continue to have a single, summary grade that is easily understood; grade point average and transcript information will be maintained; teachers, students and families will have time to adjust and see the benefits of standards-based while maintaining a component of the traditional system; and a review of other districts provided evidence that an abrupt move to a complete standards-based system at the secondary level can result in failure and loss of the entire standards-based reporting efforts" (Lisa Wachtel, personal communication, May 21, 2009).

Back to Marzano, who readily admits that we "must realize that this, or any other conversion table, is an 'artificial construct'" because the "cutoff points for the various grades are arbitrary" (2006, p. 122). So each teacher, or better yet, each building, or much better, an entire district must make the decision on what point scores equate with which letter grades. Meanwhile, why not try this out and see how it works in your own classroom? Perhaps you will discover a great modification that works just right. If so, please consider sharing it with us.

One last consideration in this conversion process: what happens when a student earns a set of scores—for a set of performance tasks over the course of a grading period—and one of those scores is obviously lower than the others? For example, what should a teacher do if one (or more) of her 9th grade physical science students earn 3, 4, 4, 2, and 4 for the five assigned performances?

Option 1, of course, would be to average them: 3 + 4 + 4 + 2 + 4 = 17. The total score of 17 divided by five tasks = 3.4 mean score, which converts into a solid *A* grade. No problem.

But what about five scores from another student: 2, 1, 2, 4, 2 = 2.2 = a low *C*. Does that 4 score skew the letter grade by artificially dragging it up?

If your answer is "no," then you are comfortable using a Compensatory System, which is a straight averaging of the various assessments' scores into a mean score. On the other hand, if you see a problem, you can use a Conjunctive System, which requires a passing performance for each task/test in the battery.

For example, the assessor employs some restrictions:

A No single task score can be below 3.0.

B No single task score can be below 2.5.

C No single task score can be below 2.0.

D No single task score can be below 1.5.

F Some single task score is below 1.5.

There are benefits to both approaches, and we recommend that you carefully experiment with both, then seek a buildingwide consensus on which approach to employ. Clearly, having a consistent grading policy increases confidence in the fairness of the system.

Now let's take a look at a third option.

Holistic 4-Point ChecBric

We took Marzano's generic 4-point rubric and converted it into our ChecBric format to come up with a third possible option for merging performance task scoring and letter grades: the Holistic ChecBric. Our earlier ChecBrics were analytical; that is, they assessed multiple traits with individual point-values—each trait on the ChecBric's right-hand side was scored independently.

The new Holistic ChecBric scores student performance with one overall score, like the one we shared in Chapter 2 for the SnapShots reading-visualizing task. Recall that the students were instructed to "take quick pictures" of what they saw in their mind's eye while reading a folk tale. (See Figure 2.4 on p. 21.)

In the Holistic ChecBric's right-hand Teacher's Rubric column, you will recognize Marzano's useful, generic 4-point scale. We find it useful to allow ourselves to add a + or a – to the scores as needed. Then, we can employ Marzano's grade conversion system. For example, if a student earns a 2+, then her grade would be B-. (See above.) We believe that these Marzano-inspired Holistic ChecBrics have potential for both teachers and students.

Five Quick Additional Suggestions to Consider When Scoring Student Effort

Weight the Traits Differently

For example, on the Study Guide Booklet ChecBric, Targets 1 and 2 (the two key traits of an excellent Study Guide) can be valued at, say 40 percent and 40 percent, while Target 3 "Being Productive"—a very useful "learning skill"/classroom habit—is worth 20 percent. Or allocate 50 percent, 40 percent, and 10 percent. Many of us weight the traits differently to highlight their respective value in our eyes.

Factor Out the "Learning Skills"/Classroom Habits Trait in the Assessment Score

We can score them to give students feedback on our observation of their behaviors during a task, but then *not factor that score* into the task's point-scale total. Some schools/districts encourage teachers to factor out behavior when scoring academic tasks.

Begin by Scoring the Effort

At the beginning of the semester or term, when we are working hard to demonstrate to our new students the key learning skills/classroom behaviors for success in the course, we tell them that as they are getting acquainted with the ChecBric, we will only score them on the first two academic Targets/Traits, and *they* get to score themselves on the last Target/Trait. Or we work collaboratively to score the last trait. Or you can have small groups score group members on the last trait,

like we suggested in Chapter 6 with the Civil War News Articles.

Redesign the ChecBric.

A reformatted Study Guide Booklet ChecBric might look something like Figure 8.2. In Column 1, instead of listing the performance requirements separately (as Targets 1 and 2 above), merge them together into one large target, and then add the effort characteristics below as the next target. Then, in Column 2, score all performance indicators and all effort indicators using the 6-point scale that totals, in this case, 84 possible points. This makes a mega-analytical scoring device that offers students lots of specific feedback—and requires lots of teacher scoring time. If it appears to be more than you need or want, we understand.

Employ Susan Kovalik's Three C's to Evaluate Student Work

Susan Kovalik, in her book *ITI: The Model Integrated Thematic Instruction* (1993), suggests the following three components of assessment:

- Comprehensive: Did the student cover the material as thoroughly as possible? Any key information missing, or it is all there?
- Correct: Is the response true/accurate? Are both sides of an issue covered?
- Complete: Was the assignment completed as stated? Is it of such quality that it is ready to be turned in?

Notice that the first two deal with performance while the third one addresses the effort category.

Betty has, in some cases, turned this model into the 4 C's by adding:

- Creative: Does the work demonstrate creativity/creative thinking?

Figure 8.2	**Reformatted Study Guide Booklet ChecBric**	
Student Checklist for TARGETS		**Teacher Rubric for TRAITS**
Key Requirements of my Study Guide booklet. Check off (√) on the left below all parts you have accomplished. My Study Guide:		Trait 1: Understanding of the **Key Content.** Each scored on a 6-point scale.
	has information that is accurate and detailed.	6 5 4 3 2 1
	identifies the chapter in the textbook it refers to.	6 5 4 3 2 1
	has three or four clearly identified sections.	6 5 4 3 2 1
	has examples in each section.	6 5 4 3 2 1
	has practice items in each section.	6 5 4 3 2 1
	uses illustrations/graphics when needed.	6 5 4 3 2 1
	has been edited for spelling, punctuation, and grammar.	6 5 4 3 2 1
	uses words that can be understood by students.	6 5 4 3 2 1
	is bound and has a cover.	6 5 4 3 2 1
My **effort** on this assignment is evident because. . .		Trait 2: **Productive and Responsible Behavior.** Each scored on a 6-point scale
	I included all assignment targets listed above.	6 5 4 3 2 1
	I turned in the parts and whole assignment on time.	6 5 4 3 2 1
	I turned in a booklet that is ready to be scored—it is organized, neat, and clean.	6 5 4 3 2 1
	I used my time wisely in class.	6 5 4 3 2 1
	I was respectful to my neighbors as they worked.	6 5 4 3 2 1
		Total Score Out of a Possible 84

Why add creativity? Well, it is a nice blend of *performance* in that is shows the student extended his or her understanding beyond the basics, and at the same time, it shows *effort* in that the student went the extra mile to do something really classy! And we like "smart and classy student work!"

So, there are lots of possibilities for separating performance from effort, as discussed in this section. Clearly, we can "heal the unsightly blemish" of student (and parent)

confusion by scoring both—turning it into a sparkle!

Blemish 3: The Time Crunch

Because it takes time to create solid tasks with accurate scoring mechanisms and to score the tasks uniformly, how are teachers expected to do this during an already hectic school day? Big problem, right?

With all the philosophical debate around the potential benefits of performance assessment, will its success boil down to dependency on time? Our position has been, and remains, that if teachers don't have adequate time to implement classroom-based performance assessment, then it won't happen.

The issue looms before us: *will we get enough time to do it right?*

The answer, quite honestly, is no. The economic collapse of 2008–2009 robbed states of critical revenue to support public education. Many school districts in the United States have suffered serious losses in funding. As one of countless negative results of the financial crisis, budgeting for training in performance assessment, as well as release time for developing and scoring performance tasks, is just not happening.

Our Proposed Solutions

The big-picture solution to this monster blemish would involve a massive reform of the global financial system to prevent the dangerous experimentations practiced by financiers that contributed mightily to the economic crisis. While we would love to pontificate on this issue, we are not qualified.

So we must leave this issue with a call for a renewed commitment to performance-based assessment when the world economy stabilizes and we can return to functioning in a noncrisis mode. This would include state- and district-level funding for in-service training, along with release time for teachers to develop, score, and interpret their classroom-based task results, and to swap great task ideas through the development of online task banks.

Blemish 4: The Reliability Issue

If performance tasks are to gain acceptance from students, parents, and the public as well as from educators, they must be shown to be reliable indicators of student abilities. But what happens if they are not shown to be scored in a fair, accurate, and consistent manner?

To ensure reliability, teams of teachers will need time to practice scoring tasks together with accurate scoring mechanisms so that they can calibrate their scoring, much like judges do in sports competitions. Students in Mrs. Miller's 5th grade classroom likely will earn different scores on the same assignment than Mr. Gonzales's 5th graders across the hall. The challenge for this new performance assessment system is to make it overt—that is, public, obvious, and consistently applied—to correct the subjectivity of the older assessment methods by building in objectivity through common tasks with shared rubrics.

In our first edition, we asked, *Will teachers get the training, practice, and technical support on how to score tasks objectively, fairly, consistently—that is, reliably?*

In the 12 years since we first asked this question, we have not found any widespread funding to ensure training, practice, and support for teacher training. In fact, the opposite appears to be the case. With the rise of the No Child Left Behind Act of 2001, and the economic collapse beginning in late 2008, there is now *less* support for performance-based assessment.

So the new question becomes, *What will it take for the educational pendulum to swing back toward teacher-designed, classroom-based assessment that is fully supported at the national, state, and local levels?*

Frankly, we cannot answer this question with a proposed solution. Time will tell.

Blemish 5: The Territorial Issue

Great performance tasks that prove to be reliable will become valuable property. Just as certain paperback novels are often "claimed" by certain grade levels or certain instructional units deemed to "belong" to certain teachers, some tasks will likewise be staked out by individuals or teams. Ownership of great tasks then becomes territorial: "You can't use the comic strip task in 3rd grade because I already use it with my 4th graders."

The challenge will be to allocate effective tasks across the grades, to adapt the good ones for different subjects, and even to allow some tasks to be repeated across some grades.

The issue is, *Can we avoid turf wars as performance assessment gains popularity?*

Suggested Solution for the Territorial Issue

To avoid turf wars over successful performance tasks, we recommend initiating an honest conversation among colleagues. The key is to recognize two competing interests.

The first view, a philosophical one, holds that teachers should not be denied access to excellent performance tasks that would allow students to reveal what they know and are able to do. Therefore, the staff cannot take a position that certain tasks will be "sacred" to certain grade levels or individual teachers.

The second view, a pragmatic view, holds that some tasks *do* lend themselves strongly to the content of specific units of study. Many times, at specific grade levels, teachers invest a great deal in developing tasks tied to particular units. In this case, it makes sense to encourage others to avoid using those tasks in other instructional settings.

Keeping both of these points of view in mind, we encourage staff who use particular tasks in specific units of instruction at a particular grade level to work with others in their building to make agreements about the exclusive use of these tasks, and to be willing to collaborate with colleagues on modifications that will make the tasks different enough so that they can be used in other settings.

This language is borrowed from agreements reached in two Oregon school districts, Bend and North Douglas public schools, who struggled with turf wars over recommended literature at various grade levels. We find it to be appropriate and useful in the context of performance task development.

Blemish 6: Unmotivated Performers

Performance tasks are designed to highly motivate students to reveal what they know and what they can do with that knowledge, but what if the tasks do not inspire some students to reach their highest possible level?

A huge incentive for moving to performance tasks is that they are new, novel, and fun—they entice kids to want to perform well. But in reality, how can performance assessment possibly become a panacea for the segment of disinterested, underperforming, and sometimes lost children who come to our schools? Their problems vary, and the responsibility for finding solutions to those looming problems remains elusive. Performance assessment will reach some of these kids by clearly informing them of what they are to do, how well they are expected to do it, and most important, how to accomplish it. But it won't reach, let alone rescue, all of them.

The issue before us becomes, *Will the performance task assessment system increase the performance of students who are presently underperforming? Will this system then narrow the achievement gap that plagues our country, or will it further divide our nation's children into haves and have-nots?*

In our first edition, we worried about the possibility of performance assessment failing to motivate the growing population of unmotivated learners. While we were confident that performance tasks have a leg up on the drier, more traditional assessment measures such as quizzes, tests, and essay questions, we were realistic to be concerned about their ability to routinely turn on our underperforming students. And, we surely recognize the iniquities in funding across the country. (See Blemish 8, The Equity Issue.)

**Suggested Solution for
Unmotivated Performers**

After 12 years, we feel even more confident about the positive impact of employing alternative assessments. Here are two good reasons. First, we have seen how the limitations of close-ended traditional measures restrict student opportunity to reveal what they know and are able to do. Second, performance tasks not only are more open-ended, allowing more room for student response, but also enlarge the *realm* of response by varying the output modes, what we call Info Out.

Turns out, varying the Info In and Info Out modes is one element of differentiated instruction. Back in 1998, not many of us were aware of differentiated instruction, but that has changed dramatically in the last few years. Performance assessment and differentiated instruction intersect at two key places:

• Using multimodal teaching as well as multimodal assessing: When teachers use alternative teaching materials like video clips, hands-on explorations, or music, as opposed to overusing lecture and textbooks, they are employing this key principle of differentiation. Likewise, when it is time to assess students, we can break the mold of quizzes, tests, and essay questions by assigning visualizations (Chapter 3), alternative writings (Chapter 4), oral presentations (Chapter 5), and large-scale projects (Chapter 6).

• Offering students a larger degree of choice. This is another key principle of differentiation, as well as a key factor in increasing motivation to read (Guthrie & Humenick, 2004). In the area of assessment, this can mean occasionally letting our kids select from a menu of assessment tasks. This menu can be fairly narrow, as in "Write a memo to the author critiquing her characterization decisions or to the protagonist critiquing the decisions that determined his actions." By varying the writing audience, students are afforded more ownership—which obviously improves student outlook and increases energy.

Some teachers are comfortable offering their students a much wider menu of task choices: "Act out a scene from this historical event depicting the major importance, or rewrite the textbook's account of this event adding another point of view, or create a computer slide show for 5th graders that will teach them the key events of this event." As you can see, the mode is no longer constant. To us, the degree of choice afforded to our students should depend on

• teacher interests, time constraints, and comfort level;
• student interests and maturity levels;
• student experiences with self-directed learning; and
• time to provide instruction in the various modes offered as choices.

Blemish 7: Missed Targets

Even when students are motivated to perform well, what happens to those students who fail to hit a target when it's time to move on to the next target?

Say the teacher has created a solid task that meets the five criteria noted earlier with a clear performance task instruction sheet and an accurate scoring device, and that teacher has provided task models to evaluate, good coaching, and ample target practice. What should he or she do with the two to three or even more kids in the class who earn scores below the standard and it's time to begin instruction and assessment of the next targeted standard?

It's like when the big show in town is over, the troupe has packed up, and it's headed to the next town. But a significant number of performers didn't "get it right." What do you do with them? What reteaching can occur in the context of "moving on"?

Rick Wormeli, an expert on differentiating instruction, says, "It is unrealistic and unreasonable to expect learners, who enter class with differing backgrounds, skills, interests, and abilities, to *arrive at the same place at precisely the same time*" (2006; italics added). Yes, that's very true.

Teachers have always faced this issue: What happens to students who fail the test? Do they receive reteaching and retesting? How? When? Performance task assessment promises better feedback to students so they can improve their performance. How is this pulled off in an overcrowded classroom with an overcrowded curriculum?

The issue is, *What are we going to do with those kids who don't hit the targets?* Will teachers really be able to use task results to do a better job of recoaching those students to lead them to higher levels of performance?

Suggested Solution for Missed Targets

Betty suggests the use of flexible scheduling that she calls "hodgepodge time." Hodgepodge is a 25- to 30-minute block of time built into the schedule so that students can receive individualized or small-group help in areas where they need help. These mini-courses are offered by invitation and last anywhere from two to four weeks.

For example, an elementary school could identify which 4th and 5th grade students are struggling with writing paragraphs and invite them to a tutorial class during language arts time taught by a skilled writing teacher for a full week.

Of course, you are probably wondering what happens to the other students during this hodgepodge time? Where do they go and what do they do? The answer is they attend a different mini-course at the same time but on a different topic with a different teacher. Or they get the same topic, but instructed at a differentiated level. At the secondary level, hodgepodge time can be institutionalized into the daily schedule across the entire school.

Possibilities for regrouping at the secondary level include

• schedule a "zero" period in middle or high school that begins early each day,

• schedule an after-lunch period, or

• schedule a "flexible" period that allows for regrouping students on an "as needed" basis.

For example, Hamlin Middle School in Springfield, Oregon, recently modified its schedule to include the third option. The daily schedule now includes a flex third period for 8th graders. This period is creatively used by teachers to address student needs. The teachers decide which of them will be working with which students on which particular needs. This provides an excellent opportunity for regrouping kids based on their need to relearn something and be reassessed. Of course, planning for effective use of the flex period is critical, as is the decision-making process on who teaches what.

Likewise, a high school could pull together 9th grade physical science students who have not yet demonstrated understanding of Newton's Laws of Motion into a temporary, two-day "short course" on this topic. The teacher should be someone who not only understands Newton's Laws but who also understands why kids fail to grasp these concepts.

This is pure differentiation: flexibly and temporarily grouping kids according to their current readiness level and instructing them in different ways.

Blemish 8: The Equity Issue

If students are to be held to high standards of performance, will all students be given an equal attempt at hitting the targets? And if not, is performance task assessment really an improvement over the traditional assessment measures?

Performers are supposed to be given an even playing field so they have an equal opportunity to perform well. But in reality, we know that this is far from true. Some kids lack good coaching; some teachers are better coaches than others at providing adequate guidance on hitting the targets. Some student performers lack adequate training facilities. Not all schools have adequate classrooms, labs, books, and so on. Some kids lack appreciative and supportive fans—that is, parents and significant others who feel welcome at and are connected to their children's school, pro-education community organizations, and supportive businesses who volunteer in the schools or give resources without strings attached.

These conditions transcend educational issues and cross into socioeconomic issues. Who do we suppose are the students who lack an even playing field and therefore are more likely to underperform? If the answer reflects racial, gender, or class differences, then performance task assessment is dead in the water. It cannot fix the social inequities that need fixing before kids are able to perform well in school.

We would never promote any assessment system without addressing the equity issue. Well into the new century, this equity issue still remains a daunting challenge in the United States. Many citizens still somehow believe that funding for education can and should vary by school, neighborhood, part of town, and state. That is, "As long as my kid's school gets the bucks, I am happy. I can't worry about other schools."

The main culprit in the United States is local property taxes, which are the key ingredient in school funding. (See "Unequal School Funding in the United States," page 149.)

The issue remains, *Will advocates of performance assessment be vocal participants in the continuing struggle for educational justice?*

Our Suggested Solution for the Equity Issue

For all the talk about school reform, and the companion high-stakes testing on the standards along with the punishments for low scores, there has not been an ongoing, honest discussion about America's haves and have-nots. We draw upon the recommended strategies from Biddle and Berliner (2002) on "How to Support Funding Equity" from their article "Unequal School Funding in the United States":

• Become familiar with the facts and issues associated with equity and funding in U.S. schools, the unsupportable claims about funding effects sometimes made by those who oppose equitable funding, and the research findings that contradict those claims.

Unequal School Funding in the United States

Bruce J. Biddle and David C. Berliner (2002) address this critical issue. In the summary, "What Do We Now Know?" they write:

Taken together, research evidence now available suggests a number of conclusions about unequal funding and its effects:

• Public schools in the United States receive sharply unequal funding. Among the nation's school districts, annual funding per student can range from less than $4,000 to more than $15,000, and although the "typical" school district with 1,000 or more students receives roughly $5,000 per year for each student, affluent districts may receive $10,000 per student or more.

• Large differences in public school funding appear both among the states and within many states.

• Funding differences appear, in part, because much of the financial support for public schools comes from local property taxes, which means that the amount of funding that communities are able to provide for their schools varies according to community affluence.

• Although most people in the United States are not aware of it, other advanced nations do not fund public schools with local property taxes. Instead, they provide equal per-student funding from general tax revenues for all schools throughout the country. Some nations also provide extra funding for disadvantaged students.

• Most people in the United States say they support equal funding for public schools, but affluent and powerful people often oppose efforts to correct funding inequities. Opposition to equity in school funding reflects several factors: ignorance about funding differences; unthinking acceptance of traditional methods for funding education; selfish desires to keep personal taxes low; and inappropriate beliefs about the causes of poverty that reflect individualism, essentialism, or the culture of poverty thesis.

• Claims from flawed research and reviews of research have asserted that levels of funding for schools have little or no effect on student outcomes.

• Strong studies indicate that level of student advantage within the home or community matters a great deal to outcomes in education, but sizable (although smaller) net effects are also associated with differences in school funding.

• The joint effects of school funding and student advantage are sizable. Achievement scores from U.S. school districts with substantial funding and low student poverty are similar to those earned by the highest-scoring countries in international comparative studies, whereas scores from districts where funding is inadequate and poverty is high are similar to those of the lowest-scoring countries.

• New demands placed on public schools have driven aggregate increases in school funding during recent years. These increases have not been used for additional resources that would generate increases in average student achievement.

• Two types of resources associated with greater school funding have been tied to higher levels of student achievement: stronger teacher qualifications and smaller class sizes in the early grades.

• The achievements of disadvantaged students are more likely to suffer in response to inequities in school funding for two reasons: Those students are more likely to attend poorly funded schools, and they are more likely to be hurt by lack of academic resources when schools are under funded.

• Legal and political efforts to reform funding inequities have been weak at the federal level, but considerable activity concerned with unequal funding has taken place in state courts and legislatures. The latter efforts have provoked some increases in state funds for poorly funded districts while leaving funding for rich, suburban districts largely in place.

• Become politically active in support of funding reform. Work with the media to raise public awareness of funding inequities and their implications in education, lobby your representatives in Congress to make the case for more federal support of impoverished schools, and work with others at the state level to support legal and legislative actions favoring greater funding equity.

• If you are an educator serving in a public school with inadequate funds, focus efforts on strategies, more often found in well-funded schools today, that are now known to be associated with greater student achievement, such as recruiting, motivating, and retaining qualified teachers and reducing class sizes in the early grades.

Blemish 9: The "When-Hell-Freezes-Over" Problem

We certainly are aware that not all teachers are willing or able to make the change from traditional assessment to performance assessment. Even with all the sparkles, the blemishes prohibit some of our colleagues from taking the plunge. Perhaps they are wary of yet another educational reform, or maybe they perceive the change as an increase in teacher workload and/or accountability. These are valid concerns; we recognize their effects on potential of implementation.

The difficulty arises when a school (or district) wants to go forward with performance assessment, but a significant number of players don't want to play. What can be done? The question is, *What do we do if an entire staff is not able to commit to performance assessment?*

Our Suggested Solution for the "When-Hell-Freezes-Over" Problem

Hell is freezing over. Performance assessment has not advanced nearly as far as we would have predicted in the 12 years since the publication of the original version of this book.

We are not advocating forcing this assessment system on anyone. Rather, we want to move forward with those colleagues who are ready and willing. *But realistically, can a school move forward with only some teachers implementing performance assessment?*

Yes, it can. We call on educators—teachers, paraprofessionals, principals, central office administrators, pre-service college students, and university professors—to keep on fighting for performance-based assessment. We trust that our arguments in favor of this approach, by now, are obvious. We urge you to use this book, as well as those listed in the references, to assist you in advancing the cause.

Additionally, we offer our help and support by providing you with our e-mail addresses in the "About the Authors" section at the end of the book. We would love to hear from you.

Our Last (Happy) Story

This story was told by a teacher in a workshop we gave on classroom-based performance task assessment in her district. During a break, she came up and thanked us for sharing our ideas. She went on:

"I really like to use performance tasks in my classroom to measure student understanding, and the kids are really catching on. Last month, when I was assigning them a paper to compare two different novels they had read, one student raised her hand, and asked, 'Where's the rubric?'

"I answered, 'Uh, it's not yet finished . . . but I'm working on it, I'm working on it.' I couldn't tell them it was due to bus duty that week.

"Another kid persisted, 'But don't you think we need one?'

"'Yeah,' more students chimed in. So I was forced to create a rubric, with their help,

on the spot. It took a few minutes, but once we had agreement on 'what good looks like,' the first kid, now satisfied, said, 'Good, it wouldn't be fair without one.'"

When students get to this level of understanding what the expectations are—of what their targets are—they are ready to produce Great Performances.

And your students will be, too.

A Snapshot of Chapter 8

In this chapter, we reviewed the sparkles (strengths) and blemishes (weaknesses) of a classroom-based performance assessment system.

• The sparkles include increased student motivation, clear alignment to the actual curriculum, increased teacher confidence in assessment, content-process linkage, Info In and Info Out linkage, and distinguishing effort from performance.

• The blemishes include student confusion over grades and performance, the time factor for busy teachers, the reliability issue, the territorial issue, unmotivated students, dealing with students who miss the targets, the resource equity issue, and moving forward even when some colleagues choose not to.

We also provided you with our suggested solutions for healing the blemishes, so your, and your colleagues', comfort level with performance-based assessment will continue to grow.

Your students will be the beneficiaries.

appendix

Figure A.1	**Folded File Folder**

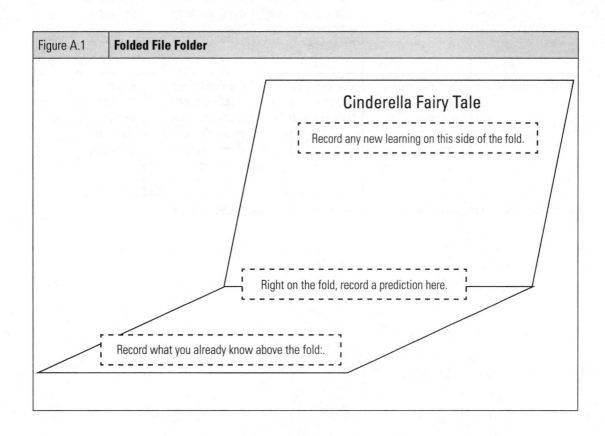

Cinderella Fairy Tale

Record any new learning on this side of the fold.

Right on the fold, record a prediction here.

Record what you already know above the fold:.

Figure A.2	**Relationship of Threads to the Dimensions in the 2005–2007 Scientific Inquiry Scoring Guides**			
	Scoring Guide Dimensions			
Threads	Forming a Question or Hypothesis	Designing an Investigation	Collecting and Presenting Data	Analyzing and Interpreting Data/Results
A—Application of Scientific Knowledge	Background information or observations are relevant to investigation.	Logical, safe, and ethical procedures are proposed.	Reasonable and accurate data are collected in a manner consistent with planned procedure.	Scientific terminology is used correctly to report results.
N—Nature of Scientific Inquiry	Question or hypothesis can be answered or tested.	Practical design is presented that provides sufficient data to answer the question or test the hypothesis.	Data transformations are valid and complete and are useful in making interpretations.	Procedures and results are critiqued. (Not applicable to 5th grade)
C—Communication	The question or hypothesis and background information are clearly expressed.	The design and procedures are communicated.	Organized displays of data (e.g., tables or other formats) communicate observations or measurements.	Results support conclusions and conclusions address the question or hypothesis.

Source: Adapted from work of Beaverton School District and Sue Squire Smith, Salem-Keizer School District in Oregon.

Figure A.3	**Scientific Investigation Scoring Guide**

Name _____ Date _____

Score	Trait
1 2 3 4	We developed a hypothesis.
1 2 3 4	We tested our hypothesis in an experiment.
1 2 3 4	We interpreted our data.
1 2 3 4	We stated our conclusions.

1 = Not present: We did not do this.

2 = Beginning work: We did this, but it looks like the work of a beginner.

3 = Progressing work: Our work is fine in this area.

4 = Accomplished work: Our work shows that we developed this trait very well.

Comments _____

_____

_____

_____

_____

_____

Figure A.4	**Performance Task Assessment List for a Scientific Drawing**			
			Assessment Points	
		Points Possible	Earned Assessment	
	Element		Self	Teacher
1.	Appropriate and accurate details of structure are shown.			
2.	The drawings show an appropriate number of views of the objects so that all of it is represented in the drawings.			
3.	All drawings use the same scale, which is clearly shown. The scale is metric.			
4.	Appropriate and accurate details of color, pattern, texture, and/or other physical characteristics are shown.			
5.	If appropriate, the relationship of the object of attention to its surroundings is accurately shown.			
6.	If appropriate, the relationship(s) between the structure of the object of attention and its function is/are accurately shown.			
7.	Labels are used accurately.			
8.	An accompanying text accurately explains the science intended to be shown in the drawing.			
9.	Drawings are neat and presentable.			
10.	Drawings use the space of the paper well.			

Source: From *A Teacher's Guide to Performance-Based Learning and Assessment* (p. 120), by Educators in Connecticut's Pomperaug Regional School District 15 (1996), Alexandria, VA: ASCD.

Figure A.5	**ChecBric for Assessing a Historical Comic Strip**

Name _____ Date _____

TRAIT ONE   **Comprehension:** Understands the historical passage ("Christmas Day, 1492" [Figure 3.1])

_____ Identifies the main ideas
_____ Identifies significant detail
_____ Has correct sequence of events
_____ Makes literal interpretations
_____ Makes inferred interpretations
_____ Gets overall meaning

> **6** Exceptional
> **5** Excellent
> **4** Proficient
>
> **3** Inadequate
> **2** Limited
> **1** Missing

TRAIT TWO   **Extends Understanding:** Goes beyond the passage

_____ Draws connections
_____ Sees relationships between

    _____ selection AND:
    _____ other texts OR
    _____ experiences OR
    _____ issues OR
    _____ events

> **6** Exceptional
> **5** Excellent
> **4** Proficient
>
> **3** Inadequate
> **2** Limited
> **1** Missing

TRAIT THREE   **Communicates Ideas Visually:** Effective comic strip

_____ Uses cartoonists' tools
_____ Is neat
_____ Presents ideas in a visually pleasing way
_____ Controls language conventions:

    _____ Capitals
    _____ Punctuation
    _____ Spelling

> **6** Exceptional
> **5** Excellent
> **4** Proficient
>
> **3** Inadequate
> **2** Limited
> **1** Missing

STUDENT Comments: TEACHER Comments:

Figure A.6	**Performance Task Assessment List for an Idea Web/Organizer**

ELEMENT	ASSESSMENT POINTS		
		Earned Assessment	
	Points Possible	Self	Teacher
1. Geometric figures are used. A large central figure is surrounded by smaller shapes.	_____	_____	_____
2. Geometric shapes are used throughout the web to convey relationships among elements in the web.	_____	_____	_____
3. The topic is listed in the central figure, and the main ideas connecting to the topic are placed in the qualifiers.	_____	_____	_____
4. An appropriate number of details support each main idea.	_____	_____	_____
5. The graphic information shows that the student has included enough information to indicate a thorough understanding of the concepts.	_____	_____	_____
6. The information is accurate.	_____	_____	_____
7. Space, shapes, textures, and colors provide information themselves and add to the overall effectiveness of the web.	_____	_____	_____
8. The web is creative: pictures, drawings, and other illustrations make it interesting.	_____	_____	_____
9. The web is neat, clear, and presentable.	_____	_____	_____
10. There are no mechanical mistakes (spelling, punctuation, grammar, word choice).	_____	_____	_____
TOTAL	_____	_____	_____

Source: Educators in Connecticut's Pomperaug Regional School District, 1996.

Figure A.7	**ChecBric for a Graphic Organizer**
STUDENT CHECKLIST	**TEACHER RUBRIC**
TARGET 1: I Understand the Novel Chapter	**TRAIT 1: Understands Content Information**
___ I present the most important information in the chapter. ___ I include information about the theme of book. ___ My information is accurate, correct, free from errors. ___ My information is thorough and complete enough to show that I understand the chapter, but I don't try to "pad" with nonessential information. ___ I include important details to support the main ideas.	**6 Exceptional** degree of content understanding goes beyond grade-level expectations. **5 Excellent** degree of content understanding represents high-quality grade-level work. **4 Proficient** degree of content understanding fulfills grade-level standard. **3 Inadequate** degree of content understanding falls a bit short. **2 Limited** degree of content understanding falls below grade level. **1 Missing** degree of content understanding completely misses the mark **0 No attempt** to complete task as assigned.
TARGET 2: I Recognize the Relationships in the Novel Chapter	**TRAIT 2: Recognizes Relationships Within Content Information**
___ My graphic organizer clearly shows that I see how the main ideas of the chapter connect to the key supporting details. ___ My graphic organizer clearly shows that I see how the characters relate to each other—positively or negatively. ___ My graphic organizer clearly shows that I see how the setting(s) relate to the characters' actions. ___ My graphic organizer clearly shows that I see how the characters' actions and thoughts relate to the BIG IDEA of the novel (the theme).	**6 Exceptional** degree of relationship recognition goes beyond grade-level expectations. **5 Excellent** degree of relationship recognition represents high-quality grade-level work. **4 Proficient** degree of relationship recognition fulfills grade-level standard. **3 Inadequate** degree of relationship recognition falls a bit short. **2 Limited** degree of relationship recognition falls below grade level **1 Missing** degree of relationship recognition completely misses the mark. **0 No attempt** to reveal relationships as assigned.

Figure A.7	**ChecBric for a Graphic Organizer** (*continued*)

TARGET 3: I Use Graphics Successfully	**TRAIT 3: Uses Graphics Effectively**
My graphic organizer. ____ has a visually appealing layout. ____ has a neat, clear, presentable look. ____ has a central figure/shape that stands out and is larger than the smaller figures that surround it. ____ uses appropriate, instead of random, figures or shapes; they are used consistently. ____ uses colors, shadings that are eye-appealing. ____ uses connector lines/arrows consistently to reveal relationships. ____ applies correct mechanics for language—spelling, capital letters, punctuation.	**6 Exceptional** degree of use of graphics goes beyond grade-level expectations. **5 Excellent** degree of use of graphics represents high-quality grade-level work. **4 Proficient** degree of use of graphics fulfills grade-level standard. **3 Inadequate** degree of use of graphics falls a bit short. **2 Limited** degree of use of graphics falls below grade level. **1 Missing** degree of use of graphics completely misses the mark. **0 No attempt** to use graphics as assigned.
Student Self-Reflection on Task:	**Teacher Comments:**

Figure A.8	**ChecBric for a Technical Training Manual**

TRAIT 1: Provides Clear and Accurate Explanation of Steps

_____ Statement of purpose is easily identified.
_____ All key steps are described.
_____ The order of steps is accurate.
_____ Each step is detailed enough for the reader.
_____ Extra, unneeded information is removed.

6 **Exceptional** presentation of how-to-do-it; guide exceeds grade-level expectations.

5 **Excellent** presentation of how-to-do-it; guide reveals high-quality grade-level work.

4 **Proficient** presentation of how-to-do-it; guide succeeds at clear explanation and shows grade-level work.

3 **Inadequate** presentation of how-to-do-it; guide attempts to explain, but has weaknesses.

2 **Limited** presentation of how-to-do-it; information is unclear/inaccurate; work is below grade level.

1 **Missing** presentation of how-to-do-it; no attempt to complete task as assigned.

TRAIT 2: Includes Diagrams/Illustrations to Support the Text

_____ Visual tools are clearly drawn.
_____ Visual tools are labeled.
_____ Visual tools are appropriately placed in the text.

6 **Exceptional** use of visual support tools; professional quality that impresses the reader.

5 **Excellent** use of visual support tools; high quality at grade level.

4 **Proficient** use of visual support tools; diagrams/illustrations succeed at supporting your words.

3 **Inadequate** use of visual support tools; attempt at visual support, but weaknesses hurt overall presentation.

2 **Limited** use of visual support tools; work is messy, misplaced, or unlabeled; work is below grade level.

1 **Missing** use of visual support tools; no attempt to include visuals as assigned.

Figure A.8	**ChecBric for a Technical Training Manual** (*continued*)

TRAIT 3: Uses Language and Conventions That Help the Reader

_____ Vocabulary is precise.
_____ Vocabulary is appropriate for the readers.
_____ Conventions make information understandable.

     _____ Spelling
     _____ Capitalization
     _____ Punctuation
     _____ Paragraphs

6 **Exceptional** control of language and conventions: vocabulary and conventions go beyond grade-level expectations.

5 **Excellent** control of language and conventions: vocabulary and conventions represent high-quality grade-level work.

4 **Proficient** control of language and conventions: contains a few errors, but vocabulary and conventions fulfill grade-level standard.

3 **Inadequate** control of language and conventions: attempted vocabulary and conventions, but errors interrupt reading.

2 **Limited** control of language and conventions: too many vocabulary and convention errors cause confusion.

1 **Missing** control of language and conventions: no attempt to repair vocabulary and conventions errors as assigned.

Figure A.9	**Holistic ChecBric for a RAFT for Fiction**

Student Checklist

1.____ On my own, I could not find the story basics or the more complicated story ideas, but **with help,** I

- stayed in character.
- wrote to my audience.
- wrote in the format.
- stuck to the topic and showed that I understand the story.

2.____ On my own, I was not able to find the more complicated story ideas, but I could find the **story basics** by identifying the story's

- characters.
- setting.
- problem.
- ending.

3.____ On my own, I could find both the story basics, **plus the more complicated story ideas:**

- I identified the story's characters, setting, problem, and the ending.

PLUS

- I made connections in the story that were not directly stated by characters or the narrator.
- I figured out the author's message.

4.____ On my own, I could do all of #3 above, plus I also was able **to go beyond** what was taught because
- I made connections to events in the story to events outside of the story, like other stories, movies, or personal experiences
- I figured out how the author's life may have affected the writing of the story.
- I commented on the author's style of writing, and/or the author's strengths and weaknesses

Teacher Holistic Rubric

Score 1 Only with help, the student demonstrates a partial understanding of some of the simpler, basic story components and some of more complex, complicated elements.

Score 2 Student independently makes no major errors or omissions regarding the simpler, basic story components.

Score 3 Student independently identifies the basic and the more complicated story elements that were explicitly taught with no major errors or omissions.

Score 4 In addition to a 3 performance, student independently exceeds what was taught by adding additional information, ideas, or commentary.

Based on Scoring Scale by Robert Marzano in *Classroom Assessment and Grading That Work* (2006); ChecBric ©2009, 2007 Larry Lewin Educ. Consulting, larry@larrylewin.com.

Figure A.10	**Holistic Scorecard Rubric for RAFT**

RAFT Scorecard

My RAFT shows that I **learned** about the topic

- My information is accurate/correct.
- My information is thorough/has details.

My RAFT follows the **requirements**

- I stay in the character/personality of my Role.
- I address my Audience.
- I write in the given Format.
- I stick to the Topic.

4 = Accurate, meets all requirements, plus entertaining, engaging, amusing.

3 = Accurate, thorough, meets all requirements.

2 = May be inaccurate or have some missing info; a missing requirement.

1 = Missed-the-boat errors of understanding, requirements ignored.

Figure A.11	**Literature RAFTs**

A Cinderella Tale from Vietnam
"The Story of Tam and Cam"

ROLE	AUDIENCE	FORMAT	TOPIC
1. Tam, the older daughter	to her father	a note under the door to his room	why you should treat me differently
2. Cam	to her older sister Tam	an apology note	for my mistreatment of you
3. Father	to his two daughters	a private talk	what I have learned
4. Tam	her dead mother	plea for help	Number Two Wife (her stepmother)
5. Hens	Tam	directions	why you should dig up little fish's clay pot
6. Tam	to Cinderella	a friendly letter	what we have in common

Source: Tom Cantwell Cal Young Middle School Eugene, OR

Figure A.12	**RAFT Choices for Math**		

Select one of the following roles. Follow across the row and complete the audience, format, and topic portions.

Role: Who are You?	**Audience:** To whom is this written?	**Format:** What form will it take?	**Topic:** What is the topic?
One parallel line	The other parallel line	A (love) rejection letter	Why we just don't connect.
A vertical line	A horizontal line	Advice column	How not to be so flat?
Origin (0,0)	Any other coordinate	Riddle	Why am I so special?
Linear equation	Itself	Journal	Why do I always take the straight and narrow path?
Standard form ($Ax + By = C$)	Slope-intercept form ($y = mx + b$)	A friendly letter	We are just alike.

Figure A.13	**Dear Character Letter Rubric**

Trait 1: Content

5 = I wrote about the story completely, describing the characters, setting, and plot.

3 = I shared the main idea of the story, but I missed some key parts.

1 = I had trouble sharing the basic idea of the story.

Score:

Trait 2: Conventions

5 = My final copy shows that I made corrections in my spelling and punctuation.

3 = My final copy shows that I corrected most of the spelling and punctuation.

1 = My final copy shows that I didn't correct my spelling and punctuation errors.

Score:

Figure A.14	**Lewis and Clark Simulation Task Sheet**

Name _____ Date _____

Your group has been invited to become members of the Lewis and Clark Expedition. As a team you will simulate keeping a travel journal of impressions of your experiences, managing the supplies and money in an accounting log, and creating a color expedition map documenting your journey.

The commander and second in command, Lewis and Clark, are ultimately responsible for documenting this expedition; however, they cannot succeed without your help and information.

Each group member should choose one of the following roles:

• The topographer keeps track of (sketches and describes in writing) the landscape and vegetation.
• The surveyor maps the journey—maintains the longitude and latitude of various locations along the journey—and records the climate, weather, and animals encountered.
• The medic maintains the health of the crew and learns as much as possible about Native American diseases and remedies.
• The linguist studies the cultures, languages, and customs of the native peoples you meet.
• The quartermaster maintains records of supplies and costs, solves problems, and records significant events.

This project is worth 100 points. Below is a breakdown of how to earn points. Read carefully and remember to strive to create work that is accurate, insightful, and complete.

Travel Journal   **50 Points**

The president of the United States, Thomas Jefferson, wants you to keep detailed records of the journey and what you learned.

• Turn in a neat-looking journal with at least five journal entries. These entries should correspond to the five locations labeled on your map (see map assignment in the final section).
• Date each entry.
• Note the longitude and latitude.
• Describe the terrain, vegetation, climate, and animals.
• Share any creative or exciting events that occur along the way.
• Include the different cultures, languages, and customs of the peoples you encounter.

The more detailed your journal entries, the better. Feel free to use pictures, descriptive language, and feelings in this journal.

Expedition Accounting Log   **25 Points**

Keep detailed records of the costs of the expedition.

• Maintain a chart showing supplies taken and money spent. Beside each item, describe why you chose to take it.
• Describe the mode of transportation you selected and why, and keep track of transportation costs.
• Include your itinerary: your intended route, the number of days your journey will take, and your anticipated time of arrival.

Figure A.14	**Lewis and Clark Simulation Task Sheet** (*continued*)

Expedition Map   **25 Points**

Create a color map of the expedition that contains

- Five locations at which you stopped along your expedition.
- Major rivers, mountains, and so forth, labeled with their names.
- A marked route.
- A legend or key.
- A scale.

Agree on a plan that involves everyone equally in getting the work done. I will check in with your group every other day to monitor your progress.

- -

Detach this form, complete it as a group, and turn it into me by _____ . Under the header "Work Projects," list which of the above project parts each person will be working to complete.

Name	Role	Work Projects
	TOPOGRAPHER	
	SURVEYOR	
	MEDIC	
	LINGUIST	
	QUARTERMASTER	

Remember, you can all support one another in doing the work. There is always something valuable you can be doing with your time!

Figure A.15	**Group/Self-Assessment for Lewis and Clark Simulation**

Your group earned _____ out of the 100 points possible on your project. You know, better than I, who put out the most effort. I would like you to allocate individual points to your group members. Everyone in the group must agree with your allocations. You may not adjust any one person's points by a point value of more than 10. For example, if your group earned 90 points, one person could not get more than 100 or less than 80. If the group feels one person's score should increase by 7, another person's or persons' must decrease by 7.

Follow this step-by-step procedure:

1. Multiply your score by the number of people in your group. If you received a 90, and there were four in your group, that would equal 360 total points.

2. Next, determine if your group feels that anybody's score needs to change. This would happen if somebody didn't follow through with his or her part, or one person did all or more than his or her share of the work (map, journal, illustrations, research, chart).

3. Determine how much any person's score should increase or decrease. If one person's score moves up, that means he or she has put out a great deal of effort. It also means that someone else in the group should have done more, and that that person's score should decrease. If you increase one score by 6, you must decrease another by 6.

4. When you've finished, record the reason why the person received what he or she did in the "Reason for the New Score" column.

5. Add up your new scores. They must equal the number that you calculated in #1.

Name of Group Member	Score	Reason for the New Score
1.		
2.		
3.		
4.		
5.		
Total Score:		

Figure A.16	**Magazine Evaluation Scoring Guide**

Name _____ Date _____

1. Organization	**1**	**2**	**3**	**4**	**5**	**6**

You structure your ideas in a logical sequence.

Comments:

• Are your ideas, details, and examples presented in an order that makes sense?

• How effective is your introduction?

• Do you end your paper well?

2. Voice	**1**	**2**	**3**	**4**	**5**	**6**

You express ideas in an engaging and credible way.

Comments:

• Does your writing convey your personal voice?

• Did you put something of yourself into the paper?

• Is the writing lively?

• Did you write what you really thought and felt?

3. Word Choice	**1**	**2**	**3**	**4**	**5**	**6**

You select words carefully to make your message clear.

Comments:

• Did you choose words that helped make your message both interesting and easy to understand?

A score of **6** means exceptional: my work is really great.

A score of **5** means excellent: my work is strong.

A score of **4** means proficient: my work is OK, and I am getting better all the time.

A score of **3** means inadequate: my work is weak but getting better.

A score of **2** means limited: my work is like that of a beginner.

A score of **1** means missing: I did not do this.

Figure A.16	**Magazine Evaluation Scoring Guide** (*continued*)

Name _____ Date _____

4. Ideas	**1**	**2**	**3**	**4**	**5**	**6**
You communicate knowledge of your topic. • How well did you develop your ideas? • Did you know your topic well, and did you choose details that helped make it clear and interesting?	Comments:					

5. Sentence Fluency	**1**	**2**	**3**	**4**	**5**	**6**
Your paper is easy to read and understand. • Does it flow smoothly from one idea to the next?	Comments:					

6. Conventions	**1**	**2**	**3**	**4**	**5**	**6**
There are no glaring errors in writing conventions, and the paper is easy to read and understand. • Did you proofread carefully and correct spelling errors and punctuation?	Comments:					

A score of **6** means exceptional: my work is really great.

A score of **5** means excellent: my work is strong.

A score of **4** means proficient: my work is OK, and I am getting better all the time.

A score of **3** means inadequate: my work is weak but getting better.

A score of **2** means limited: my work is like that of a beginner.

A score of **1** means missing: I did not do this.

| Figure A.17 | **Sample Scoring Guide for Primary-Level Animal Oral Report** |

Name _____ Date _____

Knowledge About My Animal

	I told what my animal looks like as an adult.
	I told what my animal looks like as a baby to show how it changes over time.
	I told where my animal lives and what its home is like.
	I told what my animal eats when it is a baby, when it is young, and when it is an adult.
	I told what my animal does in different seasons (spring, summer, winter, and fall) and how it changes based on the weather.
	I answered questions from the audience.

Delivery

	I looked up at the audience.
	I spoke loud enough for everyone to hear.
	I spoke clearly.
	I spoke at a good rate, not too fast or too slowly.

Organization

	I had a good beginning to my speech.
	My ideas made sense and flowed one to the other.
	I had a good ending for my speech.

+ = I did a really great job in this area.

√ = I am doing OK in this area.

− = I need to work on this.

Figure A.18	**Business Systems Social and Environmental Responsibility Project**

Name _____ Date _____

Members of my group: _____

My group will research this company: _____

Research

Each person in your group will research this company in order to answer the following questions:

1. What do we mean when we say social responsibility? Environmental responsibility?

2. What does this company manufacture and market?

3. What are its gross sales and profit for the last five years?

4. How many employees does the company have?

5. How does the company operate (franchise, public corporation, etc.)?

6. Who owns the company? What other companies does it own?

7. Where is the company located, and is it a local, regional, national, or multinational company?

8. Is this company socially responsible? Why or why not?

9. Is this company environmentally responsible? Why or why not?

After completing your individual research, you can work together as a group to combine and strengthen your ideas for your upcoming team debate on this company. You must be prepared to speak either in support of or in opposition to the company's environmental and social record. You will need to cite a minimum of five sources in support of your position. You must also cite a minimum of five sources to discount or refute that position.

Figure A.18	**Business Systems Social and Environmental Responsibility Project** (*continued*)

Oral Presentation

The day before your presentation, the flip of a coin will determine which team will speak in the affirmative and which team will speak in opposition. The presentation format will be as follows:

Both Teams:	Respond briefly to the above questions 1 through 7 to introduce the rest of the class to your company (6–7 minutes).
Team One:	Present your case citing sources to show that this company is environmentally and/or socially responsible (5 minutes).
Team Two:	Present your case citing sources to show that this company is not environmentally and/or socially responsible (5 minutes).
Team One:	Refute the arguments of Team Two and reinforce your position (3 minutes).
Team Two:	Refute the arguments of Team One and reinforce your position (3 minutes).
Team One:	State your conclusions (3–5 minutes).
Team Two:	State your conclusions (3–5 minutes).
Both Teams:	Respond to questions submitted by the audience (6–7 minutes).

Completing This Work

You will complete this project over the next three weeks, working both in class and outside class.

Everyone in your group must participate in the debate by presenting at least one point or counterpoint. You will also be expected to respond to questions from the teacher about your sources: where you found them, whether they are primary or secondary sources, and whether you consider them to be reputable.

You will be given time to work in the library here at Willamette High School and in the library at the University of Oregon. You will also have an opportunity to pursue information on the World Wide Web. Your team must develop a plan for using your group time and for recording and organizing your data.

Scoring Your Work

Your work will be scored in three ways:

1. You will evaluate your own work by completing the attached ChecBric [Figure A.18].
2. Your classmates will evaluate your work using the ChecBric.
3. Your team will conference with the teacher, working from the Peer Evaluation Scoring Guide [Figure A.20, p. 174], to determine a grade for the project.

Figure A.19	**Social and Environmental Responsibility Project ChecBric**

Name _____ Date _____

Check the appropriate column yes or no. Then give yourself one overall score from 6 to 1 in the bottom "Overall Score" box. A score of 6 equals a strong performance; a 1 represents a weak performance.

Content

Yes	No	
		Were the focus questions answered in the presentation?
		Were five sources identified in support of/in opposition to the issue?
		Were responses to the opposing arguments handled well?
		Were the ideas supported adequately by evidence?
		Was research evident (i.e., was the presentation not based upon personal experience and supposition)?
		Were questions from the audience handled well?
		Overall Content Score

Organization

Yes	No	
		Could the main ideas be easily identified?
		Was the presentation put together in such a way as to make it easy for the audience to understand?
		Were details placed in the speech for optimum impact?
		Did the presentation have a credible introduction?
		Did the presentation have a strong conclusion?
		Overall Organization Score

Figure A.19	**Social and Environmental Responsibility Project ChecBric** (*continued*)

Language

Yes	No	
		Was language carefully selected to emphasize the main points and impress the audience?
		Were the usage and grammar correct?
		Was concise, vivid, and varied language used?
		Overall Language Score

Delivery

Yes	No	
		Was eye contact maintained throughout the presentation?
		Was the use of gestures, movements, and other nonverbal techniques effective?
		Did the presenters speak clearly and fluently?
		Overall Delivery Score

Figure A.20	**Peer Evaluation Scoring Guide**

Name _____ Date _____

As an individual, complete this chart. First, list the names of those persons in your group on the left. Then, assign each person a score from 1 to 4 in each area identified. The score should reflect your perception of that person's contribution to the group work. Be sure to include yourself on the chart. Your individual responses will not be revealed to the others in your group.

I will take the charts from all group members and summarize the results before I conference with you as a group. At that time, we will review the ChecBric scores from yourself and others, along with this Peer Evaluation Scoring Guide, and agree on an appropriate grade for each team member.

Use the following scoring guide to assign points:

4 = Was very helpful, had great ideas, made important contributions, readily volunteered to do work, and always carried through with the work.

3 = Was helpful, had good ideas, made helpful contributions, volunteered to do work, and consistently carried through with the work.

2 = Was a little helpful, contributed some ideas, and did some work.

1 = Was not helpful, did not share ideas, made no contribution, did not carry through with work.

Name	Brainstorming Discussions	Research	Development of a Work Plan	Written Report	Debate

Figure A.21	**Thinking Strategies and Questioning Prompts**
Thinking Strategy	Question Prompts
Focusing Strategies are used to selectively attend to information.	• What subject/topic will we be discussing? • Did you identify any problems? • What is most important to understand about your topic? • What are the key points about your topic?
Remembering/Retrieving/ Summarizing Strategies are used to store and retrieve information.	• In your own words, what did you learn? • What can you remember about ___? • How would you describe ___? • If you could use three or four sentences to pull this all together, what would you say? • Overall, what is the situation?
Analyzing Strategies are used to examine parts and relationships, compare and contrast, and facilitate perspective taking.	• How is ___ like or different from ___? • What are the attributes of ___? • How is ___ an example of ___? • What evidence can you list for ___? • What is your point of view about this? • Are there other points of view about this subject?
Generating Strategies are used to produce new information, meanings, or ideas.	• How would you create/design a new ___? • What solutions would you suggest for ___? • What ideas do you have to ___? • If you were ___, how would you have handled ___?
Evaluating Strategies are used to assess the reasonableness and quality of something.	• What do you think about ___? Why? • Which ___ is most significant and why? • What are your sources? • How do you know they are credible? • Did you detect any biases? • What criteria did you use to come to this conclusion?

Figure A.22	**Substantive Dialogue Scoring Guide**

Student _____ Date _____ Rater _____

Thank you for helping to assess each student's core knowledge understanding through substantive dialogue.

A. Select and use one or two of the question prompts in each area.
B. Highlight those used and then jot notes on the student's responses.
C. Score the work using the 4-point scale developed by Marzano, Pickering, and McTighe[1] (p. 102).

Question Prompts	Student Responses
Focusing: • What is the subject/topic we will be discussing? • Did you identify any problems? • What is most important to understand about your topic? • What are the key points about your topic?	
Remembering/Retrieving/Summarizing: • In your own words, what did you learn? • What can you remember about _____ ? • How would you describe _____ ? • If you could use three or four sentences to pull this altogether, what would you say? • Overall, what is the situation?	
Analyzing: • How is _____ like or different from _____ ? • What are the attributes of _____ ? • How is _____ an example of _____ ? • What evidence can you list for _____ ? • What is your point of view about this? • Are there other points of view about this subject?	
Generating: • How would you create/design a new _____ ? • What solutions would you suggest for _____ ? • What ideas do you have to _____ ? • If you were _____, how would you have handled _____ ?	
Evaluating: • What do you think about _____ ? Why? • Which _____ is most significant and why? • What are your sources? • How do you know they are credible? • Did you detect any biases? • What criteria did you use to come to this conclusion?	

Figure A.22	**Substantive Dialogue Scoring Guide** (*continued*)

General Comments:

_____

_____

_____

_____

Overall Score: _____

4 = Demonstrates a thorough understanding of the generalizations, concepts, and facts specific to the task or situation and provides new insights into some aspect of this information.

3 = Displays a complete and accurate understanding of the generalizations, concepts, and facts specific to the task or situation.

2 = Displays an incomplete understanding of the generalizations, concepts, and facts specific to the task or situation and has some notable misconceptions.

1 = Demonstrates severe misconceptions about the generalizations, concepts, and facts specific to the task.

[1]R.J. Marzano, D. Pickering, and J. McTighe (1993). *Assessing student outcomes; Performance assessment using the Dimensions of Learning model,* p. 30 (Alexandria, VA: ASCD).

| Figure A.23 | **An 8th Grader's UmbrellaTella About Watersheds Before Instruction in the Unit** |

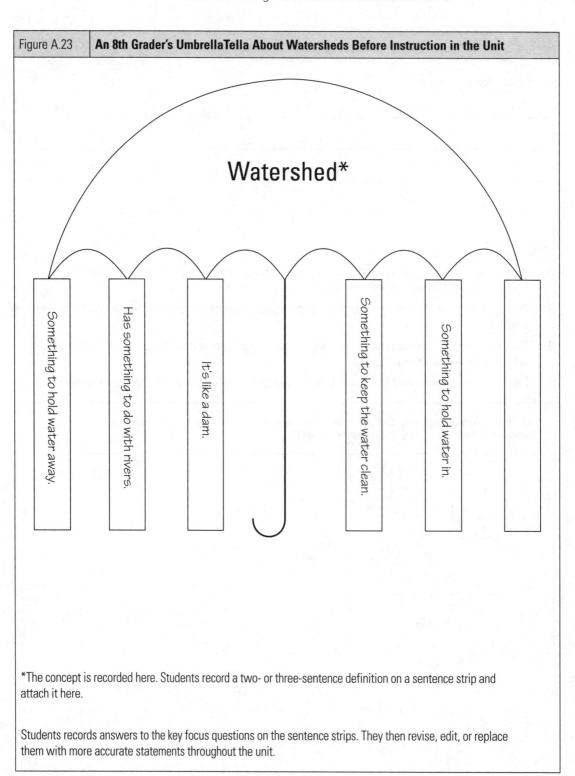

*The concept is recorded here. Students record a two- or three-sentence definition on a sentence strip and attach it here.

Students records answers to the key focus questions on the sentence strips. They then revise, edit, or replace them with more accurate statements throughout the unit.

| Figure A.24 | **The Same 8th Grader's UmbrellaTella During Instruction in the Unit** |

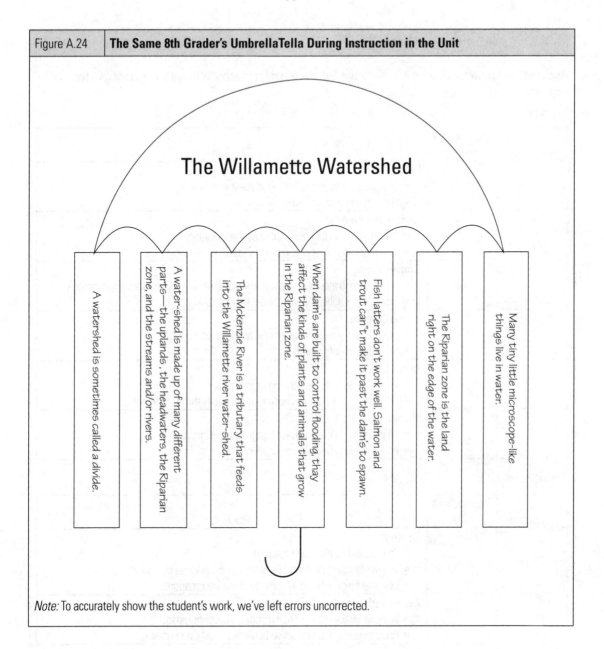

The Willamette Watershed

A watershed is sometimes called a divide.

A water-shed is made up of many different parts—the uplands , the headwaters, the Riparian zone, and the streams and/or rivers.

The Mckenzie River is a tributary that feeds into the Willamette river water-shed.

When dam's are built to control flooding, thay affect the kinds of plants and animals that grow in the Riparian zone.

Fish latters don't work well. Salmon and trout can"t make it past the dam's to spawn.

The Riparian zone is the land right on the edge of the water.

Many tiny little microscope-like things live in water.

Note: To accurately show the student's work, we've left errors uncorrected.

Figure A.25	**Homelessness Project Rubric**

Please rate your performance using a 6-point scale. The teacher will conference with you and also assign a score in each area.

1. Position Paper

My Scores	The Teacher's Scores	The Trait
		Word Choice • Your words convey the intended message. • You use a rich, broad range of words.
		Sentence Fluency • The sentences you chose enhance the meaning. • Your paper has a flow and rhythm to it.
		Conventions • You demonstrated that you use standard writing conventions appropriately (grammar, paragraphing, punctuation, capitalization).
		Ideas/Content • You present your ideas with clarity, focus, and control. • Your main points stand out.
		Organization • You use effective sequencing in your paper. • The order and structure move readers easily through the text.
		Voice • Your writing is expressive, engaging, and sincere. • Your writing reflects an awareness of your audience.

2. Oral Presentation

My Scores	The Teacher's Scores	The Trait
		Content • Your speech is clear and focused. • You made your purpose clear, and your main ideas stand out. • You effectively use visual tools to share information.
		Organization • You use effective sequencing suited to your purpose. • Your speech has an effective beginning, body, and ending.
		Language • You effectively use speaking conventions. • Your words are specific and accurate.
		Delivery • You maintain effective eye contact. • The rate at which you speak and the volume you use is appropriate.

Figure A.25	**Homelessness Project Rubric (*continued*)**

3. Overall Content Knowledge and Social Science Analysis

My Scores	The Teacher's Scores	The Trait
		Knowledge About Homelessness and Related Issues • You address the key questions in your presentations. • You identify substantive themes and issues.
		Issue Analysis • You examine multiple perspectives on the issue. • You use critical thinking to analyze the issue.
		Action Proposal • You take, support, and communicate your position. • You propose relevant actions that can be implemented.

Scoring Scale

6 Exemplary — Your work at this level is both exceptional and memorable. It shows a distinctive and sophisticated application of knowledge and skills.

5 Strong — Your work exceeds the standard. It shows a thorough and effective application of knowledge and skills.

4 Proficient — Your work at this level meets the standard. It is acceptable work that demonstrates application of essential knowledge and skills. Minor errors or omissions do not detract from the overall quality.

3 Developing — Your work at this level does not yet meet the standard. It shows basic but inconsistent application of knowledge and skills. Minor errors or omissions detract from the overall quality. Your work needs further development.

2 Emerging — Your work at this level shows a partial application of knowledge and skills. It is superficial (lacks depth), fragmented, or incomplete and needs considerable development. Your work contains errors or omissions.

1 Not Present — You presented no work in this area.

Figure A.26	**Concept Acquisition Development Continuum**

Read the continuum[1] from the bottom to see a progression of concept acquisition.

Stage Seven: Expert	• In presenting a breadth and depth of relevant and accurate facts, concepts, and generalizations about the subject, the student focuses on substantive themes, problems, and issues. • The student analytically evaluates the information and makes qualitative and quantitative judgments about the subject according to set standards. • The student synthesizes and extends facts, concepts, and generalizations about the subject to solve problems, develop position papers, and the like, requiring original, creative thinking. • The student effortlessly presents acquired knowledge about the subject in a number of different forms moving from concrete to abstract. • The student is able to clearly articulate his or her point of view if appropriate. • The student clearly shows original thinking and creativity in approaching the data and in presenting them to others.
Stage Six: Accomplished	• The student presents a breadth and depth of relevant and accurate facts, concepts, and generalizations applicable to the subject. • The student investigates the subject through an analysis of its component parts. • As appropriate, the student identifies interested parties and presents their multiple perspectives on the subject. The student articulates and evaluates the reasoning, assumptions, and evidence supporting each perspective. • The student begins to show original thinking in approaching the data and in presenting them to others.
Stage Five: Progressing	• The student demonstrates comprehension of pertinent facts and concepts applicable to the subject by drawing data from a variety of sources, including primary and secondary sources. • The student begins to demonstrate an understanding of principles, laws, and theorems related to the subject. • The student interprets information and solves simple problems using the information.
Stage Four: Developing	• The student presents some relevant and accurate information (facts, rules, or details) applicable to the subject. • This information is based on fact as well as increasingly informed opinion. • If the student presents an argument, it is weak or implausible. • Where issues exist, the student is able to identify the central issue but states it in general terms. • The student is capable of changing information given by the teacher into a different symbolic form.
Stage Three: Beginning	• Information is based on a narrow frame of reference and uninformed opinion and is from a limited number of sources. • The student presents irrelevant, simplistic, or inaccurate information about the subject.
Stage Two: Readiness	• There is an attempt to address the subject, but no detail is provided/no breadth of information is present.
Stage One: Not Present	• The student presents no information about the subject. There is no attempt to address the subject in any meaningful way.

[1] We want to acknowledge the work of George Westergaard, social studies teacher at South Eugene High School, who has worked with his Advanced Placement students in using similar content continuums.

Figure A.27	**Student Achievement Convention**

Project Fair Guidelines and Participation Checklist
Lane County Education Service District
Eugene, Oregon

The **Project Fair** provides an opportunity for students to display a major learning experience that combines content knowledge with process skills to produce a product or demonstration of learning. All projects[1] will be evaluated by a judging team trained to look for and score these specific project elements:

- Topic and Treatment
- Learning Development and Process
- Presentation/Communication

Careful presentation of the following items will help judges identify the purposes and strengths of a project:

A. PROJECT NOTEBOOK:

____ 1. *The Registration Form* (two copies)

____ 2. *Progress Journal:*
Record daily any ideas, thoughts, observations, questions, resources, problems, impressions, or discoveries you encounter while working on the project. Sketches, diagrams, data tables, photographs, or other information important to the project are encouraged.

____ 3. *Annotated Resource List:*
Include books, magazines, experiences, equipment—anything that contributed to the success of the learning experience—and tell how each was successful.

____ 4. *A Self-Evaluation of the Project:*
Use the scoring guide to assess elements of the learning experience and to comment on academic benefits. (See Example of a Scorecard Rubric [Figure A.29].)

____ 5. *Optional Letters of Support:*
Parents, teachers, or others who are aware of the effort and progress of the student(s) involved in the project may add their comments and commendations.

B. EXHIBIT:

____ The process, products, and results important to the project are displayed visually in a 40" x 30" x 73" space. This exhibit may take any combination of forms—display, video, final report, model, and so on.

C. INFORMATION PRESENTATION AND INTERVIEW:

____ Student should come prepared to talk with judges and explain how the project was chosen, the learning processes and procedures used, the important outcomes, and the learning value of the project.

For group projects, all group members should complete a journal and self-evaluation explaining their interest and involvement with the project.

[1]Projects may be entered for display only and will not be judged.

Figure A.28	**Student Achievement Convention Registration Form**

Project Fair Registration Form
Lane County Education Service District
Eugene, Oregon

Submit two copies per project.[1]
Due at the time of registration.

This form is completed for each project, and two copies are placed in the front of the project notebook.

Project Title _____ Registration No. _____
(assigned at registration)

Class/Subject _____

Project Duration _____ Date Started _____ Date Completed _____

Student/Group _____ Grade _____
(List all students. Use back if necessary.)

Teacher _____ Phone _____

School _____ District _____

In registering this project for the Project Fair, we agree to the following (check each item that is true):

_____ 1. All guidelines for the Project Fair (specified on the Student Achievement Convention Project Fair Guidelines and Participation Checklist) have been met, including completion of the self-evaluation Scorecard Rubric.

_____ 2. We have arranged for the project to be set up by 12 noon on Tuesday and removed following the Awards Reception, Thursday evening.

_____ 3. One or two students will be available for an oral interview about the project between 1:30 and 3:30 p.m. on Tuesday.

_____ 4. We accept full responsibility for the security of the items displayed.

_____ 5. The work on this project has been done primarily by the student(s).

Figure A.28	**Student Achievement Convention Registration Form** (*continued*)

I grant my permission to the Lane County Education Service District and _____ School District to release my child's name, photograph, address, and any other information about him or her for public information purposes to the extent in such manner and for such public information as deemed appropriate by the Lane County Education Service District and _____ School District. Parents/guardians will be informed of each release.

Signed _____ Date _____
                       (Parent/Guardian)

                                                              Phone _____

Signed _____ Date _____
                     (Student(s))

Signed _____ Date _____
                     (Sponsoring Teacher)

Signed _____ Date _____
                     (School Principal)

[1]One copy is displayed with the project; when students remove their displays, this copy goes home. The other copy is filed with the project fair staff in case there are challenges to submissions.

Figure A.29	**Example of a Scorecard Rubric**

I. Topic and Treatment: What did you study, and how well did you learn it?

Score	A. The project provides opportunity for important and challenging learning.				
	5 = Outstanding	4 = • Evidence of real interest • Sense of ownership • Topic/purpose well stated • Wholehearted effort • Represents new area of learning	3 = Balanced	2 = • Lacking interest, challenge • Routine response • Purpose unclear • Halfhearted effort • Familiar, easy topic • Compliance without commitment	1 = Incomplete

Comments

_____

_____

_____

Score	B. Project outcome provides evidence of detailed, deep thinking about the task or topic.				
	5 = Outstanding	4 = • Factual understanding • Insightful interpretations • Logical conclusions • Creative, conceptual observations • Multiple points of view	3 = Balanced	2 = • Some inaccuracies • Routine observations • Illogical or trite comments • Confusing or unreasoned statements • Limited, common, obvious observations • Accepts without inquiry	1 = Incomplete

Comments

_____

_____

_____

Figure A.29	**Example of a Scorecard Rubric** (*continued*)

Score	C. Student demonstrates development of academic understanding and expertise.				
	5 = Outstanding	4 = • Confident and knowledgeable • Depth of understanding • Explains in detail • Curious, persistent • Seeks specifics • Pride of accomplishment	3 = Balanced	2 = • Limited understanding • Memorized responses • Superficial treatment • Fails to pursue answers • Generalizes, avoids detail • Satisfied with minimum	1 = Incomplete

Comments

_____

_____

_____

II. Learning Development and Process: How did you go about learning, and what did you use?

Score	A. Project reflects purposeful planning and effort.				
	5 = Outstanding	4 = • Process appropriate to topic • Accurate procedures • Logical sequence of steps • Monitors and adjusts plan • Good time and resource management • Focused, controlled purpose	3 = Balanced	2 = • Inaccurate or inappropriate plan • Nondeliberate trial and error • Follows directions without understanding • Pursues original plan regardless of results • Lack of time and resource management • Unsure about intent of project	1 = Incomplete

Comments

_____

_____

_____

Figure A.29	**Example of a Scorecard Rubric** (*continued*)

Score	B. Project documents reveal resourcefulness.				
	5 = Outstanding	4 = • Variety of resources, technologies • Develops resources • Uses community/group resources • Seeks out expertise, advice • Independent learning • Annotated listing	3 = Balanced	2 = • Limited resources, nontechnical • Lacks initiative • Avoids input from others • Fails to recognize or use resources • Extensive dependence on others • Listings without annotations	1 = Incomplete

Comments

_____

_____

_____

Score	C. Student provides evidence of problem solving and adjusting for quality.				
	5 = Outstanding	4 = • Careful control/ monitoring • Self-directed thinking • Creative problem solving • Analytic evaluations • Considered/tested alternatives • Revisions improve results	3 = Balanced	2 = • Haphazard management • Dependent on directions from others • Gives up easily or takes easiest way • Oversimplifies or states the obvious • Relies on best or random guesses • Accepts errors, excuses problems	1 = Incomplete

Comments

_____

_____

_____

Figure A.29	**Example of a Scorecard Rubric** (*continued*)

Score	D. Student provides reflective evaluation of learning.			
	5 = Outstanding	4 = • Recognizes strengths, quality of work • Aware of weaknesses, faults • Understands criteria, goals • Assesses process and progress • Sets own learning goals • Accepts academic challenges	3 = Balanced	2 = • Does not accurately identify strengths • Minimizes weaknesses, faults • Seems unclear about criteria, goals • Unclear about learning process and progress • Lets others set learning goals • Avoids academic challenges	1 = Incomplete

Comments

_____

_____

_____

III. Presentations/Communication: In how many ways and how well can you communicate to others what you did and what you learned? (Audiovisual/computer stations will be available.)

Score	A. Written progress journal and other written products and records are effective.			
	5 = Outstanding	4 = • Clear explanations • Attention to details • Interesting to read • Well organized, formatted • Helpful terminology, vocabulary • Strong conventions	3 = Balanced	2 = • Confusing explanations • Lacking detail, clarity • Safe, bland, trite comments • Organizations, format weak • Technical, unnatural, or ambiguous terms • Language, mechanics interfere	1 = Incomplete

Comments

_____

_____

_____

Figure A.29	**Example of a Scorecard Rubric** (*continued*)

Score	B. Visual display and other visual compositions are effective.			
	5 = Outstanding	4 = • Labels/explanations help draw attention to important points • Display is — balanced, colorful, attractive — purposefully designed — carefully crafted • Artistry enhances effect	3 = Balanced	2 = • Labels, explanations are lacking • The intent is unclear and confusing • Color, line, balance detract • Constructed without purposeful design • Imprecise, poor craftsmanship • Artistic elements lacking	1 = Incomplete

Comments

_____

_____

_____

Score	C. Oral presentation and interview are effective.			
	5 = Outstanding	4 = • Clear, easy to follow • Enthusiastic, interested • Helpful, responsive to listener • Thoughtful, informative • Detailed, authoritative • Fluent, natural responses	3 = Balanced	2 = • Rambling, confusing explanations • Robotic, memorized responses • Routine, unresponsive. • Halting, unsure • Too superficial or too domineering • Short, one-word responses	1 = Incomplete

Comments

_____

_____

_____

Projects may vary by age, type, and purpose.
Judges are instructed to look at all evidence to determine a final score.

SCORE _____

TOTAL POSSIBLE POINTS = 50

Figure A.29	**Example of a Scorecard Rubric (***continued***)**

PROJECT REFLECTION

You may wish to make additional comments about your project that will help judges understand the following:

- Why you chose this project.
- Any unusual or difficult things that happened during the project.
- How you feel about the results of the project.
- How others feel about your project.

_____

_____

_____

_____

_____

_____

_____

_____

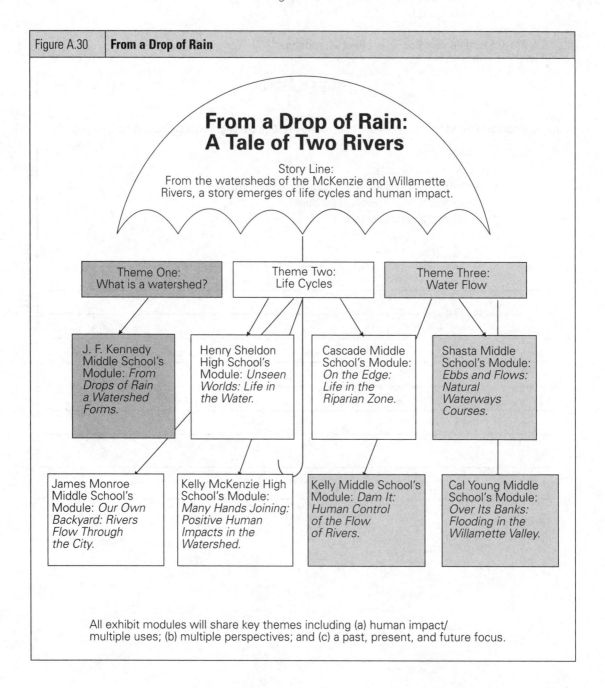

Figure A.30   **From a Drop of Rain**

From a Drop of Rain:
A Tale of Two Rivers

Story Line:
From the watersheds of the McKenzie and Willamette
Rivers, a story emerges of life cycles and human impact.

Theme One:
What is a watershed?

Theme Two:
Life Cycles

Theme Three:
Water Flow

J. F. Kennedy
Middle School's
Module: *From
Drops of Rain
a Watershed
Forms.*

Henry Sheldon
High School's
Module: *Unseen
Worlds: Life in
the Water.*

Cascade Middle
School's Module:
*On the Edge:
Life in the
Riparian Zone.*

Shasta Middle
School's Module:
*Ebbs and Flows:
Natural
Waterways
Courses.*

James Monroe
Middle School's
Module: *Our Own
Backyard: Rivers
Flow Through
the City.*

Kelly McKenzie High
School's Module:
*Many Hands Joining:
Positive Human
Impacts in the
Watershed.*

Kelly Middle School's
Module: *Dam It:
Human Control
of the Flow
of Rivers.*

Cal Young Middle
School's Module:
*Over Its Banks:
Flooding in the
Willamette Valley.*

All exhibit modules will share key themes including (a) human impact/
multiple uses; (b) multiple perspectives; and (c) a past, present, and future focus.

Figure A.31	**Characteristics of Seven Performance-Based Scoring Devices**
Analytical Trait Scoring Rubric	• This rubric includes a combination of single rubrics corresponding to each dimension, or trait, being scored. • Each trait rubric contains a scale and descriptors of each level of performance. • The scaling system contains from 3 to 6 points and assesses a range of performances from weak to strong. • This rubric can be task-specific (crafted for a particular project) or generic (designed to evaluate one type of performance, for example, writing across the curriculum).
Developmental Scoring Rubric	• This rubric is designed to be longitudinal—showing progress over time. • Generally, a number of traits are embedded in one scale. • A large number of stages or bands assess a range of performance from "like a beginner" to "like an expert." • Younger students score on the lower bands of the scale, and older students score in the higher ranges.
Checklist	• A checklist specifies traits that must be present in a performance. • The assessor simply checks off the presence or absence of critical traits listed.
Assessment List	• An assessment list is similar to a checklist in that it indicates to students the essential traits of excellence. • A weighted scoring value is assigned for each trait.
Scorecard Rubric	• This rubric contains analytical traits and a scoring scale. • A point system provides an overall score, which can then be converted into a percentage or letter grade.
ChecBric	• A ChecBric is a combined scoring rubric and checklist. • The presence or absence of a particular trait is noted in one column. The assessment of that trait's quality is in the other column.
Holistic Scoring Rubric	• A holistic rubric includes one general descriptor for performance as a whole. • One scale is present, and one score is assigned for the entire performance.[1]

[1]We have not provided specific examples of holistic scoring rubrics in this text. We rarely use them. However, others report that they do and are pleased with the results.

Figure A.32	**Museum Exhibit Assessment List of Traits and Key Questions**

1. Story Line	Yes	No	Points Possible	Points Earned
• Is there a clear title, and does the title make the content and focus of the exhibit clear?			3	
• Do the text and labels relate to what is seen?			3	
• Do the words encourage the visitor to view the exhibit?			3	
• Does the text provide basic information in an easy-to-read format?			3	
• Is the text in small chunks (fewer than 100 words) with headings, captions, and instructions?			3	
• Can the main points of the exhibit be easily identified?			3	
• Were the main ideas presented using objects, written information, and interactives?			3	
• Did the method of presenting the main ideas in this exhibit help convey the main ideas?			3	
			Total Score	

2. Interpretive Brochure	Yes	No	Points Possible	Points Earned
• Can the main points of the exhibit be easily identified in the brochure?			3	
• Is the text in small chunks (fewer than 100 words) with headings, captions, and instructions?			3	
• Does the text provide basic information in an easy-to-read format?			3	
• Do the graphics contribute to the overall understanding of the main ideas in the exhibit?			3	
			Total Score	

Figure A.32	**Museum Exhibit Assessment List of Traits and Key Questions (*continued*)**

3. Objects	Yes	No	Points Possible	Points Earned
• Do the objects help illustrate the exhibit?			3	
• Are they interesting?			3	
• Can the objects be touched? Does touching or not touching the objects affect the overall exhibit?			3	
• Are the objects displayed in such a way as to attract the visitor's attention?			3	
			Total Score	

4. Interactives	Yes	No	Points Possible	Points Earned
• Are there interactives, portions that require the visitor to do something in order to participate?			3	
• Is each interactive durable and in good working order?			3	
• Are the instructions for using the interactives clear and easy to understand?			3	
• Does the interactive directly relate to the main theme of the exhibit?			3	
			Total Score	

5. Work Plan and Time Lines	Yes	No	Points Possible	Points Earned
• Did your group have a work plan, and did you follow it?			6	
• Were you able to meet the time lines identified in your work plan?			6	
			Total Score	

Figure A.32	**Museum Exhibit Assessment List of Traits and Key Questions** (*continued*)

6. Collaboration	Yes	No	Points Possible	Points Earned
• Were you able to solve conflicts when they arose in your group?			6	
• Did you all share the workload, or did some members of the group do more work than others?			6	
			Total Score	

7. Prototype Development	Yes	No	Points Possible	Points Earned
• Did your group draft a number of ideas, possibilities, and sketches?			4	
• Did you keep a processfolio of your work?			4	
• Did you revise and edit your work?			4	
• Did you develop a prototype and present it to the class?			4	
			Total Score	

Overall Score

Student Reflection:

Make additional comments here that will help the judges understand your work better.

Judges' Comments:

Figure A.33	**Grade 3 Reading Assessment**

P. B. Noodles and the Story of the Purloined Paper

TESTER READ:

This is a story of a very unusual cat named Pizza Noodles and how he solved the mystery of the purloined newspaper. "Purloined" is a word you may not be familiar with. If something is purloined, it means it was stolen or nabbed.

WRITE THE WORD "Purloined" ON THE BOARD AND REPEAT THE WORD WHILE POINTING TO IT AND PRONOUNCING IT.

Hello! My name is Pizza Noodles, but my family calls me "Pizza Bugs." I am the head of home safety for the Noodles family.

When the Noodles found me at the shelter, I was in pretty bad shape. I was the tiniest kitten they had ever seen. My orange fur was thin and matted. I reached out my paw to touch the Noodles. Right then, they decided to make me a member of the family. When the Noodles brought me home they named me "Pizza." I sort of looked like a slice of cheese pizza wearing white cowboy boots.

There are a few things you need to know about working in home safety. One, you can't look like a wimp. The first thing I had to do to get this job was to get fat. This is VERY important if you are in charge of keeping a family safe from harm, loss, or crime.

I insisted that they give me the very best cat food that money can buy. This is the moist, fish-flavored stuff that comes in cans. Now I am the biggest cat around. Some people say that I am too fat to save anybody. As you will learn, I sure proved them wrong.

Two, as the head of home safety, I must look like the boss. To do that, I simply spread myself out on the sofa in front of the window. Some folks might think that I am just sleeping. But don't you be fooled. My eyes may look closed, but I always keep them open a pinch to check the street. That is how I first noticed something strange on the doorstep. More about that later...

Three, to be in home safety, you must be able to do special tricks. I can open doors by myself and turn on lights. I can also get myself a drink of water. I just keep batting at the handle of the faucet until it turns on.

For sure, I am someone you would not want to mess with! Let me tell you how my smarts helped me solve the crime of the purloined paper.

It all started when I noticed something odd. In the early, dark morning, a newspaper was dropped on our front step. And soon it disappeared! Can you believe it? Well, I could not have this go on with me in charge of home safety. I set out to find the thief.

| Figure A.33 | **Grade 3 Reading Assessment** (*continued*) |

My expert mind guessed that the mean dog across the street was stealing the Noodles' paper. He was one of those yapping weenie dogs. He wagged his tail constantly trying to scare everyone off. His name was Oscar. I decided to trap Oscar in the act.

Using my great brain, I came up with a plan. I decided to prop a bucket of water over the front door that night. My idea was to catch Oscar as he swiped the paper. When he grabbed it, I would flash the porch light on. Then I would tip the bucket of water on him. That would show everyone who was in charge at our house.

So I set my plan in motion. I got a bucket from the lawn shed and hid it under the sink. In the middle of the night, I filled it with water. It was very hard to lug that thing out to the front door. But, as I said, I **am** very strong. I used all my might to prop it in place above the door. That's what I call super strength!

Then I crept onto a shelf by the door. I tied a string on the light switch. I dropped it down to the floor and rolled it over to the sofa. I held one end in my paw as I flopped down on the back of the sofa to wait.

| Figure A.33 | **Grade 3 Reading Assessment** (*continued*) |

I heard the paper drop on the steps. I crouched quietly. As soon as Oscar entered the yard, I would be ready.

I waited and waited, and then—just to give my eyes a rest for a minute—I closed them. The next thing I knew, I heard a noise by the door. I yanked on the string, which turned the light on. The door opened and the bucket came crashing down on Mr. Noodles's head. Oscar was nowhere to be found.

For that daring plan, I got a special reward from the Noodles. They let me sleep in the dark, cold basement the rest of the week. They figured that with me in the basement, the house had never been safer!

USE YOUR SCAN SHEET TO MARK YOUR ANSWERS. <u>DO NOT</u> MARK ON THIS SHEET.

1. Pizza Noodles got his name because he
    a. liked to eat cheese pizza.
    b. was an orange tabby cat.
    c. looked like a piece of pizza.
    d. liked to solve mysteries.

2. Pizza noticed that
    a. the dog across the street was a thief.
    b. things disappeared from in the house.
    c. it was nice to lie on the back of the sofa.
    d. the paper seemed to disappear each day.

3. According to Pizza, to be the head of home safety, it is important to
    a. be fat and do tricks.
    b. do tricks and stay awake.
    c. be fat and boss dogs.
    d. sneak around and watch.

4. Pizza describes Oscar as a
    a. big, cruel dog from across the street.
    b. dog who steals and threatens others.
    c. mean weenie dog who yaps all the time.
    d. big, dumb dog who lives next door.

Figure A.33	**Grade 3 Reading Assessment** (*continued*)

5. Pizza didn't realize who was at the door because he
    a. had fallen fast asleep.
    b. wasn't paying attention.
    c. hadn't smelled the dog.
    d. looked out the window.

6. Pizza was "rewarded" for his work by
    a. getting special treats to eat.
    b. being kept in the basement.
    c. being in charge of home safety.
    d. sleeping on the back of the sofa.

7. You could say that Pizza liked to eat
    a. dry cat food and scraps from the table.
    b. anything good that he could find to eat.
    c. cat food that tasted like cheese pizza.
    d. moist cat food that smelled like fish.

8. Pizza had special skills that included
    a. opening the door and turning on the lights and faucet.
    b. turning on the water and the lights and opening cans.
    c. bragging about himself and showing off his fat body.
    d. catching the thief and carrying a bucket of water.

9. The word "purloined" means
    a. rolled up.
    b. wrapped.
    c. newspaper.
    d. stolen.

10. Pizza believes if you want to look like the boss, you should
    a. eat well and do exercises every day.
    b. spread out on the back of the sofa.
    c. teach others the special tricks you do.
    d. scare all of the neighborhood pets.

| Figure A.33 | **Grade 3 Reading Assessment** (*continued*) |

11. The story leads you to believe that Pizza
    a. lies around and sleeps a lot.
    b. is very smart and capable.
    c. likes to eat and chase dogs.
    d. is a big, scary, mean cat.

12. The story tells us that Pizza
    a. will eat any canned food.
    b. likes expensive cat food.
    c. is a very picky eater.
    d. wants hard, crunchy food.

13. To capture the thief, Pizza collected
    a. a ball of yarn and a small bucket of water.
    b. a very small bucket and a roll of newspaper.
    c. some expensive cat food that smelled like fish.
    d. a ball of string and a bucket from the lawn shed.

14. To turn on the faucet, Pizza
    a. pulled the handle with his teeth.
    b. sat on the handle with his body.
    c. batted the handle with his paw.
    d. jumped on the handle with his feet.

15. Pizza Noodles might be described as a
    a. genius who can solve any neighborhood crime.
    b. big wimp who is afraid of the neighbor's dog.
    c. big, fat cat who thinks he is very important.
    d. clever thief who can steal and get away with it.

| Figure A.33 | **Grade 3 Reading Assessment** (*continued*) |

16. If the Noodles took Pizza to the vet for a checkup, what do you think the vet would tell them about his health? Write down all of your ideas here.

17. Why might the neighbors have named their dog "Oscar"?

| Figure A.34 | **Grade 9: *My Antonia* Maze** |

Name _____ Date _____ Section _____

Part One:

This type of assessment is somewhat different than ones you may have completed in the past. Every so often, a blank is left in the text. Four words that might fit in the blank are underneath. As you read, choose the word that will make the most sense in this particular place in the story. It is OK to read ahead and then go back and change an answer. Once you are confident that you have made the best selections, transfer all of your answers onto the scan sheet.

What you are about to read is from the book My Antonia *by Willa Cather. It tells the story of Jim Burden and his friendship with a young immigrant woman named Antonia (pronounced An-toe-NEE-ah) Shimerda. The story is set in the late 1800s, and the Shimerdas have recently immigrated to the United States from Bohemia. They are not doing well in their new country trying to make a living by farming. Antonia's father dies soon after the family's arrival. She and her brother Ambrosch step in to help their mother run the farm. Jim, over many months, tutors Antonia in reading and helps her learn English. As you read, think about what you know about farming and use that information to help select the best word to fill in the blank.*

Much as I liked Antonia, I hated the superior tone that she sometimes took with me. She was four years older than I, to be sure, and had seen more of the world; but I was a boy and she was a girl, and I resented her protecting manner. Before autumn was over, she began to treat me more like an equal and to defer to me in other things than reading lessons. This change came about from an adventure we had together.

One day when I rode over to the Shimerda's I found Antonia starting off on foot for Russian Peter's house, to borrow a spade Ambrosch needed. I offered to take her on my pony, Dude, and she got up behind me. There had been another black frost the night before, and the air was clear and heady as wine. Within a week all the blooming roadsides had been despoiled, hundreds of miles of yellow sunflowers had been transformed into brown, rattling, burry stalks.

We found Russian Peter digging his potatoes. We were glad to go in and ___ warm

1.   a. have
      b. huddle
      c. get
      d. wrap up

by his kitchen ___ and to see his squashes and Christmas ___, heaped in the

2.   a. window
      b. door
      c. lantern
      d. stove

3.   a. melons
      b. lights
      c. presents
      d. candy

Figure A.34	**Grade 9: *My Antonia* Maze** (*continued*)

storeroom for ___. As we rode away with the ___ Antonia suggested that we

4. a. summer
b. autumn
c. winter
d. spring

5. a. spade
b. book
c. hay wagon
d. bowl

stop at the prairie-dog-town and dig into one of the holes. ___ could find out

6. a. They
b. We
c. I
d. He

whether they ran ___ down, or were horizontal, like mole-holes; whether they

7. a. crooked
b. up
c. steep
d. straight

had underground connections; whether the ___ had nests down there, lined with

8. a. owls
b. cats
c. sunflowers
d. wasps

feathers. We might get some puppies, or owl ___, or snakeskins.

9. a. ears
b. droppings
c. claws
d. eggs

The dog-town was spread out ___ perhaps ten acres. The grass had been nibbled

10. a. above
b. over
c. around
d. beside

short and even, so this stretch ___ not shaggy and red like the surrounding

11. a. was
b. could be
c. is
d. began

country, but grey and velvety. The ___ were several yards apart, and were

12. a. horses
b. holes
c. acres
d. dogs

Figure A.34	**Grade 9: *My Antonia* Maze** (*continued*)

distributed with a good deal of regularity, almost as if the town had ___ laid out

13. a. once
b. always
c. begun
d. been

in streets and avenues. One always felt that an orderly and very sociable kind of life was going on there. I tied Dude down in a draw, and we ___ wandering about,

14. a. talked
b. chased
c. went
d. glanced

looking for a hole that would be easy to dig. The ___ were out, as usual, dozens

15. a. moles
b. stars
c. dogs
d. blossoms

of them, ___ up on their hind legs over the ___ of their houses. As we ___,

16. a. laying
b. reaching
c. sitting
d. scratching

17. a. chimneys
b. windows
c. floors
d. doors

18. a. approached
b. screamed
c. ran away
d. scrambled

they barked, shook their tails at us, and scurried underground. Before the mouths of the holes were little patches of ___ and gravel, scratched up, we supposed,

19. a. weeds
b. sunlight
c. sand
d. water

from a ___ way below the surface. Here and ___, in the town, we came on

20. a. long
b. crooked
c. short
d. distant

21. a. about
b. there
c. now
d. gone

larger ___ patches, several yards away from any ___. If the dogs had

22. a. grass
b. weed
c. sunlight
d. gravel

23. a. hole
b. water
c. grass
d. bushes

| Figure A.34 | **Grade 9: *My Antonia* Maze** (*continued*) |

scratched the gravel up in ___, how had they carried it so ___? It was on one

24. a. playing
    b. fighting
    c. burying
    d. excavating

25. a. easily
    b. far
    c. close
    d. quickly

of these gravel beds that I met my adventure.

references

ABCTeach. (n.d.). Solving word problems. Retrieved December 17, 2010, from http://www.abcteach.com/free/p/poster_strategiesforwordproblems.pdf

Beatty, P. (1981). *Lupita mañana.* New York: Beach Tree Books.

Biddle, B. J., & Berliner, D. C. (2002). Unequal school funding in the United States. *Educational Leadership, 59*(8), 48–59.

Bloom, B. (Ed.). (1956). *Taxonomy of educational objectives.* New York: David McKay.

Christensen, L. (1991 May/June). Unlearning the myths that bind us. *Rethinking Schools, 1,* 3–7.

Christmas Day, 1492. (1984). In E. R. May, *A proud nation* (p. 38). Evanston, IL: McDougal, Littell, and Company.

Conrad, P. (1991). *Pedro's journal.* New York: Scholastic Books.

Cortiella, C. Response-to-intervention: An emerging method for LD identification. Available: http://www.greatschools.org/special-education/LD-ADHD/emerging-method-for-ld-identification.gs?content=883

Cranney, A. G. (1972–73). The construction of two types of cloze reading tests for college students. *Journal of Reading Behavior, 5*(1), 60–64.

Cunningham, P. M. (1990). The Names Test: A quick assessment of decoding ability. *The Reading Teacher, 44*(2), 124–129.

Dorris, M. (1992). *Morning girl.* New York: Hyperion Books for Children.

Duffelmeyer, F. A., Kruse, A. E., Merkley, D. J., & Fyfe, S. A. (1994). Further validation and enhancement of the Names Test. *The Reading Teacher, 48*(2), 118–128.

EasyCBM [Website]. (2008). Available: http://easycbm.com/

Educators in Connecticut's Pomperaug Regional School District 15. (1996). *A teacher's guide to performance-based learning and assessment.* Alexandria, VA: ASCD.

Eugene Public School District 4J. (1995). *Education 2000 K–5 integrated curriculum*. Eugene, OR: Eugene Public School District 4J.

Florian, L. (Ed.). (2007). Curriculum-based measurement in reading and math: Providing rigorous outcomes to support learning. In *The SAGE handbook of special education* (Chapter 23). Thousand Oaks, CA: SAGE Publications.

Fuchs, L. S., Hamlett, C. L., & Fuchs, D. (1990). *Monitoring basic skills progress: Basic reading.* Austin, TX: PRO-ED.

Ginsburg, H., & Opper, S. (1998). *Piaget's theory of intellectual development.* Englewood Cliffs, NJ: Prentice-Hall.

Good, R. H., & Kaminski, R. A. (Eds.). (2002). *Dynamic Indicators of Basic Early Literacy Skills* (6th ed.). Eugene, OR: Institute for the Development of Education Achievement. Available: http://dibels.uoregon.edu

Granowsky, A. (Ed.). (1993). *Point of view* [series]. Austin, TX: Steck-Vaughn.

Guthrie, J. T. (1973). Reading comprehension and syntactic responses in good and poor readers. *Journal of Educational Psychology, 65,* 294–300.

Guthrie, J., & Humenick, N. (2004). Motivating students to read: Evidence for classroom practices that increase reading motivation and achievement. In P. McCardle & V. Chhabra (Eds.), *The voice of evidence in reading research.* Baltimore, MD: Paul H. Brookes Publishing Company.

Haladyna, T., & Hess, R. (1999). An evaluation of conjunctive and compensatory standard-setting strategies for test decisions. *Educational Assessment, 6*(2), 129–153.

Hasbrouck, J., & Tindal, G. (2005). *Oral reading fluency: 90 years of measurement.* (Tech. Rep. No. 33). Eugene, OR: University of Oregon, College of Education, Behavioral Research and Teaching.

Huck, C., Hepler, S., & Hickman, J. (1987). *Children's literature in the elementary school* (4th ed.). New York: Holt, Rinehart, Winston.

Illinois State Board of Education. (2004). Illinois Snapshots of Early Literacy (ISEL). Available: http://www.isbe.net/curriculum/reading/html/isel.htm

Inspiration Software, Inc. (n.d.). Inspiration [Computer software]. Beaverton, OR: Author.

Invernizzi, M., Juel, C., Swank, L., & Meier, J. (2005). *Phonological Awareness Literacy Screening.* Charlottesville, VA: The Rector and the Board of Visitors of the University of Virginia. Available: http://pals.virginia.edu/

Kingston, A. J., & Weaver, W. W. (1970). Feasibility of cloze techniques for reaching and evaluating culturally disadvantaged beginning readers. *The Journal of Social Psychology, 82,* 205–214.

Kovalik, S. (1993). *ITI: The model integrated thematic instruction.* Los Angeles: Discovery Press.

Lewin, L. (2009). *Teaching comprehension with student questioning strategies.* New York: Scholastic.

Marzano, R. (1994). *The systematic identification and articulation of content standards and benchmarks.* Aurora, CO: Mid-continent Regional Educational Laboratory.

Marzano, R. (2004). *Building background knowledge for academic achievement.* Alexandria, VA: ASCD.

Marzano, R. (2006). *Classroom assessment and grading that work.* Alexandria, VA: ASCD.

Marzano, R. J., Brandt, R. S., Hughes, C. S., Jones, B. F., Presseisen, B. Z., Rankin, S. C., & Suhor, C. (1988). *Dimensions of thinking: A framework for curriculum and instruction.* Alexandria, VA: ASCD.

Marzano, R., Pickering, D., Arredondo, D., Blackburn, G., Brandt, R., Moffett, C., Paynter, D., Pollock, J., & Whistler, J. S. (1997). *Dimensions of Learning teacher's manual* (2nd ed.). Alexandria, VA: ASCD.

Marzano, R. J., Pickering, D., & McTighe, J. (1993). *Assessing student outcomes: Performance assessment using the Dimensions of Learning model.* Alexandria, VA: ASCD.

Mather, N., Sammons, J., & Schwartz, J. (2006). Adaptations of the Names Test: Easy-to-use phonics assessments. *The Reading Teacher, 60*(2), 114–122.

Morsy, L., Kieffer, M., & Snow, C. E. (2010). *Measure for measure: A critical consumers' guide to reading comprehension assessments for adolescents.* New York: Carnegie Corporation of New York.

National Institute of Child Health and Human Development. (2000). *Teaching children to read: An evidence-based assessment of the scientific research literature on reading and its implications for reading instruction.* Summary report of the National Reading Panel. (NIH Publication No. 00-4769). Washington, DC: U.S. Government Printing Office. Available: http://www.nichd.nih.gov/publications/nrp/upload/smallbook_pdf.pdf

National Research Center on Learning Disabilities. (2007). *Responsiveness to intervention in the SLD determination process* [Brochure]. Lawrence, KS: Author. Available: http://www.nrcld.org/resource_kit/tools/RTIinSLDProcess2007.pdf

Newmann, F. M. (1991). Linking restructuring to authentic student achievement. *Phi Delta Kappan, 72*(6), 458–463.

Ogle, D. (1986). K-W-L: A teaching model that develops active reading of expository text. *The Reading Teacher, 39*(6), 564–570.

Oregon Department of Education. (n.d.). Oregon English/language arts grade-level standards: Comparing 1996 to 2003. Retrieved October 1, 2010, from http://www.ode.state.or.us/teachlearn/subjects/elarts/curriculum/comparison1996to2003standards.pdf

Oregon Department of Education. (n.d.). Scientific inquiry scoring guides [Website]. Retrieved September 2009 from http://www.ode.state.or.us/search/page/?=1414

Oregon Department of Education. (n.d.) Standards by design [Online tool]. Retrieved September 2009 from http://www.ode.state.or.us/teachlearn/real/standards/sbd.aspx

Oregon Department of Education, Office of Assessment and Evaluation. (1996). *Writing scoring guide: Middle school student version.* Salem, OR: Oregon Department of Education.

Parker, R., Hasbrouck, J. E., & Tindal, G. (1992). The maze as a classroom-based reading measure: Construction methods, reliability, and validity. *The Journal of Special Education, 26*(2), 195–218.

Paulsen, G. (1998). *Soldier's heart.* New York: Dell-Laurel Leaf.

Popham, J. (2008). *Transformative assessment.* Alexandria, VA: ASCD.

Raphael, T. E., & Au, K. H. (2005). QAR: Enhancing comprehension and test taking across grades and content areas. *The Reading Teacher, 59*(3), 206–221.

RTI Action Network. (n.d.). Learn about RTI. Retrieved December 17, 2010, from http://www.rtinetwork.org/learn

Santa, C. M. (1988). *Content reading including study systems: Reading, writing and studying across the curriculum.* Dubuque, IA: Kendall Hunt Publishing.

Sayers, D. L. (1947). *The lost tools of learning.* Essay delivered at Oxford University. Available: http://www.gbt.org/text/sayers.html

Scieszka, J. (1989). *The true story of the three little pigs.* New York: Viking.

Shoemaker, B. J., & Lewin, L. (1993). Curriculum and assessment: Two sides of the same coin. *Educational Leadership, 50*(8), 55–57.

Shuster, K., & Meany, J. (2005). *Speak out! Debate and public speaking in the middle grades.* New York: International Debate Education Association.

Snyder, T. (n.d.). TimelinerXE [Computer software]. Watertown, MA: Author.

Stiggins, R. J. (1997). *Student-centered classroom assessment* (2nd ed.). Upper Saddle River, NJ: Merrill.

The story of Tam and Cam. (2001). In McDougal Littell, *The language of literature.* Orlando, FL: McDougal Littell.

Texas Education Agency & University of Texas System. (2006). *Texas Primary Reading Inventory (TPRI) early reading assessment.* Available: http://www.tpri.org

Tindal, G., et al. (2008). easyCBM. Available: http://easycbm.com/

White, E. B. (1952). *Charlotte's web.* New York: Harper and Row.

Wiggins, G. (1995, September). CLASS Workshop, San Antonio, Texas.

Wormeli, R. (2006). *Fair isn't always equal.* Portland, ME: Stenhouse.

index

The letter *f* following a page number denotes a figure.

about the authors

Betty Jean Shoemaker recently retired after serving as a curriculum and staff development coordinator for Eugene Public School District 4J in Eugene, Oregon. She has taught in both regular and special education classrooms since 1965. As a curriculum coordinator, she worked districtwide to provide instructional leadership and to develop curriculum and assessment resources for staff. In addition, she provided professional development to administrators, teachers, and instructional assistants.

Betty earned her Ph.D. in curriculum and instruction at the University of Oregon. She consults nationally in the areas of literacy, integrated thematic curriculum, performance-based assessment, and teaching methodology. She has published work in *Educational Leadership, Phi Delta Kappan,* and *Roeper Review.* She and coauthor Larry Lewin have also written two books— one on performance assessment titled *Great Performances: Creating Classroom-Based Assessment Tasks*, and one on teaching strategies titled *Innovative Instruction*. Betty can be reached at dr.betty.shoemaker@comcast.net or by mail at 2978 Dry Creek Road, Eugene, OR 97404.

Larry Lewin taught at the elementary, middle, and high school levels for 24 years in Oregon. He now presents staff development workshops to teachers in the United States and Canada on such topics as performance-based assessment, differentiated instruction, strategies to assist struggling readers and writers, and teaching comprehension with student-based questioning.

He is the author, with Betty Shoemaker, of *Great Performances* and *Innovative Instruction*, and he has also authored *Paving the Way in Reading and Writing, Reading Response That Really Matters to Middle Schoolers,* and *Teaching Comprehension with Questioning Strategies*. Larry has written for *Educational Leadership* and *The Reading Teacher*. Larry can be contacted at larry@larrylewin.com or by mail at 2145 Lincoln Street., Eugene, OR 97405.

Related ASCD Resources: Performance Assessments

At the time of publication, the following ASCD resources were available (ASCD stock numbers appear in parentheses). For up-to-date information about ASCD resources, go to www.ascd.org.

ASCD EDge Group
Exchange ideas and connect with other educators interested in performance assessments on the social networking site ASCD EDge™ at http://ascdedge.ascd.org/.

Print Products
- *Checking for Understanding: Formative Assessment Techniques for Your Classroom* by Douglas Fisher and Nancy Frey (#107023)
- *Educational Leadership,* September 2004: *Teaching for Meaning* (#105028)
- *Educational Leadership*, December 2007/January 2008: *Informative Assessment* (#108023)
- *Enhancing Professional Practice: A Framework for Teaching* by Charlotte Danielson (#106034)
- *Exploring Formative Assessment* (The Professional Learning Community Series) by Susan Brookhart (#109038)
- *How to Give Effective Feedback to Your Students* by Susan M. Brookhart (#108019)
- *Increasing Student Learning Through Multimedia Projects* by Michael Simkins, Karen Cole, Fern Tavalin, and Barbara Means (#102112)
- *Improving Student Learning One Teacher at a Time* by Jane E. Pollock (#107005)
- *Learning on Display: Student-Created Museums That Build Understanding* by Linda D'Acquisto (#105018)
- *Problems as Possibilities: Problem-Based Learning for K–16 Education,* 2nd edition, by Linda Torp and Sara Sage (#101064)
- *Transformative Assessment* by W. James Popham (#108018)
- *Understanding by Design,* expanded 2nd edition, by Grant Wiggins and Jay McTighe (#103055)

Video and DVDs
- *Giving Effective Feedback to Your Students* (#609104)

THE WHOLE CHILD The Whole Child Initiative helps schools and communities create learning environments that allow students to be healthy, safe, engaged, supported, and challenged. To learn more about other books and resources that relate to the whole child, visit www.wholechild education.org.

For more information: send e-mail to member@ascd.org; call 1-800-933-2723 or 703-578-9600, press 2; send a fax to 703-575-5400; or write to Information Services, ASCD, 1703 N. Beauregard St., Alexandria, VA 22311-1714 USA.